CAPE FEAR
CONFEDERATES

Cape Fear Confederates

The 18th North Carolina Regiment in the Civil War

James Gillispie

McFarland & Company, Inc., Publishers
Jefferson, North Carolina, and London

Frontispiece: This flag was the last issued to the 18th North Carolina Regiment. The regiment received it in the second half of 1864, most likely toward the end of the year. It was captured on April 2, 1865, as the regiment's thin ranks were overwhelmed in a massive Union attack that morning (North Carolina Museum of History).

LIBRARY OF CONGRESS CATALOGUING-IN-PUBLICATION DATA

Gillispie, James Massie, 1969–
    Cape Fear Confederates : the 18th North Carolina regiment in the Civil War / James Gillispie.
       p.   cm.
    Includes bibliographical references and index.

    ISBN 978-0-7864-4847-0
    softcover : acid free paper ∞

    1. Confederate States of America. Army. North Carolina Infantry Regiment, 18th.   2. United States — History — Civil War, 1861–1865 — Regimental histories.   3. North Carolina — History — Civil War, 1861–1865 — Regimental histories. 4. United States — History — Civil War, 1861–1865 — Campaigns.   5. North Carolina — History — Civil War — 1861–1865 — Registers.   6. United States — History — Civil War, 1861–1865 — Registers.   7. Soldiers — North Carolina — Registers.   I. Title.
E573.518th .G55 2012
973.7'456 — dc23   2011047360

BRITISH LIBRARY CATALOGUING DATA ARE AVAILABLE

© 2012 James Gillispie. All rights reserved

No part of this book may be reproduced or transmitted in any form or by any means, electronic or mechanical, including photocopying or recording, or by any information storage and retrieval system, without permission in writing from the publisher.

Front cover print *Battle of Cold Harbor* created by Kurz and Allison, 1888 (Library of Congress); background flag: 18th of NC flag captured July 1864 (North Carolina museum of history)

Manufactured in the United States of America

McFarland & Company, Inc., Publishers
   Box 611, Jefferson, North Carolina 28640
   www.mcfarlandpub.com

Table of Contents

Introduction and Acknowledgments   1

1. The 18th North Carolina's Road to War   5
2. Secession and the Formation of the 18th North Carolina   20
3. Seeing the Elephant: Hanover Court House, Gaines's Mill, and Frayser's Farm   37
4. Stonewall Salutes the 18th: The Battle of Cedar Mountain   59
5. Battling the "Miscreant" Pope: Second Manassas and Chantilly/Ox Hill   78
6. More Hard Marching: The Maryland Campaign   97
7. A Difficult Way to End a Year: Fall and Winter of 1862   112
8. The Regiment Loses Its Colonel and Its Colors: The Bloody Battle of Chancellorsville   126
9. Difficult Days: The Gettysburg Campaign and the Winter of 1863-1864   149
10. Desperate and Relentless Fighting: Wilderness to Cold Harbor   174
11. Petersburg: The Final Campaign   195

Appendix A: 18th North Carolina Regiment Members Who Surrendered at Appomattox Court House, April 9, 1865   215
Appendix B: Biographical Sketches of 54 Men Who Served the Longest with the Regiment   217
Chapter Notes   225
Bibliography   237
Index   241

Introduction
and Acknowledgments

Well before the Old North State officially seceded from the Union on May 20, 1861, men in the southeastern section of the state began preparing to join the Confederacy. While a significant number of North Carolinians were somewhat reluctant secessionists, pro-secession sentiment was more pronounced in the Cape Fear region. Socially, politically, and economically this section of the state had more in common with the Deep South states than did other parts. There, slaveholding was more common and the number of African Americans higher than in other parts of North Carolina. Consequently, concerns that Lincoln and the victorious Republican Party were determined to abolish a labor system that was profitable to many whites in the region and elevate black people to social and political equality with whites were more acute. Republican ascendancy in Washington, as far as many whites in the Cape Fear region were concerned, represented a very real and very dire threat to their world as they understood and accepted it.

Men across the region began forming local military organizations like the Bladen Guards, Robeson Light Infantry, and the Moore's Creek Riflemen in New Hanover. In Richmond County local men formed the Scotch Boys, and in Columbus County they organized the Columbus Vigilants, which was also known as Columbus Guards Number 1. Others were already members of existing militia groups like the German Guards and the Wilmington Light Infantry. During April and May 1861 companies from New Hanover, Bladen, Columbus, Richmond, and Robeson joined forces; these companies drilled together and formed the 8th North Carolina Volunteers, the designation they retained until November when they were re-designated the 18th North Carolina State Troops. In those early, romantic days of the war when victory seemed so certain and just over the horizon, these Cape Fear Confederates had no idea of the long, hard journey ahead. When it came to an end exactly four years later, those who were left could take well-earned pride in having been members of the 18th North Carolina.

Early in the war it certainly did not look as if the regiment would ever get the opportunity to make a name for itself. Until March 1862 most of the regiment guarded the *South* Carolina coast while three of the companies constituted artillery support at Fort Fisher. Yankees were occasionally spotted offshore but there was little chance for glory for the regiment's members for most of its first year. In March 1862, though, things began to change rapidly for the Eighteenth as it became part of General Lawrence O'Brian Branch's North Carolina brigade along with the Seventh, Twenty-eighth, Thirty-third, and Thirty-seventh North Carolina regiments. And, Union General George McClellan was moving his huge Army of the Potomac to the peninsula between the York and James Rivers in Virginia and making for the Confederate capital. Richmond needed all the protection it could get, and soon the 18th North Carolina was bound for Virginia and its baptism by fire.

During the spring and summer of 1862, the regiment not only entered the conflict as a combat unit but joined two famous Confederate military machines. On May 27 the Eighteenth got its first taste of battle at Hanover Court House, and it was a truly bloody introduction. The regiment drew the job of attacking an artillery position with infantry support across an open field; the results were predictable with the regiment losing significant numbers of casualties. In fact, Hanover Court House remained one of the regiment's bloodiest and most costly battles of the entire war. Shortly after the debacle at Hanover Court House, the Confederacy decided (with good reason) that it would be more effective to place the many independent brigades under more trained and experienced division commanders. When this happened the 18th North Carolina, along with the rest of Branch's brigade, became part of newly promoted Ambrose Powell Hill's Light Division. Hill's division was the largest in what would become Robert E. Lee's Army of Northern Virginia and, thanks to "Little Powell's" pugnacious personality, the division forged a reputation for one of the hardest-hitting divisions in the East. As part of Hill's Light Division the 18th North Carolina fought, and fought well, at Gaines's Mill and Fraser's Farm during the Seven Days Battles that pushed McClellan from the gates of Richmond. The regiment was also lightly engaged at Mechanicsville and Malvern Hill during that historic week.

Following the Seven Days Battles, General Hill and General James Longstreet, his immediate commander, fell out to the point that dueling was a very real possibility. To avoid that rather counter-productive situation, Lee reassigned A.P. Hill to General Jackson's command and the 18th North Carolina became part of Jackson's famous "foot cavalry." Under Jackson and Hill the regiment's members became hardened veterans throughout the rest of 1862 at places like Cedar Mountain, Second Manassas, Ox Hill, Harpers Ferry, Sharpsburg, Shepherdstown, and Fredericksburg. At each and every battle the regiment performed well and did all that was asked and expected of it.

In 1863 the Eighteenth unfortunately became famous and best known for accidentally wounding Stonewall Jackson during the Battle of Chancellorsville. That event, understandable though ultimately tragic for the Confederate cause the regiment was dedicated to, given the terrain and the time of day, was just the beginning of one of the worst campaigns in the regiment's history. The following morning the regiment helped renew the attack on General Joseph Hooker's Federals and was mauled by their enemy who had spent the night fortifying and entrenching their position. In the fierce early-morning fight the Eighteenth lost its leader, Colonel Thomas Purdie, who was much loved and respected by those he led. The regiment also suffered the indignity of losing its colors to the enemy. Chancellorsville has been viewed as Lee's finest hour, but for the men of the 18th North Carolina the battle held nothing but bad memories, memories that only got worse when they discovered that they were the ones responsible for Jackson's wounding.

Life and the war had to go on. During the second half of the Civil War, the 18th North Carolina continued to do its duty to the best of its ability and to add battle honors to its flag. The regiment was lightly engaged at Gettysburg, but as the 1864 campaign season opened it saw significant action as Grant seized the reigns of the Federal war effort and determined to batter the Confederates in Virginia into submission once and for all. The Eighteenth saw action during the Wilderness in May and was virtually destroyed at Spotsylvania Court House where it lost roughly half its numbers and another battle flag. While the regiment's numbers were somewhat augmented with new recruits and conscripts, after Spotsylvania the 18th North Carolina dwindled down to a company-sized unit that was a regiment more in name than in reality.

During the Petersburg Campaign, the Eighteenth moved back and forth across the James to deal with various Union threats to Lee's flanks. During the second half of 1864 and into 1865, General Grant stretched Lee's defenses constantly during several distinct offensives designed to either pierce or extend the Confederate defenses around Petersburg. During most of these offensives the 18th North Carolina was on hand to deflect Grant's assaults. Unfortunately for the regiment, though, Grant successfully stretched Lee's lines to the point that by April the Eighteenth formed a skeletal defensive position along the Boydton Plank Road near the center of Lee's Petersburg defenses. On April 2, 1865, Grant sent a multi-division wave at the heart of the regiment's position and overwhelmed it. What was left of the regiment, barely 125 men, broke under the blue wave, losing its battle flag for the last time. A week later the remnants, barely 100 men, many of whom were stalwart members who had been with the regiment since Hanover Court House, surrendered at Appomattox Court House and were paroled to begin the long walk home to southeastern North Carolina to rebuild their lives.

It is appropriate to take a moment and thank those who played a significant role in helping me complete the story of the 18th North Carolina. Mark Rushing and Sherry Best of Sampson Community College in Clinton, North Carolina, never failed to get books, articles, microfilm, and anything else I needed to conduct my research. Mark and Sherry, many thanks. John Coski, a scholar and friend, once again came through for me and found letters and records pertaining to the 18th North Carolina at the Brockenbrough Library of the Museum of the Confederacy in Richmond, Virginia, and made them available. I have yet to do serious research that John has not proven to be a valuable source for records and helpful suggestions. Tom Belton of the North Carolina Museum graciously provided me with photographs of the 18th North Carolina's battle flags, for which I am very grateful. And last but by no means least, John Varner at Auburn University Special Collections and Archives could not have been more helpful in making available records and images relating to General James Lane, the Eighteenth's brigade commander from September 1862 through the rest of the war.

Chapter 1

The 18th North Carolina's Road to War

One thing that most people interested in the Civil War can agree on is that the war started because eleven states declared themselves independent of the United States and members of a new Confederate States of America. Disagreement does exist about whether North Carolina and the other Confederate States possessed the constitutional right to do such a thing; but that their secession led the Lincoln administration to resort to military means to reassert legal and political control of those states is accepted as the answer to why the military clash between North and South erupted in the spring of 1861. The bigger and more hotly debated question is: What caused states like North Carolina to secede in the first place? Most professional Ph.D.-holding historians cite white Southerners' fears that a "Black Republican" administration, controlled and driven by rabid abolitionists, would use every means at its disposal — no matter how illegal and unconstitutional — to end slavery in the United States. According to this model, Tar Heels and other white Southerners seceded to escape one government with an abolitionist domestic agenda in order to live under one dedicated to preserving and protecting the region's "peculiar institution." On the other side of the debate about what caused North Carolina and other states to proclaim themselves independent of the United States are those who vehemently denounce the idea that the protection of slavery had anything to do with the formation of the Confederacy. Partisans of this model insist, often with a considerable amount of heat, that the only reason the South left the Union was to preserve the sacred political principle of states' rights from corrupt Northerners who sought to centralize governmental authority and reduce the states to political colonies of the national (Yankee-dominated) government in Washington.

Too often, discussions about what caused those eleven states to secede have taken on an "either-or" quality where the participants plead one factor *or* the other. To be sure, there have been historians who have pointed out that this question is more complex than "slavery *or* states' rights," but anyone familiar with this question knows that most of the time people addressing it stress one cause or the other as *the* major factor with the other one playing a distant second fiddle. When the evidence is consulted and viewed with an unbiased eye, one finds that the objective reality is that when North Carolinians became Confederates they did so to maintain the institution of slavery *and* to protect broader political principles that they and other Southern citizens believed were critical to their ability to maintain their individual freedom and equality. In the years leading to the election of Lincoln, the evidence is that Tar Heels were quite obviously and vocally pro-slavery and were determined to prohibit outside forces from tampering with the institution. Equally clear is that antebellum North Carolinians viewed Northern meddling with slavery in the territories as part of a broader and more dangerous plot to seize control of the national government and reduce them and their fellow slaveholding brethren to second-class citizenship in the Union, something they would not and could not submit to.

Traditionally North Carolina has been portrayed as a state that had little real stake in the slavery question because most of the state's citizens were not slaveholders themselves and the state was certainly not known for large plantations. In 1963 John G. Barrett published *The Civil War in North Carolina*, which has influenced generations of Tar Heels interested in the state's history during this period. It has earned the right to be called a "classic" and is still an excellent piece of historical writing. On the first page Barrett painted a picture of antebellum North Carolina that has rarely been questioned:

> Since the soil of the state was not well suited for the growing of cotton, there were relatively few wealthy planters with large slaveholdings to agitate for a break with the Federal government. The non-slaveholders from the mountain districts of the west and the swamp regions of the east, and certain Quaker and small farm elements in the central region, saw no reason to become vitally concerned with the preservation of a slave system in which they had little part. These non-slaveholding whites had considerable influence in the state, and their attitude toward slavery and secession had to be reckoned with.

This image of North Carolina being populated mostly by non-slaveholders and therefore having little direct interest in preserving slavery is not without foundation but it is greatly oversimplifying the case. There is also considerable evidence that the non-slaveholding majority Barrett pointed to were very much interested in that current and future status of slavery.[1]

A key problem with the argument that North Carolinians were mostly in the non-slaveholding class and therefore ambivalent about the institution's present and future protection is that it underestimates the significant number of the state's citizens who did derive economic benefits from slavery and would understandably have resisted attempts by outsiders to put limits on or even take them away entirely. A study of antebellum North Carolina politics revealed that in 1860 29.1 percent of North Carolina families were slaveowning families, a minority but a very significant minority. That was only slightly less than the percentage in the Deep South states of Louisiana, where 31 percent of families owned at least one slave, and Alabama, where 35.1 percent of families owned slaves. One must also remember that there were a number of families that did not own slaves themselves but were closely related to those who did. It is highly doubtful that this group would have been nonchalant about outsiders intruding on their relatives' right and ability to use slaves if and for as long as they chose. It should be understood too that at certain times of the year non-slaveowners rented slaves to help bring in the harvest, for example. So there were certainly times when that large group of non-slaveholders derived direct economic benefits from slavery. Furthermore, Barrett's position, which has been echoed for generations, suggests that because one did not own slaves one never hoped to enter that class is questionable at best. Everyone in the South, and that certainly included North Carolinians, understood that the road to wealth and power in the region was paved by slavery. The richest men in the South and some of the richest in the country were slaveowners. The value of slaves was increasing throughout the 1850s and by 1860 over half of the country's exports were those grown on lands owned by slaveowners. To put it another way, slavery paid and many an ambitious yeoman sought to put himself in a position to be part of a profitable system; that yeoman on the make was certainly not blasé about slavery because he did not yet own one. The notion that he would sit back while Northerners tried to take future economic opportunities away from him seems difficult to believe.[2]

That the protection of slavery was a key motivator for secession in the seven Deep South states that created the Confederate States of America is impossible to deny. South Carolina, which, given the number of fire-eating radicals it produced, not surprisingly led the way in December 1860, explaining its actions by pointing out that when the Republicans believed that "a war must be waged against slavery until it shall cease throughout the United States." Georgia secessionist and soon-to-be Confederate general Robert Toombs was the author of his state's declaration of causes of secession; in the declaration he cited very clearly what the people of his state perceived to be the Republicans' diabolical dedication to subjecting the people of the South "to the loss of our property." Mississippians left after stating in their declaration: "There was no choice left to us but submission to the immediate mandates of abolition, or dissolution of the Union.... We must either submit to degradation and to the loss of property worth four billions of money, or we must secede from the Union." Other Deep South secession ordinances and defenses clearly and repeatedly connect secession to the protection of slavery from the allegedly pro-abolitionist Republicans. The author of perhaps the best and clearest study of the secession movement in the Cotton South, Professor Charles Dew, has demonstrated:

> the secessionists of 1860–61 certainly talked more openly about slavery than present-day neo–Confederates seem willing to do. There are clear, unambiguous references to slavery in many of the official documents that emerged from the secession conventions of the lower South. A defense of states' rights is also there, to be sure, but no attempt was made to hide concern over the fate of the South's slave system in a United States run by a Republican majority.[3]

The new Confederate government's two top figures, President Jefferson Davis and Vice-President Alexander Stephens, certainly made no bones about the connection between secession and protecting slavery. Davis stated in the spring of 1861 that "the Southern States were driven by the conduct of the North to the adoption of some course of action to avert the danger [of abolition] with which they were openly menaced." But it was Stephens's famous "cornerstone" speech that has been most often cited as the clearest articulation by a high-ranking Confederate official of the South's views on the importance of slavery's preservation. It resonates particularly since Stephens was far from a fire-eating radical; he was about as moderate in his political views as it was possible to have been. For at least a generation before the Civil War, Northerners had criticized the South for not living up to the noble promises of the Declaration of Independence, which stated that the United States believed in universal freedom and equality. Lincoln had once said that those who deny freedom to others deserve it not for themselves. In an attempt to finally put that issue to rest, Stephens argued that any ideas expressed in the Declaration of Independence that hinted that *all* men were created equal and possessed the same basic natural rights of life, liberty, and the pursuit of happiness "were fundamentally wrong." Such bizarre ideas, he said, "rested upon assumption of the equality of races. This was an error.... Our new government is founded upon exactly the opposite idea; its foundations are laid, its cornerstone rests, upon the great truth that the negro is not equal to the white man; that slavery, subordination to the superior race is his natural and moral condition."[4]

Protecting slavery was just as important to North Carolinians as it was to those living in the Cotton South. In his excellent study of antebellum politics in the state, Marc Kruman demonstrated that in North Carolina politics the Whigs and Democrats fought hard and often to prove to the state's voters that their party was the strongest defender of slavery. "From the beginning of the second party system in North Carolina," Kruman has argued, "Whigs and Democrats each contended that they alone were the best defenders of the South's institutions and that their opponents' credentials as defenders of slavery and southern rights were somehow suspect." For example, when the Democrats argued for annexation of Texas they did so in North Carolina by pointing out that doing so would keep Texas from being taken by abolitionist England, which would then launch antislavery attacks on the South from there. Whigs, who tended to be skeptical of annexation, did so in the state by arguing that annexation actually did more harm to slaveholders' rights than good. Texas, North Carolina Whigs pointed out, could be divided into multiple states but only a minority of them would be conducive to slavery. Thus, in the long run, annexation brought in more free states and with them more enemies of slavery. The 1848 presidential election was another example of how central slavery was to state political activities. Whigs told North Carolinians to vote for their man, Zachary Taylor, because as a slaveholder with plantations in Louisiana he was safe on slavery while Democrats said to vote for their candidate, Lewis Cass, because he had proven his willingness to protect Southern slaveholders' rights by coming out against the Wilmot Proviso.[5]

Throughout the 1850s North Carolina newspapers, the political parties' mouthpieces, routinely pointed out how the "other" party was unsafe on slavery and how failure to support their party's candidate kept the South from being able to protect itself from the growing antislavery movement in the North. In 1854 Wadesboro's *North Carolina Argus*, a Whig paper, printed a series of resolutions passed a few years earlier by the Democratic Convention of Massachusetts as a way to point out the dangers of voting Democratic. The very first resolution was political treason in the state by the mid–1850s: "Resolved, That was are opposed to slavery in every form and color, and in favor of freedom and free soil wherever man lives throughout God's heritage." The fourth resolution was also shocking and illuminating: "That we are opposed to the extension of slavery to free Territories, and in favor of the exercise of all constitutional and necessary means to restrict it...." If a Massachusetts Democratic meeting could be rationalized as an aberration given that it lay in the very heart of Yankeedom, the *Argus* revealed in 1857 that similar unsafe statements were made in Virginia. There the party was credited with saying "that the Democratic party ever has been, or is now, a *pro slavery* party, we deny." Democratic papers often did the very same thing and each party's newspapers accused the other of letting the South down by refusing to support their candidate and provide a united front against abolitionist fanatics.[6]

That slavery was at the heart of political races should come as no surprise. Obviously the significant number of people directly benefiting from the institution economically were worried about the institution's future, but too often it is forgotten that slavery was believed to provide important benefits for the non-slaveholding majority that they certainly thought worth preserving. There developed in the antebellum South, as part of the general pro-slavery argument, the idea that slavery assured all whites true social equality. No matter what differences existed in wealth between planters, yeomen, and poor whites, socially they were equal. Southerners argued that the peculiar institution could provide this sort of egalitarian society because, as one proclaimed, it "promotes equality among the free by dispensing with grades and castes among them...." That ardent defender of slavery's many benefits, George Fitzhugh, claimed that unlike in the free states, whites in the slave states "are equal in privilege, if not in wealth. Our slaves ... do all the hard work, and fill all menial position." Alabama political leader William L. Yancey once proclaimed to an audience: "Your fathers and my father built this government on two ideas, the first is that the white race is the citizen, and the master race, and the white man is the equal of every other white man." In 1848 John C. Calhoun argued that in the South "the two great divisions of society are not the rich and the poor, but white and black; with all the former, the poor as well as the rich, belong to the upper class, and are respected as equals ... and hence have a position of pride of character that neither poverty nor misfortune can deprive them."

North Carolinians certainly felt no differently. In 1847 the Raleigh *Standard* had argued: "No negroes are born free and upon equality with white men, but all white men are entitled, at the proper age, to the privileges of citizenship, and all are equal." This was a full year before Calhoun's statement and fourteen years ahead of Stephens's "cornerstone" speech. The *Asheville News*, based in a part of the state where slavery was least entrenched and, according to much popular mythology, where concerns for slavery's protection were minimal, echoed the *Standard* and anticipated Stephens in 1859, arguing that in the South, "society rests upon natural distinctions, where all those whom God has created equal are placed on the same broad ground of an equal citizenship, and the inferior negro race ... [is in its] normal condition of social subordination...." In 1860 the same paper ran a diatribe against the North's inequitable free labor society where the "wage slaves" toiled in poverty and were degraded and treated as inferiors by their employers. Further east, the region where the 18th North Carolina would be raised, one of the most widely read newspapers, the *Fayetteville Observer*, also claimed that that the poor and working class whites of the North were not treated as equals by their wealthier neighbors, employers, and leaders. The lower class whites were generally exploited in the free labor states, it was claimed, where "almost universally, there is no sympathy between the servant and the master or mistress, no attachments,... no nursing of a sick servant, no employment of one except while he or she remains well enough to work. When sick they are discharged, to get well as they can, or to die or starve, as the chance may be." To antebellum North Carolinians there was a clear and qualitative difference between life (for whites) in the free states and the slave states. From their point of view true social and political equality for the non-slaveholders was intimately linked to slavery's existence, and where slavery did not exist, great social and political inequality did. Understanding that is key to understanding why the non-slaveholding majority in North Carolina was just as worried, perhaps even more worried, about outside attempts to restrict or take away entirely the one thing that made them equal to their wealthier brethren.[7]

Most whites in the state understood not only the social and political benefits of living in a slave society as opposed to a free labor one, they also tended to believe that slave labor society was far less destructive to them physically. Life in the free states was thought to be more unstable and unhealthy than life in the slaveholding states. One Raleigh newspaper in 1859 argued that in the North every political or social question "excites commotion, and is deeply imbued with an element of fanaticism." Of course the antislavery forces were the main cause of all that unhealthy "commotion." "Abolitionism, the head and front of a family of isms as numerous as the catalogues of folly and wickedness as capable of containing ... is still daily bringing forth its new progenies to excite the base passions of the human heart, and to curse the country." In 1858 the *Fayetteville Observer* reported: "We think that some of the people in the Northern cities are beginning to see, what has long been apparent to Southern people, that there is far more danger of popular commotion and violence there than here." The paper went on to chastise "those Northern fanatics, who distress themselves about Southern institutions, [who] would do well to ponder over" the more numerous and dangerous problems in their own section of the country.

From Raleigh came the concern that in the free states people were so consumed with petty financial issues that their "whole nervous system becomes morbidly excited by the daily anxiety attending the rise and fall of stocks." The result was that many became "hopelessly demented." In December 1859 the Greensboro *Patriot and Flag* echoed the idea that the South's slave based agricultural society was more conducive to good mental health than free labor capitalism. According to one article, businessmen become greedy and obsession for money "disturbs the brain by violently exciting hope and fear." The Charlotte *Western Democrat* even claimed to have evidence that life expectancy was shorter in the free states than in the slave states. "Gentlemen," which would have been defined in the story as the planter elite, lived the longest at sixty-eight years. Next were "agriculturalists" who lived to be sixty-three on average. Then, as one gets to professions most associated with the North the numbers fall precipitously; seeing even fifty years of age was but a dim hope for most Northerners according to this piece. "Traders" lived to be forty-six, "mechanics and manufacturers" to forty-three, and "machinists" could expect to keel over at the tender age of thirty-six! Here again is more evidence that one did not have to own slaves to perceive that living in a slave society had benefits for all whites living within it. To take away slavery would be to impose the Northern free labor society; to many non-slaveholders in the Old North State, this clearly meant imposing a less stable, less healthy way of life upon them.[8]

Like most other white Southerners in the mid-nineteenth century, North Carolina whites tended to be white supremacists who could see nothing but horror in the prospect of slavery's death and the possibility that with it would come that most terrifying specter, social and political equality with black people. "Races," a Charlotte newspaper argued in 1857, "have never amalgamated without virtual destruction. Wherever it has been attempted, almost without exception, the superior race has sunk to the low and degraded position of the inferior." Such a position was not unique to white North Carolinians or Southerners; at this same time Westerners — be they American or European — would have found little to quarrel with in the Charlotte paper's position on race. White Northerners certainly did not and they enacted all sorts of laws to separate the races and keep African Americans subordinate in their states; some even passed laws barring free blacks from settling down in their states. The point here is not to condemn any past generation or group of people for holding views that are disapproved of today. Rather, the point is merely to help demonstrate why maintaining slavery would have been important to virtually every white North Carolinian before the Civil War, not just those who actually owned slaves.[9]

When the term "abolitionism" was uttered, it was widely understood that it meant far more than simply the end of a particular labor system. For most whites in the state, the term was synonymous with the elevation of an inferior population to social and political equality with themselves. Such a vision of the future was truly horrifying to many at the time and most viewed the Republican Party as being in league with the more radical abolitionists to bring just such a social and cultural calamity down upon North Carolinians' heads. To many in the state, John Brown's raid on the federal arsenal at Harpers Ferry, Virginia, in October 1859, was clear evidence that the abolitionists and their political wing, the "Black Republicans" meant "to overthrow the supremacy of the white man of the South and equalize the races — in short, to compel others to disregard the distinctions of nature and fraternize with negroes as [they do]." The *North Carolina Whig* related a story illustrating just how devoted the abolitionists and their allies were to racial equality in

1859. According to this story the writer witnessed an abolitionist entering a restaurant where he was accompanied to the table by a black friend, whom he had the audacity to bring to the table with him as an equal dinner companion. The owner did remove the black man from the dining room, but after the meal this abolitionist tried to cheer his friend up over being kicked out of the dining room. As part of those efforts, he "put his arm around the black fondly caressing him," which the writer referred to as a "disgusting maneuver" because of the intimacy and social equality it represented. But, of course, such was just the sort of warped activity abolitionism encouraged. In the early days of the war, another state newspaper repeated a well-worn theme that abolitionism was dedicated to racial leveling. "The object of this Abolition war," a contributor to the *North Carolina Argus* railed in early May 1861, "is to enforce the political and social equality of the races." The war waged "against us by the Abolitionists, not only seeks to subvert our liberties, destroy our institutions and subjugate us, but it also aims to put us on an equality with negroes. It is a war of Abolitionists waged to destroy slavery and bind the races into equality."

Often the fears that equality with blacks was at the top of the abolitionists' wish list to be granted just as soon as the Republicans got control of Washington were expressed in the most intimate and therefore most lurid and terrifying terms. The charge was made that should the abolitionists ever come to control the government, their calls for social equality with black people would automatically lead to legions of black men and white women approaching marriage altars all across the South. One story in a state newspaper told the story of one Sarah Judson of Michigan who, at the tender age of eighteen, was forced by her father to marry "a black buck negro." Of course, this was because her father was a "red-hot abolitionist." He was portrayed as such a zealot in the cause of racial equality that he would force his only daughter to marry a black man; this was a strong and frightening image in the 1850s. The message was clear; if he would give his own daughter to "a black buck negro" he would have no problem giving away other people's daughters and would do so if he and his political allies ever got into a position of power. Another state news outlet pointed out that in Canada, which had abolished slavery, interracial marriages were quite common. The message: first slavery is outlawed and then the interracial marriages begin. "It is the commonest thing to find in all Canada," the paper argued, "burly, black buck African husbands actually legally married to white females. In fact it is the rule rather than the exception." Wherever abolitionism took root, one North Carolinian concluded, whites were "willing to take rank with a subordinate race, and eat, sleep, intermarry and affiliate with negroes." Again, the point is that if the non-slaveholding majority believed that such dire consequences went hand in hand with Northern-imposed emancipation, it is not difficult to see why they would have had a keen interest in avoiding such a social and cultural calamity despite not owning even one slave themselves.[10]

Of course one needs to also keep in mind that the term *slavery*—as North Carolinians and most other antebellum Southerners understood it—conjured up radically different images in their minds than it does today. Where modern readers see a brutal, exploitive institution with no redeeming qualities whatsoever, they tended to see a benign system where both whites and blacks coexisted in a mutually beneficial relationship. Whites enjoyed economic and social benefits, and the slaves enjoyed a quality of life well above what they would have had in Africa and one that was even better, most in the state believed, than the poor deluded white "wage slaves" and free blacks of the North. In other words, being pro-slavery in the 1850s and 1860s was not something one would have been ashamed of in North Carolina. Talking about the benefits of slavery was not something done in secret or whispered in hushed tones among trusted friends because the society and culture of that period did not attach any of the moral stigmas to slavery that exist today.

Most white North Carolinians were like other whites of the period in that they accepted that darker skinned people generally, and black people most specifically, were innately inferior to whites in every conceivable way. In the minds of many enslaving black people was doing them a favor because doing so exposed the slaves to a vast culture they could learn from, as well as provided them with a higher standard of living, and introduced them to Christianity. One eastern Carolinian spoke for many when he wrote in 1856:

> It is true that more than nine-tenths of the negroes at the South are still slaves; but is slavery under Christian masters in America, the same evil with slavery under heathen tyrants in Africa? Degraded as these slaves may still be compared with the sons of the pilgrims in New England, or even with the mass of laborers in some of the enlightened countries in Europe, can 3,000,000 or 1,000,000 negroes, bond or free be found in any part of the world, who can compare, for good condition, physical, intellectual, and moral, with the 3,000,000 slaves at the South?

Another North Carolina writer argued in the columns of the *Argus*:

> The institution of African slavery as it exists in these Southern states is a good thing; it improves the condition of the African. That race, as the Scriptures teach us, and as all history proves, is laboring under a curse of inferiority; ... left to themselves they make no intellectual, social, or moral improvement.

From the *North Carolina Presbyterian* came the following in 1860:

> [Slaves] have risen from extreme barbarism to a fair standard of civilization; from heathenism to Christianity. This servile condition is the best possible,

at present, for the negro; nowhere in the world and under no circumstances is the African so happy, so respectable and so *self-respecting* as the family servant in our southern homes. His situation is incomparably better than that of the African in his native jungles, or the free negro at the North.

"Contact with a white man under the restraints of our institutions," one Tar Heel asserted in 1859, "induces a material elevation in his character, but left to himself the negro relapses into his normal condition of barbarism. Involuntary servitude is the only sphere in which he can be useful, and evidently the condition God intended he should fill in contact with the Anglo-Saxon race." Just a few weeks later a Raleigh newspaper said much the same thing, expressing the widely held belief that the "true condition of the African race is that of dependence on the white man, or in other words, slavery." When North Carolinians defended slavery they honestly viewed themselves as defending a system that was humane and that sensibly recognized the so-called natural (and divinely created) deficiencies of black people and put them in a position where they could do the most good for themselves and others.[11]

If people wanted proof of how good black people had it under slavery, all they had to do was pick up their newspapers and read stories about how miserable free blacks' lives were. In 1854 a story was printed that showed that the free black population in the North was declining by eight percent every ten years while the enslaved population of the South was growing by twenty percent each decade, leading the writer to conclude: "While we hear so much said of slavery and the Slave States, the condition of the free negroes, under our own eyes, is every day becoming worse and worse." In 1858 the *Fayetteville Observer* gloated that a group of emancipated slaves in Virginia was mired in poverty. "The number of free negroes now living there is between two and three hundred, and a more miserable, destitute community is not to be found, though they have, and always had the best of opportunities for improvement." The family that freed them had made, the paper said, a well intentioned mistake given the innate limitations of black people.

One common method of proving how much better off slaves were than free blacks was to expose how horrible life was in places where governments, blinded by muddle-headed philanthropy, had set black people free. The British-owned Caribbean islands were a favorite target. One North Carolina writer related in an article that the English had discovered that freeing the slaves there led to misery for all, landowners and free blacks alike. "The negro himself, though he has become free, has not become wise or industrious. [English] planters have not found that free blacks make good laborers. [Their] colonies have not risen in prosperity and affluence above the slaveholding colonies of other States...." This would not have surprised the Fayetteville area writer who pointed out in 1858 that whenever the slave performs labor "he performs it badly and would not perform it at all if he were not compelled." Similar conditions were, not surprisingly to readers at the time, reported in Liberia, a colony in Africa set aside for free and emancipated blacks because the citizens there were "too lazy to work." Canada was also a popular target. "One hears and sees much in Canada of runaway negroes. Their condition is described by all impartial observers as pitiable in the extreme." Freeing slaves was anything but humane or generous from the perspective of many North Carolinians; it was downright cruel. By turning slaves loose, by denying them the benevolent and guiding hand of whites, abolition amounted to "sending ... negroes off to starve and die."[12]

If the state's newspapers are to be believed, those slaves that were either emancipated or escaped (usually, it was claimed, with the help of abolitionist fanatics) quickly discovered how much better life was as a piece of property in North Carolina than as a human being somewhere else. Stories of African Americans voluntarily returning to slavery or waxing nostalgic about the good life they had lost when they became free are not difficult to find and were taken to be irrefutable evidence of the peculiar institution's benign and paternalistic qualities. In one story a group of forty emancipated slaves from Virginia had been resettled with some Ohio Quakers but after only a few weeks in freedom, "One of the children had been stolen, and several had died for want of attention and the necessaries of life. They begged [to be allowed] to return ... to Virginia and go into slavery." In a brief article, "A Nut for the Abolitionists," it was reported that a slave named Watkins Love, "by his own voluntary act ... chose rather than remain a free negro, subject to all the disabilities of that unfavored class, to enslave himself again...." One former slave was reported to have contacted his former master and related that he "was tired and sick of the North; ... that nobody took care of him, and that most of the time he could not get anything to eat." A female slave, Emily, was reported to be coming back from Liberia in 1859 because she "is sick of freedom and prefers living with her mistress in the Old North State [to] being fleeced by abolition friends in Liberia." One poor deluded runaway from Ohio "soon learned of the differences between the home he had left and the disappointment to which he was doomed in the one he had found, and wished himself, as he expressed it, 'wid marsa and missus in old Kentucky again.'" From New York came the story of a manumitted slave who, "having tasted the sweets of liberty, voluntarily returned to bondage." This came as no surprise to a visitor to North Carolina who wrote to one newspaper that he observed that

> in return for food, clothing, house room, medical attendance, and support in old age, about one-third of the labor which is required of the white man in most countries is demanded of the black. He performs it badly and would not

perform it at all if he were not compelled. The rest of his time is spent singing, dancing, laughing and chattering, and bringing up pigs and chickens.

This same writer pointed out the reason that slaves had it so good despite their general laziness was that the "Southerner has been reared among them from his childhood, and in general, has a tenderness and affection for them...."[13]

Such stories may not have been fabrications; it is entirely possible that a few emancipated or runaway slaves did voluntarily return to bondage. Life in the North was no picnic for a black person in the antebellum era, and the possibility that a few former slaves determined that their material conditions were better as slaves is not ridiculously remote. But, this evidence was used in a highly selective, self-serving, and altogether misleading way. These stories were told as if they were typical examples of how former slaves reacted to freedom in order to prove that slavery was a humane institution as practiced in the South; after all, if the slaves preferred slavery then who were the abolitionists and other misguided Northern philanthropists to complain about its supposed horrors? Of course, totally ignored were the many thousands, like Frederick Douglass, who gained their freedom during the antebellum era and never even contemplated returning to bondage.

The idea that North Carolinians, even the non-slaveholding majority, were ambivalent about slavery and its future seems very difficult to sustain. A significant number of the state's white families had a direct economic interest in the institution and many of those who did not hoped to at some future point. Whites in the state saw it as the foundation of a society that offered equality for all whites and a good life for the slaves themselves, so good they seemed to prefer it to freedom. The alternative was the North's free labor society, which, if imposed as abolitionists and their Republican allies were thought to desire, would ruin North Carolinians' economic lives, destroy universal white male equality, and bring the horrors of miscegenation. When it is clear what slavery meant to North Carolinians at the time it is not difficult to understand why most would be pro-slavery and would be willing to go to great lengths to preserve the institution that produced such great and widespread benefits.

But protection of slavery is only part of the reason most North Carolina whites ultimately left the Union and were among the Confederacy's staunchest and most formidable defenders during the Civil War. To them slavery represented something more than just an economic and social system that provided them with a number of benefits; it also represented their ability to be first-class citizens with the freedom to live their lives as they saw fit. If their property rights were restricted or taken away against their will by Northerners, then they saw themselves as losing something very important; they would have lost their equal status with the free states in the Union. To many North Carolinians' way of thinking, they would become mere serfs to their "Black Republican" lords, a situation that could not and would not be tolerated. As one North Carolina newspaper put it: "This Union must be a union of coequal States, or it will cease to be a Union as formed by our fathers." In early 1860 a Raleigh newspaper articulated the feelings of most in the state that "the Union of the States can only be perpetuated so long as it continues to be a Union of equals. We are still devoted to it, and would behold its dissolution with profound regret; yet *if we cannot hold our slave property, and at the same time enjoy repose and tranquility in the Union*" North Carolinians will be forced to consider other arrangements.[14]

North Carolina newspaper coverage during the late 1850s reflects the citizens' view that tampering with slavery represented a corrupt conspiracy to undermine their constitutional rights and liberties. One called attempts to restrict slavery's expansion into the territories "open resistance to the laws which recognize [slavery's] existence and are intended to secure the rights of the South." Both the Constitution and the Supreme Court, via the Dred Scott decision, clearly recognized "the right of the people of any State to take their slaves into the territories of the United States," and any Northern interference with this right represented a diminution of North Carolinians' and other Southerners' equal rights. One newspaper warned readers in 1856 to really examine James Buchanan's statements and actions to make sure he would "protect the Southern people in their rights." Buchanan, after all, had voted not to allow Missouri to enter as a slave state back in 1819, a major red flag. From Raleigh came the position:

> Motives of philanthropy may be assigned for this <u>unwarrantable interference</u>; and weak men may persuade themselves for a moment that they are laboring in the cause of humanity, and asserting the rights of the human race; but everyone, upon sober reflection, will see that nothing but mischief can come from <u>these improper assaults upon</u> the feelings and <u>rights of others</u>.

In the wake of John Brown's attempt to wipe out slavery by force at Harpers Ferry, a leading paper asserted that North Carolina "is stronger today in its <u>rights and institutions</u> than it was before this attempt to subvert them." A Salisbury contributor warned readers that the Brown raid "was not simply an outburst of a crazy man with a few followers." Rather, it was the logical outgrowth of "the systematic and persistent efforts of men of all degrees in the Northern States, to form there a public sentiment at war with us and our institutions." From Asheville at about the same time came an article emphasizing "the great importance of [Southern Whigs and Democrats] uniting under one banner for the defense of their rights and the protection of their property under the Constitution against the progressive assaults of Black

Republican abolitionists." This same paper urged all in the state to vote for John Breckenridge, the Southern Democratic nominee because he was the only candidate "able to withstand the assaults of the Black Republicans upon the property of the South...." An eastern Carolina Whig paper countered that John Bell was the best choice for all Tar Heels because he "is perfectly safe for the South" and is alone "above reproach and above suspicion" because his "long and brilliant political record" proves that he "looks upon slavery *not* as an evil and a curse ... but that he regards it as a blessing both to master and to the slave — a blessing alike to the South, to the Union, and to the world." Whether one was a Democrat or a Whig, the bottom line was, as one put it in 1859:

> Negroes are property under the laws of fifteen States of the Confederacy, and are recognized as property by the Federal Constitution. Whatever may be the views of individuals in regard to the wisdom, morality, or policy of such laws, they are as much bound to respect that species of property as any other article which is the subject of ownership.

Northerners were absolutely free to disapprove of Southern institutions, the most common euphemism for slavery, but they were not free to take those institutions away from Southerners. If Northerners wanted to keep the Union together, one writer argued, they needed to immediately cease "their wild and unprincipled crusade against the institution of negro slavery."[15]

Clearly, in the years leading to the election of Abraham Lincoln, North Carolinians showed themselves to be firm supporters of slavery and resistant to any attempts by outsiders to restrict or abolish slaveholders' rights. This was not because they were particularly or uniquely evil people; it was because from their point of view slavery was an economic, social, and political blessing for all — slaveowners, non-slaveowners, and slaves. Taking away slavery would mean taking away all of those blessings and substituting a nightmarish new reality of economic ruin and black equality. But as has been introduced here and will be discussed in more detail in the next chapter, North Carolina citizens saw in their ability to control the status of slavery a symbol of their sacred freedom and equality in the nation. Their and the South's ability to move about the country with their slave property and to choose for themselves whether to own slaves was the political barometer measuring their freedom and equality with Northerners. If circumstances ever reached the point where Northerners (Republicans specifically) proved that they were no longer willing to work with the South to ensure that North Carolinians had all their traditional and equal rights, then they may have to leave the Union for which they expressed so much devotion. The question in late 1860 and early 1861 was whether the election of Lincoln constituted the sort of dire and direct threat to slavery and "Southern rights" that the Deep South, starting with South Carolina, determined that it was.

Chapter 2

Secession and the Formation of the 18th North Carolina

In the months between John Brown's raid at Harpers Ferry in October 1859 and Abraham Lincoln's victory in November 1860 bringing a "Black Republican" to the White House, North Carolinians expressed their concerns about the safety of slavery and their equal rights. Fire-eating secessionist radicals were in relatively short supply in North Carolina at this time, but Brown's activities, and especially the connection of at least some Republican Party members to it, caused the state's largely pro–Union citizenry to contemplate seriously for the first time the possibility of secession. As Joseph Carlyle Sitterson observed in his study of North Carolina during the secession crisis, "the John Brown raid produced among conservatives and radicals alike a determination that the rights of the South must be maintained at all hazards." On December 7, 1859, Governor John Ellis and the council of state articulated North Carolina's position regarding the Brown raid (the state legislature would have done this but was not in session at the time) in a resolution that, in part, read: "1. that North Carolina was prepared at all times to sustain Virginia in its efforts to defend the rights of the slaveholding states; 2. that 'if we cannot hold our slave property, and at the same time enjoy repose and tranquility in the Union, we will be constrained, ... to establish new forms and provide new forms and provide new guards for our security and well being.'"[1]

In the fear and excitement caused by the Brown raid, there was a noticeable increase in support for the idea of seceding should a Republican win the 1860 presidential election. This was especially true in the southeastern counties where the 18th North Carolina would draw its membership. Three of the regiment's companies were from Wilmington and in January 1860 the city's Democratic paper, the *Journal*, reflected the more fiery reactions to Harpers Ferry and its alleged connection to the Republican Party. Since the Republicans were part of the planning of the Brown raid and since they had taken a firm stand against the admission of any new slave territories, a contributor to the paper asked rhetorically, "What hope can even the most sanguine and Union-loving of us all entertain, when this fanaticism seats itself in the Presidential chair? In that case, will there be any escape from the final *catastrophe*, the *irrepressible conflict*, so often predicted and gloried in by the apostles of Abolitionism?" Could North Carolina remain in the Union, the *North Carolina Standard* asked in November 1859, if the Republicans won high office? Could it remain in the Union with men like Benjamin Wade, Charles Sumner, Joshua Giddings, and especially William Seward (assumed by most at this point as the front runner for the Republican nomination) who called the Harpers Ferry raid one of the "acts of highest heroism"? How could the state hope to enjoy its rights when the government was run by a party that believed that the quickest route to becoming a hero "is to go [to] the South and excite the slaves to rise and cut the throats of their white masters"? A New Bern writer railed that the Harpers Ferry plotters, "composed of the political leaders, preachers, press, ... and the popular mass at the North, openly applaud the criminals and the crime."

In April 1860 the Fayetteville *Weekly Courier* echoed the more radical Wilmington paper in suggesting that the election of a Republican in November portended a dire threat to the state and region. The Republican Party, it said,

> disregards alike the rights and honor of the South, and threatens her very existence — it regards the Constitution of our fathers as a violation of divine law, and therefore not to be obeyed — it tramples under foot all our Constitutional rights.... The very existence of such a party is a standing insult, and menace to the Southern States.

This same edition declared:

> The principle feature in the approaching canvass is whether we of the South shall continue as we have under the Constitution from its adoption to manage our own domestic and local affairs, or have the work done for us [by a party] whose ideas are foreign to our wants, habits and conditions of *life*.

Another frightened voice from the eastern part of the state warned that "Black Republicansism contemplates the vassalage of the South to the North." From Charlotte came the warning that the Brown situation proved that the Republicans were willing to resort to extreme physical actions to take Southerners' rights from them. If the Brown-lovers should get power in Washington it would mean "the lash upon our shoulders." There can be no doubt that John Brown had helped create a tense situation in North Carolina and made people seriously contemplate their safety in the Union and to be more open to the possibility of a future out of it.[2]

Though the Brown raid excited passions in the state to a white-hot level, it seems that once many North Carolinians had expressed their shock and outrage through angry (and sometimes extreme) rants in the newspapers, passions cooled considerably. But the lid to Pandora's box had been lifted in the sense that the state's citizens, wherever they fell on the political spectrum, were more acutely concerned about how to defeat what they saw as a very real threat to their individual liberties in the Republican Party and what actions, if any, ought to be taken should the great calamity of a "Black Republican" victory in November come to pass. As had been the case for most of the antebellum period, both Democrats and Whigs articulated differing methods of protecting North Carolinians' property rights and equal standing with Northerners in the Union, each arguing that only their party was capable of achieving these critical goals in the face of "Black Republican" attacks. Democrats in the state tended to insist that the test of whether the Republicans would recognize and respect Southern rights was by repudiating the free soil plank in their platform. For them popular sovereignty was not enough, Republicans must overtly acknowledge slaveholders' positive right to take their property into the territories in the same way that Northerners were permitted to do. Whigs tended to be less insistent on overt recognition of slaveholders' rights to take their slaves into the territories. They were willing to see it as a show of good faith if the Republicans merely backed off the strict insistence that not another foot of slave territory enter the Union. John Gilmer of North Carolina, who worked tirelessly for compromise with Republicans to avoid destroying the Union, tried to explain to New Yorker Thurlow Weed that the strict non-extension position was the biggest obstacle to meaningful dialogue between North and South. If the Republicans would give up the principle of non-extension — which Gilmer argued was a chimera in most territories anyway because of climate and soil — "this useless and foolish abstraction of Congressional protection to slavery in the Territories" would be removed. Nobody understood better than Gilmer, so moderate and astute a politician that Lincoln offered him a position in his cabinet after he was elected (which he declined), that the people of North Carolina were very agitated over what a Republican in the White House potentially meant to their definition of liberty and that their loyalty to the Union was based on their conviction that their property rights and political equality continued to be safe.[3]

When the election actually came and Lincoln emerged victorious, a new reality set in for North Carolinians. No longer was the question what would be done *if* Lincoln won; now the question was what to do now that he had actually won. On the one hand were those who believed that Lincoln's victory by itself was cause for secession. The *Wilmington Herald* spoke for many in that camp when it declared a few days after Lincoln's victory was announced that his victory

> means a sweeping away of all the guaranties of State equality in the Union — ...It also means that slave property is to be excluded from the Territories, and new slave States from the Union.— it means that the whole influence of the Federal Government is to be cast into the scale of opposition to the institutions of our section of the Union....

A secessionist from Charlotte said in November 1860 that North Carolina should join the Cotton South right away. As he saw it, the question is: "Shall we remain in the Union under Black Republican rule, and give up our property, or shall we go out with our sister States and retain it, and with it our honor and self-respect?" A North Carolina Democrat said in late November that if the state did not secede it would "see *our institutions* subverted, our wealth gradually swept away, and our fair land over-run by the Goths and Vandals of Northern fanaticism."

On Thursday, January 3, 1861, a secession flag was raised in Wilmington that afternoon at the corner of Market and Front Streets. The red flag with a single star in the center and three smaller stars in each of the big star's corners representing the fifteen slave states was raised to much cheering and celebratory cannon fire from the banks of the Cape Fear River. Later that evening Robert H. Cowan, who would lead the 18th North Carolina through its bloody baptism at Hanover Court House and throughout the long, hot, combat-filled summer of 1862, gave a pro-secession speech at a local theater that was well received. "He is a fine specimen of the popular orator," the *Wilmington Herald* reported, "and there were passages in his speech on this occasion, of genuine eloquence, such as is seldom enjoyed." But such calls for disunion because Lincoln was elected and that victory spelled utter doom for the state did not represent the majority of North Carolinians in late 1860 and early 1861. Governor John Ellis said in a letter to South Carolina Governor Gist: "Upon the whole, I am decidedly of [the] opinion that a majority of our people would not consider ... [Lincoln's election] as sufficient ground for dissolving the Union of the States."[4]

And he was absolutely correct. Many, even in the southeastern corner of the state where pro-secession sentiment was strongest, questioned both the legality and the wisdom of secession. While the Lost Cause tradition, which emerged after the war and exerted great influence on how the war era was remembered, held that the South united in what they saw as their constitutional right to secede, the reality is that strong arguments were made in North Carolina against the notion that such an action was constitutionally permissible. In November 1860 the *Wilmington Herald*, the city's more moderate

Whig newspaper, argued that the "right of one State to withdraw from the Union and to break up the Government is utterly at war with all the principles of the Constitution." Take the amendment process, for example, the paper said. If amendments can be passed over the objections of individual states, as the Constitution clearly provides for, then the notion that the states are sovereign entities is obviously flawed. A set of resolutions introduced in the legislature by Dennis Ferebee of Camden in November said the same basic thing, declaring that "the Constitution of the United States is not a compact of sovereign states [and] that no state can withdraw from the Union without revolution." A Greensboro man made a distinction between secession, which he said was not a right under the Constitution, and revolution in the name of preserving liberty, which "is an inherent right in every form of Government." Such, after all, had been the justification for the American Revolution in 1776.[5]

Generally most North Carolinians seem to have accepted the right of secession in the abstract, though it is not as clear whether they believed states had the legal, constitutional right to leave the Union if they wanted to or whether they viewed secession more as a moral right, one that offered a state a way to get away from a corrupt centralized power. While most believed that states could, if their citizens were threatened by tyranny and oppression, secede and form a new nation with other like-minded states, few Tar Heels viewed Lincoln's election by itself as sufficient cause to tear the nation apart. "Who can prepare a declaration of independence," one North Carolina official asked, "appealing to a candid world for its approbation and sympathy, upon the ground that we have been outvoted in an election in which we took the chances of success, and a candidate has been elected who, however obnoxious, we have not deemed unworthy to compete with us for our votes?" A Salisbury Whig spoke for many, saying that "while determined *not* to submit to the administration of the government on Black Republican principles, it would be our duty to give Mr. Lincoln a trial and preserve the government from disruption and destitution." A New Bern man agreed, saying he "would much prefer trying Lincoln to seeing the Government broken up, being conscious that Revolution with all its horrors must follow dissolution." A Wilkes County meeting held in the wake of Lincoln's election resolved in late December that "we do not see in [Republicans'] election alone, sufficient cause for the dismemberment of the best government vouchsafed by God to man." "We rejoice to know," a piedmont Tar Heel wrote, "that in North Carolina there are but few, very few, who regard the election of Lincoln ... a sufficient cause of disunion."[6]

That South Carolina had determined otherwise was, in most North Carolinians' opinion, a rash mistake. In fact a lot of the citizens of the Old North State were quite put out with South Carolina and the Gulf States for being so impulsive, and many were angry that they were pressuring North Carolina to leap blindly into the abyss with them. Even in a city like Wilmington, where supporters of disunion were more numerous than in most other parts of the state, the *Herald* lashed out: "People of North Carolina, shall this programme [secession because of Lincoln's election alone] be carried out? Will you suffer yourselves to be spit upon in this way? Are you *submissionists* to the dictation of South Carolina? ... Are you to be called *cowards* because you do not follow the crazy lead of that crazy state?" A Raleigh man said if "South Carolina wishes to leave the Union, let her go and welcome, but when she tries to involve States which do not choose to follow her insane example" its leaders are going too far. Another eastern Tar Heel demanded to know in November if others in the state would "*submit*, to be dragged into revolution and anarchy, and all to please the State of South Carolina, who, by her insufferable arrogance, and conceited self-importance, has been a consistent source of annoyance and disquietude to the whole country, North and South, for the last thirty years." Such sentiments were echoed in New Bern. There one newspaper criticized South Carolina for thinking that the election results were sufficient cause for secession and for trying to convince North Carolina of the same thing. The writer expressed his opinion and anger that "they are so conceited that they think South Carolina is the great centre and that as she acts so must the entire South." Sampson County, in the sandhills region many future members of the 18th North Carolina called home, resolved at a public meeting in February "that we disapprove of the hasty and inconsiderate action of South Carolina in seceding from the Union, and that we consider said action as injurious to the cause of the South and tending to plunge the country into civil war." Another exclaimed:

> The *North* Carolinian who has not State pride sufficient to make him indignantly spurn any attempt of our Southern neighbor to dragoon this State into treason and civil war, is a bastard son of the soil on which was first sounded the key-note of American liberty [reference to the Mecklenburg Resolves].

Whatever the future held, a Wilmington writer said, "the Old North State will stand firm, whatever may be her determination, that she will act for *herself*, and not for the 'Cotton States.'"[7]

So while the men who would shortly become members of the 18th North Carolina were probably not, generally speaking, fire-eating secessionists, their unionism was always conditional. From the mountains to the coast there were frequent expressions of love for the Union and criticism of the Deep South states for seceding. Many felt that if the Republicans were willing to compromise on certain issues, like backing off their hard-line stand against slavery's expansion one more inch into the territories and expressing greater willingness to enforce the Fugitive Slave Law, then there was no reason to secede; their rights would be respected. In fact, many North Carolinians believed that their rights were actually better protected in the Union than out of it, which helps explain their greater willingness to look for common ground with the new administration before bolting the Union. They understood that given their proximity to the North that a civil war would be more destructive to Upper South states like North Carolina and Virginia. Civil war would also cause such a chaotic atmosphere that it would be more difficult for slaveholders to hang onto their property. And when the slaves took advantage of the opportunity to run off to the North, there was absolutely no way to get them back again because the Fugitive Slave Law only required the United States to return slaves to states in the Union — yet one more reason why secession needed to be avoided unless it was absolutely necessary. As a Wilmington commentator noted, secession may be a right but there are many rights "which it would be very unwise and impolitic to exercise."[8]

That North Carolinians viewed secession as a cure that was worse than the disease before Lincoln took office in March 1861 could be seen throughout the state. A Wadesboro writer warned in November: "Peaceable secession is an impossibility. The State that secedes must pass through a baptism of blood, in which the garments of her surrounding sisters will be freely dipped...." From Fayetteville came the warning that civil war was "the worst of all earthly evils." "The truth is," a Greensboro article pointed out, "the man who speaks lightly of dissolving the Union, is a simpleton or a demagogue." The article went on to say what most in the state believed, which was: "We believe the Union and the Constitution, rigidly administered and guarded, are adequate to the protection of every interest they encircle."[9]

But it was always very clear that North Carolina would remain in the Union only under certain conditions. The Lincoln administration must respect slaveholders' rights in the territories and must not, under any circumstances, attempt to use force to get the seceded states back into the Union. That would prove that the Republicans were indeed the evil and uncompromising tyrants the fire-eaters claimed. Those Deep South states may have been rash in the decision to secede, but most North Carolinians believed they had the right to do so under the argument that all people have the natural right to live under a government of their choosing and to protect their property rights. After all, that exact sentiment was expressed in the Declaration of Independence and was the justification for the formation of the United States in the first place.

In November the *North Carolina Presbyterian* reported that they found most Tar Heels to be "ardently attached to the Union, and they are willing to wait further developments before they consent to a separation. They are ready to remain in the Union, provided the Northern States will repeal their unconstitutional statutes in violation of the fugitive slave law, and will exhibit hereafter a disposition to adhere to that solemn compact." A contributor to the *North Carolina Argus* offered in March:

> Let the Northern people understand that North Carolina, Virginia and all other Border states, regard the present as a time to demand the acknowledgement of every right under the Constitution, the removal of all State legislation which interfere with the laws made by the Federal Government, [personal liberty laws] ... for the protection or defense of our rights....

At a meeting in Robeson County, which would furnish one of the 18th North Carolina's companies, came the resolution "recommending a repeal of all obnoxious laws in regard to fugitive slaves ... [and] that we cannot give up the Constitution and Union until all efforts are made to get justice and these efforts fail." Sampson County citizens resolved that "much as we love our present Constitution and Government, we will not submit to any rule, by which the South or her institutions [slavery] would be dishonored." The Sampson meeting further resolved in early 1861 that "we most earnestly condemn the action of some of the Northern States, in passing certain laws in conflict with the constitution of the U. States, known as personal liberty laws." Company K of the 18th organized in Bladen County where the citizens proclaimed on February 2, 1861, that they were "opposed to secession at this time," but that they viewed Lincoln's victory as evidence "on the part of those who supported him to deprive the Southern States of their Constitutional equality and just rights...." The Bladen men further adopted the following resolution:

> That in order to effect a peaceable and honorable settlement we have been willing and are now willing to adopt the compromise measures recently introduced by Mr. Crittenden; or any other compromise, whereby the honor and rights of the South may be kept untarnished and inviolate, and the Union of the States continued to be unbroken and unimpaired.

The Crittenden Compromise the Bladen meeting referred to, if passed, would have inserted an amendment to the Constitution barring the federal government from abolishing slavery in the states where it existed and permitting the expansion of slavery into the territories by reviving the old Missouri Compromise Line and extending it to the Pacific Ocean. The *Fayetteville Observer* reprinted another county's resolutions (Wilkes) as they did for others and these expressed very well the conditional unionism that existed in North Carolina. The Wilkes resolves said quite clearly that "we are in favor of exhausting all conciliatory means consistent with our honor and rights" and remaining in the Union. However, if after exhausting such means as are consistent with our rights and common safety, we are unable to secure safety in the Union, we are as ready as any people to sacrifice our blood and treasure to maintain <u>and preserve our institutions</u> out of the Union.[10]

For most in the state, when Lincoln called for 75,000 volunteers to put down the rebellion, he had gone too far. To many this was a simple abuse of coercive power against people who were merely exercising their right to self government, to protect their inalienable rights to "life, liberty, and the pursuit of happiness." "Coercion" as many referred to the call for 75,000 soldiers, was unmistakable proof that Southerners' rights would not be respected in a Republican-dominated Union. A Bladen County meeting would "object to coercive means being used ... as it would widen the breach already existing and destroy all hope of conciliation." "Coercion means civil war, and [while we have previously repudiated secession], we would never, as a Southern man, suffer a Southern State to be driven into subjection by armed force, as long as we could stagger under a musket." The only argument, a Wilmington Whig said, was "the argument of the sword." If Lincoln actually tried to attack the South, "our citizens will unite and make common cause with the assailed. We have yet to see an individual who would tolerate an invasion of the South." The *North Carolina Standard* said the "soil of North Carolina must not be polluted by the tread of armed men sent to make war on the 'Confederate States.'" Another writer said that Lincoln's call for troops to coerce the South to live under a government they no longer wanted to be part of left the state "no alternative but resistance or unconditional surrender. The Southern man who would quietly submit ... is fit only for a slave." From the eastern part of the state came this angry proclamation:

> The mask has fallen and the Black Republican administration stands forth in all its hideous deformity. A war of *coercion* has been openly proclaimed and each State has been called on to furnish men to put down what the President is pleased to call a "rebellion" in the seceded States. A free people unwilling to submit to wrong and oppression and fighting for their rights are to be butchered by the power of this great Government. We have differed about political matters but now our section, <u>our property, our rights</u> and our honor call us to arms.

The *Fayetteville Observer* ran an article in late April that captured very well the sentiments of many in the state after learning of the call for men to force the seceded states back into the Union:

> Not a man can leave her borders upon such errand, who has not made up his mind to war upon his own home and all that he holds dear in that home. For ourselves, we are Southern men and North Carolinians, and are at war with those who are at war with the South and North Carolina.

2. Secession and the Formation of the 18th North Carolina

When North Carolina's governor, John Ellis, responded to Lincoln's call for troops from North Carolina, he effectively marked the end of unionism in the state. Ellis informed Lincoln:

> Your dispatch is received, and if genuine, which its extraordinary character leads me to doubt, I have to say in reply, that I regard the levy of troops by the administration for the purpose of subjugating the states of the South, as in violation of the Constitution, and as a gross usurpation of power. I can be no party of this wicked violation of the laws of the country and to this war upon the liberties of a free people. You can get no troops from North Carolina.[11]

At that point the only thing to be determined was when North Carolina's secession would be official. Everyone knew the state was leaving after Lincoln's April call, and throughout the state military companies organized to defend the state. A week to the day after Governor Ellis sent his reply to Washington, Confederate Secretary of War Leroy P. Walker congratulated Ellis on his and North Carolina's stand and welcomed the state into the Confederacy, though that had yet to become official. In an April 24 communication to Ellis, Walker said,

> Your patriotic response to the requisition of the President of the United States for troops to coerce the Confederate States justifies the belief that your people are prepared to unite with us in repelling the common enemy of the South.

Walker also told Ellis that troops were needed as soon as possible to help defend Virginia, which was certain to be the Yankees' primary target because the capital was there and because of the city's industrial capacity. To Walker's request Ellis responded at the end of April that he could expect "from one to ten thousand volunteers in a few days, with arms, ... " Politicians could work out the details of the state's official Ordinance of Secession but the Old North State was, for all practical purposes, out of the Union.[12]

The companies that ultimately made up the 18th North Carolina were mustered in New Hanover, Columbus, Bladen, Richmond, and Robeson counties. One of the New Hanover companies, the "German Volunteers" was a preexisting militia company that enlisted at Wilmington on April 15 and would eventually become Company A. With officers like Christian Cornehlsen, Charles Ackerman, Gerhard Runge, Engelhardt Schulken, and Hanke Vollers, it is not hard to see where the name "German Volunteers" originated. One of the two companies from Bladen County was the "Bladen Light Infantry," which organized at Elizabethtown on May 3, became Company B. Part of what would become Company C enlisted at Bugg Hill and part at Whiteville on April 24 and was known as the "Columbus Guards Number 3." At Lumberton on May 8 the company that was known by two names, "The Robeson

Rifle Guard" and the "Robeson Light Infantry" organized to defend the state and became Company D. Company E was made up of another group from New Hanover County that also went by a couple of different names, the "Moore's Creek Rifle Guards" and the "Moore's Creek Riflemen." The "Scotch Boys" from Richmond County organized on June 1 and formed Company F. The "Scotch Boys" stood out, according to the regiment's adjutant, for their height. According to him the company had numerous members well over six feet tall and that the average height was six feet, one inch, which put them a good four to six inches taller than the average Civil War soldier. Company G was formed from another preexisting Wilmington-area militia group, the "Wilmington Light Infantry." Columbus County men rallied to the Old North State's defense and formed the "Columbus Vigilants," which was also known as the "Columbus Guards Number 1" on April 23 and wound up as Company H. The "Wilmington Rifle Guards," yet another pre-war militia organization, enlisted at Wilmington on April 15 and became Company I. The final company, Company K, enlisted at Elizabethtown on April 26 and was the second company drawn from Bladen County and was known as the "Bladen Guards."[13]

The three Wilmington companies were the first to have any excitement. Since North Carolina was leaving the Union the coastal forts needed to be in Confederate hands, so to that end Colonel J.L. Cantwell, the military commander at Wilmington, ordered out the volunteer militia companies to take forts Caswell and Johnston on April 15, 1861. The following day elements of the Wilmington Light Infantry, described as something of a club for local aristocrats and admiringly referred to in one newspaper as "the very flower of our chivalry," arrived for the mission. The Wilmington Rifle Guards and the German Volunteers quickly joined them at the corner of Market and Front streets. From there they marched the short distance to the Cape Fear River and boarded the steamer *W.W. Harlee*, which took them to Smithville (present-day Southport) and Fort Johnston. As they glided up the river, "a large number of ladies stood waving handkerchiefs until the vessels disappeared downtstream." The companies arrived at Smithville around four o'clock that afternoon and Fort Johnston was turned over to them without incident, another early and misleading bloodless "victory" for the Confederacy.[14]

After securing the forts around Wilmington, those three companies remained in the lower Cape Fear region drilling and strengthening fortifications around this critically important port city. Throughout the war Wilmington would be a key port of entry for supplies from abroad; for much of the war the supplies that kept Lee's army going came through Wilmington. In July those three companies were joined by the others that would form the regiment (except for the Bladen Guards, which was assigned to support artillery at Confederate Point below Wilmington) at Camp Wyatt and became the 8th North Carolina Volunteers. Twenty-eight-year-old James D. Radcliff was elected the regiment's first colonel, though it is unclear what his qualifications may have been besides his having been the principal of a Wilmington military school before the war.[15]

While at Camp Wyatt the varied companies from the southeastern corner of the state began the work of becoming a regiment. This was more complicated than it may at first sound. Many of the men who had signed up no doubt thought they would grab their guns, join another group of like-minded Southern patriots, go off and shoot a few Yankees and come home with tales of glory. The reality was that the era's tactics required hours of daily training to turn companies of raw recruits (and inexperienced officers) into a cohesive and disciplined battlefield unit. There was, these eastern Tar Heels quickly found out, a whole lot more to soldiering than knowing how to fire a gun. They had to learn how to move in formation; they had to learn how to deploy quickly from a marching column into a battle line; they needed to learn how to change fronts quickly as well as how to withdraw in a disciplined way so as to avoid being routed and captured; they had to learn how to properly charge the enemy as a unit rather than as a pell-mell group of screaming individuals who would wind up shot to pieces; they had to learn the multiple commands for delivering fire; and they had to be able to do these things under fire, as a unit, without thinking about them. Since these volunteers had not been in battle they probably did not see any use in the hours of drill besides looking pretty on the parade grounds or doing anything but providing officers with an excuse to give orders all day in the hot sun. But at least one of the men of the regiment thought Colonel Radcliff's efforts were paying off, writing that the colonel "soon had the regiment in good shape." Another wrote approvingly that summer that the men had "advanced rapidly in the drill and discipline." They were apparently right. Though the men in the ranks may not have appreciated it at the time, and they probably did not, when the regiment went into combat for the first time they performed very well and would continue to do so throughout the war.[16]

In the late summer and early fall of 1861, most of the regiment continued to drill while three companies (F, I, and K) performed duty as artillery support at Fort Fisher. They were assigned to Anderson's Battery, Gatlin's Battery, and Baily's Battery, respectively. Lieutenant William Wooster of Company I wrote to his mother that the new camp was an improvement over Camp Wyatt. "Our camp is pitched upon the top of a grassy hill, commanding a fine view of both the river and ocean." He went on to relate: "We have large waterproof quarters, and our only complaint now as regards them, is that we have to spread our beds on the ground for want of boards with which to make floors.

This however will be remedied I hope." When describing the new location, Wooster said that he found "working the large Columbiads ... [to be] hard labor." There was not much "action" for the artillery companies, though they did see the enemy from time to time off the coast. In one letter a member saw a Federal steamer anchored "so near, in fact that with an opera glass here men may be seen looking over her sides. I hope she may come near enough to the battery for us to tender her our compliments with a sixty-four pound ball."[17]

In late summer and early fall 1861 the regiment went through several changes. On August 20 the regiment was transferred from state to Confederate service. In November the regiment's numerical designation changed as well. Since North Carolina officially seceded on May 20, there were two sets of infantry regiments sharing the same numbers, which was very confusing obviously. The companies that formed before May 20 were one-year regiments and had been designated as North Carolina Volunteers whereas those brought in after the state seceded were three-year or the war regiments designated North Carolina State Troops. Since the State Troops had signed on for longer terms of service they kept their numerical designation while the Volunteers all added ten to theirs. Thus the 8th North Carolina Volunteers became the 18th North Carolina State Troops in November 1861.[18]

These were not the only changes. The regiment was also ordered to collect itself and head for South Carolina to help defend there. The only exception was Company K (Bladen Guards), which remained in North Carolina providing artillery support at Fort Fisher and then on Zeke's Island in the Cape Fear River. The transfer to Camp Stephens, South Carolina, in Pocataligo, which is about halfway between Charleston and Savannah, was not particularly popular with the regiment. First and foremost these men felt they had volunteered to defend their state, not someone else's. Not only that, but the 18th's members were from counties most likely to be targets of Federal operations. They were extremely upset about the possibility that Yankees would come ashore along the state's southern coast, probably near Wilmington given its strategic importance, and pose a direct threat to their homes and families while they were not there to protect them. The traditional animosity towards South Carolina did not help make the decision any more palatable. Furthermore, at this stage of the war especially, most Southerners' first loyalty was to their state anyway. William Bellamy, who had enlisted at the tender age of seventeen, was a Wilmington native serving in Company I, recorded in his diary that "there is great feeling existing concerning our getting home and defending the coast of North Carolina chiefly around the Cape Fear district." Any sort of nationalistic ideas that one's duty was to defend the Confederacy first and one's state second just did not compute for most. Some historians have even argued that there was no such thing as true Confederate nationalism during the Civil War capable of transcending state loyalty. That position is debatable, but it is clear that the 18th North Carolina was less than pleased with being ordered to South Carolina in the fall of '61, so much so that Colonel Radcliff warned officials that there was so much irritation over being stationed in South Carolina that the regiment would likely disband when its year was up if it were not brought home.[19]

Life at Camp Stephens, South Carolina. continued and was uneventful and monotonous. As Lieutenant Wooster wrote home in December: "In the vocabulary of the soldier there is no such word as Friday you know — all days to him are alike." Life was all drill and camp duties but no martial action or glory. Christmas 1861 offered a nice and much-needed break from routine. Wooster told his mother that Christmas Day in camp was "a perfect Saturnalia; the whole camp was in an uproar; drilling was cast to the dogs; and pleasure was the order of the day." He told "Mother" that there was no whiskey in the camp, but one wonders if that was accurate or to reassure her that the frivolity was not overly sinful. Aside from Christmas, though, the morale among the Tar Heels in the Palmetto State was low. When Colonel Radcliff began encouraging the men to re-enlist for the war, which the Confederacy wanted all of its one-year units to do to ensure sufficient manpower for the upcoming spring and summer battle season, he found very little of the patriotic zeal that had been present back in April and May. "Reenlistment for the war," Wooster told his father in February, "is already beginning to be the topic of discussion. I have however taken my position, and intend to hold it moreover. I argue thus. Reenlistment now is premature. Three months hence will be ample time to discuss it. Our term will then be near its end, and should our cause imperatively demand our services, no man can hesistate...." Probably like a lot of other members of the regiment who had seen that army life was a bit different than they thought it would be. He expected to reenlist "but will not now pledge myself. There will doubtless be many and important changes by June next [when the regiment was accepted into state service], and I intend to view the question in all its bearings before I bind myself by an irrevocable oath. I shall look before I leap certainly and look long and carefully." Wooster did look and did reenlist for the war, serving as a lieutenant in Company I until he was killed at Frayser's Farm that June.[20]

As the spring of 1862 approached, the 18th got its wish to return to the Old North State, but not because of any lobbying by Colonel Radcliff. Union General Ambrose Burnside had been doing a good bit of damage to the North Carolina coast, taking Roanoke Island in February and then threatening to take New Bern in early March. The regiment was told on March 13 that they would be leaving for Kinston, North Carolina, news that Private Bellamy said "was hailed with great joy." The regiment got back to North Carolina in the days immediately after the Battle of New Bern and was rejoined by Company K, bringing the 18th North Carolina back up to its full strength. On March 17, 1862, the regiment passed through Wilmington where many of the New Hanover men, like Bellamy, got the chance to have a small visit with friends and family before continuing by train to Goldsboro and then to Kinston.

In the wake of the Battle of New Bern, several regiments pulled back to Kinston to resupply and to replenish and build their ranks. The 18th North Carolina's green men and officers had never seen such a large military site before. "I am in the midst of a tremendous camp," Lieutenant Wooster wrote home. He also commented on the fact that the term "uniform" was not a particularly accurate term for the North Carolina soldiers, rather, "Officers and soldiers [are] dressed in every conceivable style of uniform...." Probably at no other time in the war were these soldiers so mismatched in terms of uniform. Some wore the five-button gray sack coat that came to just above mid-thigh that North Carolina provided; some wore militia garb; others wore items of home manufacture based roughly on military patterns. Wooster probably noticed too that, as in his own regiment, there was also a variety of weaponry as well as uniforms. Some fortunate few carried the .57 Springfield or Enfield rifle musket but many more Tar Heels were carrying older .69 smoothbore muskets that had been converted from flintlock to percussion and fired a nasty round of "buck and ball," which consisted of three musket balls and a buckshot slug. Over time the 18th North Carolina was able to procure more rifle muskets for issue to its troops but for much of the first year of the war many of the soldiers carried their "conversion" muskets and wielded them with deadly effect.[21]

While at Kinston the 18th North Carolina also became part of a brigade along with four other North Carolina regiments. They were originally brigaded with the 25th, 28th, 33rd, and 37th North Carolina regiments but shortly after the order was read, the Twenty-fifth was reassigned and replaced by the 7th North Carolina under the command of Lawrence O'Byran Branch. Branch was a Princeton graduate, class of '38 and had been president of the Raleigh and Gaston Railroad before entering politics in the 1850s. For most of the decade prior to North Carolina's secession, Branch had served in the United States House of Representatives and posted a record as a defender of Southern rights but, as with most North Carolinians, he was something of a moderate as opposed to being a fire-eater like Asheville's Thomas Clingman. Branch had opposed secession until the Fort Sumter crisis when he offered his services to his state. Originally, given his administrative record, he was made a quartermaster and paymaster but Branch wanted field command. Whether this was purely out of patriotism or because he was well aware of what a boon battle honors and glory were to a political career is not entirely clear; it was most likely a combination of the two. His first command was as colonel of the 33rd North Carolina, and his first battlefield command had come in the loss at New Bern.[22]

Becoming part of Branch's Brigade was not the only, or even the most momentous, change that affected the regiment in the early spring of 1862. In April the Richmond government enacted the first conscription act in American history, and it required all members of twelve-month regiments (like the 18th North Carolina) between the ages of eighteen and forty-five to remain in the service for an additional two years. Officials were quite concerned, and rightly so, that volunteerism had fallen off and they were no doubt aware that some of the twelve-month units were in danger of disbanding when their terms of service were up. In the 18th North Carolina this was certainly the case. Some members felt they had done their duty and intended to either go home or join other units. Some expressed an interest in changing to a different branch of service; the cavalry seemed very appealing to many infantrymen after a year marching around in bad shoes. One member of the regiment said he though that "from all appearances the original 18th will be extinct on the 15th of June [the date it was accepted into state service]."

Many were annoyed at the conscription law for a variety of reasons. Some, especially those who had organized in April, felt that they were free to do as they liked at that point — that was their twelve months. But the new law made June 15 the date that soldiers had to reenlist or be conscripted into Confederate service. Richmond did put a carrot in the deal to go with the stick; if a regiment reenlisted before June 15 the soldiers could get a furlough and the right to reorganize their units through new officer and non-commissioned officer elections. This caused some rather extreme bitterness in the ranks because they felt they had been betrayed by their new government. In their eyes they had done their duty and intended to still — on their terms. The government was taking that freedom away from them and they resented it. They expressed their anger the only way they could, by their votes when they reorganized the regiment and held new elections in April 1862. The whole brigade had these same elections but the 18th North Carolina had by far the most turnover among officers and NCOs — twenty-six total changes in the rank structure of the regiment. Colonel Radcliff was defeated and was replaced by Wilmington businessman Robert H. Cowan, formerly colonel of the 3rd North Carolina. Radcliff went on to become colonel of the 61st North Carolina. Thomas Purdie was one of the few existing officers who was actually promoted. Purdie, a wealthy Bladen County farmer and owner of over forty slaves in 1860, jumped from captain of Company K to lieutenant-colonel of the regiment. Except for Cowan and Purdie, most of the officers were brand new to the commissioned ranks. Twelve had had some experience with rank having previously served as non-commissioned officers, but twelve others entering the NCO and officer ranks had been privates before the reorganization. Cowan expressed concern about such radical turnover among his officers and NCOs but there was nothing he could do about it other than work closely with them to help them learn their new roles.[23]

Colonel Cowan and his second-in-command, Tom Purdie would not have very much time to work with. The 18th, along with the rest of Branch's brigade, remained in the Kinston area building up their numbers (though the 18th was only able to recruit twenty-five while the Twenty-eighth added 451 and the others added at least 200) for six weeks. With the weather warming up the war's second battle season was about to begin in earnest in the Virginia theater. General George B. McClellan had taken control of the demoralized Army of the Potomac after its defeat at Manassas and trained it and infused it with confidence. He also began moving this huge army, the largest ever seen in North America, to the peninsula between the York and James rivers. From there he could drive up the peninsula and take the Confederate capital. This would be a demoralizing loss to the Confederate civilian population as well as a loss of Richmond's significant industrial capacity. Many on both sides believed that to lose Richmond would be to lose the war so such a calamity could not be allowed to happen. To make sure that it did not, calls for all available troops were made to save the capital, and at the beginning of May 1862 the 18th North Carolina was again on its way out of the state; but this time their assignment would not be so uneventful.

Chapter 3

Seeing the Elephant: Hanover Court House, Gaines's Mill, and Frayser's Farm

In May 1862 the 18th North Carolina left its home state, again, this time as part of General Lawrence O'Bryan Branch's North Carolina Brigade. No doubt there were grumblings as the men left North Carolina again, especially with Union forces still quite close to their homes and families. They felt they had volunteered to defend their state and homes and here the government had ordered them away from both. The irritation at the Richmond government over the conscription law (which many felt was a bit of dirty pool) still lingered and certainly did not help the morale in the regiment. Duty, however, called them to the capital, so to the capital they would go; they had taken an oath and they would live up to it. They may not have been happy about the prospect of going to another state to march about and perform picket duty, but they would do it. What few in the ranks realized at the time was that their days of safe monotony were about to end as the spring of 1862 warmed up. Before the month was out, they would "see the elephant," as Civil War soldiers termed going into combat, for the first time. By the time summer came to an end, the 18th North Carolina would be transformed from green unit to fighting regiment.

Early 1862 had been difficult for Lincoln, at least in terms of events in Virginia. After the Army of the Potomac was driven back into the defenses of Washington after the Battle of Manassas/Bull Run the previous July, the president had appointed General George B. McClellan to take over putting the pieces of that massive army back together so that it could be thrown at the enemy again, but hopefully with much different results. McClellan today seems like a huge mistake but it is important to remember that at the time McClellan was an overwhelmingly obvious choice. He had posted an impressive prewar military career, had defeated Confederate forces under none other than Robert E. Lee in western Virginia, and he exuded tremendous confidence and surety as well as just looking like a successful general ought to look. People did not call him the "Young Napoleon" as a joke; many saw him in the early stages of the war as the best military commander the Union possessed, and not without very good reason. Whatever criticisms one wants to level at McClellan, and there is room for so many it is perhaps difficult to know where to start, but one thing that can be said for him is that he was a superb organizer and trainer of men. By early 1862 the Army of the Potomac had become the best outfitted organization in the country; it was much better trained; and, perhaps most importantly, its soldiers had regained their confidence in themselves. Most of that can be attributed to McClellan's leadership.

As admirable a job as he had done rebuilding an army that had taken a demoralizing whipping in their first fight, he was loathe to actually use the magnificent tool that he had worked so diligently to create. For Lincoln that was a major problem. Lincoln had a difficult time understanding how the Federals were going to win the war if the armies did not actually go fight the enemy. Lincoln, who had begun reading every military treatise and book he could lay his hands on, thought, as did General Ulysses Grant, that the only way to win the war was to destroy the enemy's armies. When the enemy had no ability to resist further the war would be over. That seemed simple enough to Lincoln and to other later Union commanders who believed the very same thing and ultimately were most responsible for bringing the war to a successful close by making the destruction of the enemy's armies the primary goal. McClellan, however, seemed very reluctant to actually do that, so reluctant that Lincoln had to use his power as commander-in-chief to essentially order McClellan to make some move to attack General Joseph Johnston's army hovering menacingly close to Washington at Manassas.

Lincoln had wanted McClellan to launch attacks on Johnston from Washington. McClellan did not like that plan at all. Whether he legitimately thought it would not work or whether he just liked creating a plan that was different from the president's (for whom he had absolutely no respect) is not clear. Whatever his reasoning, McClellan submitted an alternate proposal. He would flank Johnston's army by moving the Army of the Potomac around the Confederate right and plant it at the mouth of the Rappahannock River. Doing that would put the large Union army between Johnston and his capital, forcing him to turn and face him and fight a battle on McClellan's terms. This was better, McClellan argued, than launching bloody frontal assaults against enemy entrenchments, especially since the Confederates had over 100,000 defenders — the first time McClellan's penchant for greatly exaggerating Southern numbers reared its head. Lincoln was not totally convinced. It seemed to him that either way McClellan would have to attack Johnston and if McClellan took off from Washington did that not leave Johnston free to attack Washington? But if McClellan was going to actually do something Lincoln would support him and hope for success.[1]

These plans were altered when Johnston pulled back from the Manassas defenses in March to a position behind the Rappahannock. Since the original plan to turn Johnston along the Rappahannock was no longer an option, McClellan decided he would take his army to a different location but with the same basic plan. The Army of the Potomac would instead be taken further down the Chesapeake Bay to land at Fort Monroe at the tip of the peninsula between the James and York rivers. From there McClellan would head west and cover the seventy miles to Richmond and victory. As McClellan began landing his huge army at Fort Monroe the first week of April, Richmond sent out for more troops to protect the capital from what looked to be a major attempt to take it and deal the Confederate cause a potential death blow. So, the 18th headed for Virginia and the seat of war.[2]

During the first half of May, as McClellan was slowly moving up the Peninsula, the 18th North Carolina arrived in Virginia and camped with the rest of Branch's force north of Richmond at Gordonsville. The assignment was an important one because the town was a major railroad junction connecting Richmond to points north and west. Gordonsville was not only important to the Confederate authorities; the Federals also relied on the rail lines going through the town for supplies and communication with their forces in the Shenandoah Valley. Being there also permitted the brigade to go to Jackson's command in the Valley if needed or quickly to Richmond should the need be more urgent there. Upon arrival, the regiment got off the trains, slung off their knapsacks, and began making camp at their new home. Cowan and Purdie also resumed a drill schedule to continue teaching all those new officers and NCOs their battlefield roles.

In the middle of May the routine of life in a stationary camp changed as orders came down for the brigade to head to the Valley and join Jackson's army. Finally, the 18th was going to have its chance to strike a blow in defense of its new nation. For over a year they had been training for the event and had heard about great fights without having taken part in even one. Many were anxious for their first taste of battle, even if they were also a bit nervous about the prospect. Few wanted the great event of their lives to end without their having at least one good story to tell their friends, relatives, and children about. On May 16 the 18th North Carolina's camp came alive with excitement as the men and officers broke camp and fell in to march west over the mountains to join the already-famous Stonewall Jackson.

As it turned out, the regiment's first taste of "real war" was not battle but hard marching under difficult conditions. The weather was very warm;

when the sun was not baking the men, rains were drenching them and turning the roads into a muddy sort of paste that made marching twice as difficult. The tramping of hundreds of men, horses, and wagons through the mire only made it thicker and deeper. For this still-green regiment — marching in full gear in the rain, mud, and heat of Virginia in the springtime — this march from Gordonsville was an exhausting introduction to infantry campaigning. Lieutenant Wooster of Company I wrote home on May 23, 1862: "Had I ever been foolish enough to entertain the idea that a soldier's life was a 'primrose path of dalliance,' the experience of the last seven days would have forever put to flight [such] an absurdity." "I can say with truth," he said, "I have not been dry in a week." And no wonder, in their first real march, he went on to relate:

> For ten long hours we struggled on, through driving rain and over roads in which we sank at every step over our shoes. When night fell in on us we had only made nine miles. Footsore and weary we threw ourselves upon the wet ground, and slept as calmly and soundly with no tent above us, and the rain pattering in our faces, as if I were in my room at home. Col. Cowan declared it to be the hardest march he had ever undergone and said the 18th acquitted themselves handsomely. And so they did.

Previously the brigade was at least somewhat protected from the rain by their tents but General Ewell, who had told Branch to head for the Valley, had ordered the North Carolinians to leave all excess baggage behind to speed the movement. As he told Branch, "the road to glory cannot be followed with much baggage." The next day the regiment was "baptized again" as the heavens opened. Lieutenant Wooster had always liked to watch those storms — when he did not have to march in them. "There we were in a beautiful valley, with a sky as black as death over our heads, and the grand old peaks of the Blue Ridge frowning down upon us." That evening a member of the brigade recorded bedding down "at the foot of the Blue Ridge in a Large Clover field [with] plenty of wheat straw to lay on."[3]

Unfortunately another part of life in the infantry is enduring orders that seem to be drafted for the express purpose of exponentially increasing the stress and discomfort of the soldiers. After nearly two full days of marching under trying conditions, the brigade was told to turn around and head back to Gordonsville. One can well imagine how well that bit of news went over with the weary, wet, and footsore men in the ranks. In the months and years to come, the 18th North Carolina became used to such marches as they became veterans, but at the moment they were tired and irritated at having to turn around and go back over the very same path they just marched over. Wooster figured the regiment made twenty-two miles that day, "a tremendous march indeed, and one I never imagined our regiment capable of." When the 18th got back to Gordonsville, they boarded trains that took the men to the vicinity of Hanover Court House, about fifteen miles north of Richmond, to help protect Johnston's right/north from a gathering Federal force of some 30,000 at Fredericksburg under General Irvin McDowell, a force McClellan desperately wanted to use, along with General Fitz John Porter's V Corps, north of the Chickahominy River. "After a week of marching and countermarching through the mountains," Wooster wrote home, "we have once more pitched our tents within a half hour's ride of Richmond, Dear Mother."[4]

Lieutenant Wooster may have pitched his tent, but most other members of the regiment did not have them. As one member of the brigade grumbled on one of the many soggy May days, "This is a very wet day.... We have no tents in camp except for the officers." Another of Branch's soldiers remembered, "we had no tents neither had we slept in tents but one night in five weeks." The 18th, along with the rest of the brigade plus the temporary additions of another North Carolina regiment and one from Georgia, was camped just southwest of Hanover Court House at Peake's Station on the Virginia Central Railroad. General Branch had no idea that a large body of Federals in the form of Porter's V Corps were nearby when he sent out two companies of the 37th North Carolina and several companies of the 18th North Carolina to perform picket duty, which consisted of manning posts short distances from the main camp to act as a warning should the enemy suddenly appear. Nothing much was expected and the men performing the duty on the rainy night of May 26, 1862, slogged out to their soggy posts "with some grumbling and pretty sharp criticism" of their officers. The rest of the regiment wrapped themselves up in their blankets and, if they had them, waterproof ground sheets, and tried to get some sleep.[5]

The Federals had been receiving reports of a sizable number of Confederates in the vicinity of Hanover Court House and McClellan did not like that. He was hoping to be able to have McDowell's 30,000-man force swoop down on Richmond from the north with Porter along the Virginia Central Railroad while he moved on the Rebel capital from the east with the bulk of the Army of the Potomac. McClellan, always so convinced that he was woefully outnumbered by his opponent, was, in fact, relying on being able to have McDowell's reinforcements come down the Virginia Central to have any prospect of success. So when he received reports of 12,000 to 15,000 Confederates around Hanover Court House (in reality Branch had, at most, about 6,000 men) he ordered Porter to look into it and get the enemy force out of the way. That evening, while the 18th was performing picket duty and trying to stay dry, equally wet and irritated Yankees were issued two days' rations, sixty rounds of ammunition, and told to be ready to move out at dawn the next day, May 27.[6]

Early that morning Branch got reports from his pickets of Federal movement in the area. Unfortunately he had only a sketchy idea about the enemy in his front. He had very limited cavalry to perform reconnaissance, and the reports from the local civilians did not provide much that was of any real use. All Branch knew, or thought he knew, was that McClellan was focusing all his energies and resources on attacking Richmond from the east and that there were some scattered reports of Yankees in his immediate vicinity. He came to the conclusion that the Unionists in his area must be a small force, perhaps cavalry scouts. Unaware that, like at New Bern, he was outnumbered by his enemy by a three-to-one margin, Branch ordered James H. Lane to take his 28th North Carolina to locate the scouting party and swat it away.

Colonel James H. Lane was a twenty-eight-year-old Virginian who had graduated second in his class from the Virginia Military Institute in 1854. While there he had also had the uncomfortable experience of being one of Professor Thomas J. Jackson's students. Lane went on to study science at the University of Virginia before becoming a mathematics and tactics professor himself at his alma mater before heading the philosophy department at the North Carolina Military Institute in Charlotte. This learned and gifted commander led his regiment just south of Hanover Court House where he came upon the skirmishers of the 25th New York in a wheat field. Lane had his opponent outnumbered and he ordered his Carolinians to charge them. Given the numerical advantage Lane had, his Tar Heels quickly got the upper hand over the New Yorkers, inflicting heavy casualties and taking nearly 100 prisoners. Lane was elated at the easy and severe thrashing his men were administering. As he sat astride his horse controlling the action he waved his sword and encouraged his men, shouting to

James Lane, most likely taken while a student at the Virginia Military Instititute. Lane became the 18th's brigade commander after Lawrence Branch was killed at Sharpsburg/Antietam and led it well for the remainder of the war. Auburn University Special Collections/Archives.

them: "Charge on the scoundrels, boys!" With Rebel yells and flags waving their defiance, the 28th North Carolina confidently charged forward to finish the job, convinced their first battle was going to end in glorious victory over the Yankees.

Such was not to be, unfortunately. While Lane's men had driven the New York skirmishers back and taken many of them prisoner, as they charged the fleeing Yankees they came upon the main Federal line where a full brigade of Northerners from New York and Pennsylvania, along with two artillery batteries, were waiting. Suddenly the situation was reversed and the North Carolinians were the ones who were severely out manned and out gunned and fighting for their lives. Quickly realizing the dangerous position he was in, Lane ordered his regiment to pull back and re-form. He also pulled a staff officer to him and shouted at him to send word of the situation to Branch and have him send up artillery and infantry reinforcements — quickly.

Having heard the shelling that had erupted from the Union batteries Branch had already figured out that something more than a mere scouting or raiding party was lurking around and that Lane had run into it. The 18th North Carolina, behind the 37th North Carolina, marched in column of fours east on the Ashcake Road towards Hanover Court House in support of Lane, who was in a terrible fight when Branch saw an artillery position in a field to the right near where the Ashcake and Pole Green Church roads met and led north to Hanover Court House. While Porter sent the bulk of his force to Hanover Court House, two regiments, the 22nd Massachusetts and 44th New York were ordered to tear up portions of the Virginia Central before rejoining the rest of the corps at Hanover Court House. Branch decided to take out the artillery position and these Federal units along the Pole Green Church Road and sent the 37th North Carolina to form the far right of his battle line, facing the New Yorkers. The 33rd North Carolina were to attack the Federals' right flank. The 18th North Carolina drew the unenviable job of taking the center position and charging the Yankee guns in a frontal assault across an open field. The 18th North Carolina's first battle was certainly not going to be an easy one.

As often happened in Civil War battles, what was planned was not always what occurred on the field. The attack by the 33rd North Carolina on the Federals' right never materialized so the fight against the 2nd Maine and 44th New York and their batteries was made by the 18th and 37th North Carolina. The 18th North Carolina had formed into their battle lines in a stand of woods; Colonel Cowan had been assured that the Yankee guns were not more than 200 yards in their front. One brave rush should do the job, Cowan encouraged his men. He then gave the order to "fix bayonets." Next came the order, to march forward at "charge bayonets." This order did not mean that the 18th North Carolina came screaming out of the wood line towards the Federals. The front rank only moved forward with their bayonets pointed menacingly at the enemy followed closely by the rear rank with their muskets on their right shoulder. Though the movement "charge bayonets" sounds like an invitation for an undisciplined chaotic charging mass of steel, the reality is that during the Civil War this order was designed to be very disciplined, with the regiment moving as one at the "double quick" towards the enemy, which was supposed to be more of a mild jog than a rush. By all accounts this is exactly what the regiment did that hot May afternoon.

Cowan was misinformed about the distance to the enemy guns; they were much further than 200 yards away. In reality they were closer to 600 yards away across a totally open field. Immediately the Federal cannons opened on the eastern Tar Heels with predictably devastating results. One member remembered that the "artillery was playing upon our men the whole while— throwing shrapnel principally," until they got within musket range. Then "the Minnie rifles began to assist the artillery. Still the regiment continued to advance — the line in perfect order — withholding its fire because the range was too great for effective musketry, and thus it continued until within two hundred yards of the battery, ... brave men falling at every step." Another member of the regiment recorded that the men were being "mowed down like grass." With every step Cowan, Purdie, and the other officers were shouting above the din of the firing and screams of the wounded for the men to close the ranks and keep on their guide as men fell out in clumps every few feet. The 18th managed to get off a few volleys in self defense but in their exposed position there was little they could accomplish. Cowan reacted quickly and shouted to his officers to have the regiment drop to the ground to at least make it more difficult for the Northerners to hit them.

As the men lay there, getting off what fire they could, Cowan determined that if they remained in their current place the 18th North Carolina would be literally blown out of existence. To save his men he had them rise up and march (likely at as quick a pace as possible) by the right flank to a set of woods. From those woods the 18th, working with the 37th North Carolina took some revenge and poured in volley after volley of oblique fire into the Union left side. This fire was effective and took such a toll that the New York and Maine regiments began to falter and pull back. If it looked like the Confederates may yet take the day, reinforcements arrived late in the afternoon and turned the tide for good in the Yankees' favor. The 62nd Pennsylvania, 5th New York, and 9th Massachusetts arrived on the Confederate left and drove the 33rd and 12th North Carolina away from that sector while the 13th and 14th New York came crashing into the woods where the 18th and Thirty-seventh were making their stand. It was New Bern all over again for Branch but he had learned from that previous battle the importance of having a retreat covered so as the other regiments pulled back and headed for Ashland, the 7th North Carolina covered the rear so they could make their escape.

At the end of the day, the 18th North Carolina had finally seen the elephant and it had been a brutal baptism indeed. The regiment lost thirty-eight killed and eighty-eight wounded and another fifty-six missing or taken prisoner. A number of the prisoners were taken because they had been wounded. These numbers represented a significant amount of the brigade's total losses, which were seventy-two killed and 191 wounded. William McLaurin said the regiment earned the title that day, "The Bloody Eighteenth." While the day was a bloody one and one that did not end in victory, the regiment had entered its first true test and passed with high marks, thus beginning its record as one of Lee's fighting regiments. "Colonel Cowan," Branch wrote in his report of the battle, "with the Eighteenth, made the charge [against the Federal guns] most gallantly; but the enemy's force was much larger than had been supposed and strongly posted, and the gallant Eighteenth was compelled to seek shelter." He also reported that the regiment continued to fight from the woods after the devastating losses it had already suffered. "The steadiness with which this desperate charge was made reflects the highest credit on officers and men." At the other end of the ranks, Private William Bellamy also had praise for his colonel: "We went in battle knowing we had a patriot soldier and gallant leader ... to lead us through the Battle. We trusted in him as a God. Through the whole engagement he displayed great coolness and fortitude, did not stand idly looking on, but emptied time after time the well put in load from his Navy repeater." Perhaps the best compliment came from their supreme commander, Robert E. Lee. On the evening of June 3, the brigade was formed up at a dress parade to hear a message from Lee. In it Lee told Branch to tell "the troops of your command ... [of] my hearty approval of their conduct, and hope that on future occasions they will evince a like heroism and patriotic devotion."

Even their enemies had compliments for the 18th North Carolina. A New Yorker said several days after the battle that he "never saw a more imposing sight [than the charge of the 18th North Carolina] though the ensign of treason floated in the centre." Colonel Charles Roberts of the 2nd Maine thought the North Carolinians were impressive as well, and formidable fighters. He said in his report that they "appeared boldly in front, advancing in perfect order, the red colors of right and left general guides, also the Stars and Bars defiantly flying."[7]

As the 18th North Carolina was fighting in its first battle, authorities in Richmond were making decisions that would affect it and other regiments and brigades in the army. To utilize its manpower more efficiently, officials determined that the myriad independent brigades, like Branch's, should be organized into divisions of four to six brigades under the command of a major-general. There were several very good reasons for doing this. For one thing, many brigades were commanded by men who owed their position to their political connections or social prominence rather than military background or ability. Branch was a prime example. True, he had been outnumbered three-to-one at both New Bern and Hanover Court House but at both places he had made mistakes that were directly related to his inexperience. Communication would be easier and more efficient as well with the commanding general being able to issue commands not only to more experienced officers who would be most likely to comprehend his plans and execute them, but to fewer commanders. Orders would go to division commanders who would then deal with the various brigades under their command rather than orders having to go to every single brigade commander who was to be part of a given operation. Another added benefit was having multiple brigades act as a unit rather than as independent commands doing their own things on battlefields. A unified division could pack a much more powerful punch than several disjointed brigades.

Branch's North Carolinians became part of a new brigade on May 27, 1862, under the command of Ambrose Powell Hill. Hill had been recently promoted to major-general, the youngest to hold that rank in the Confederate armies, after effective leadership on the peninsula. Hill designated his new command the Light Division, possibly to instill unit pride in his brigades and regiments by giving it the same name as the famous British unit that had fought so fiercely for the Duke of Wellington. The name may also have reflected the idea that Hill intended to move fast and fight hard, which

The 18th fought under Hill from the middle of 1862 through the end of the war as part of Hill's "Light Division" and then as part of Hill's 3rd Corps of the Army of Northern Virginia. Library of Congress.

was certainly in keeping with Powell Hill's pugnacious nature. Whatever the reasoning, the Cape Fear Confederates in the 18th North Carolina had just become a cog in what was to become a very famous machine.

Becoming part of Hill's Light Division was not the only change affecting the 18th North Carolina. Four days after the fight at Hanover Court House, Joseph E. Johnston attacked the Army of the Potomac at the Battle of Seven Pines (Fair Oaks to the Yankees). During the battle Johnston was severely wounded and Jefferson Davis turned to his most trusted military advisor, Robert E. Lee, to assume command of the Army of Northern Virginia. With Lee came a change in outlook and basic strategy for securing Southern independence. Johnston's Fabian approach saved lives, something that the outnumbered Confederacy had to consider, and would avoid major military catastrophes such as having an entire army destroyed. These were legitimate concerns but at the same time, Lee reasoned, that method of prosecuting the war would certainly prolong the war, something that favored the resource-rich North. In the new commander's view, the South had to do more than just keep from being defeated, its armies had to seize the initiative and actively defeat the enemy. The Army of the Potomac had to be dealt a stinging blow, and Northern civilians needed to be given a reason to fear that the Confederate military was far from on the brink of collapse and could hold on for years and perhaps even win. Only when the majority of Northern citizens believed that Southern armies could consistently punish Unionist armies would they pressure their government to sue for peace and let the Confederates have their independence.[8]

Lee let Davis know right away that he had no intention of sitting back and letting McClellan move closer to Richmond. Such a course of action only left the date Richmond fell to be determined, not whether the capital and its industrial capacity would fall to the enemy. As soon as he took command, Lee worked on how to save Richmond and destroy the Army of the Potomac. In keeping with the way he planned his moves, Lee devised a plan to get his enemy to react to him, forcing him to fight on ground and terms Lee chose to maximize the destruction to McClellan while minimizing his own losses. Lee did not intend to just rush out and attack McClellan's breastworks; that was suicide and would cost too much for questionable results. He was, rather, working on a plan to maneuver the Army of the Potomac out of its formidable entrenchments and into the open so Lee could thrash it. If he left McClellan alone, he explained to Davis, he "will take position from position, under cover of his heavy guns, and we cannot get at him without storming his works, which with our new troops is extremely hazardous" as was amply demonstrated at Seven Pines. There had to be a way to save Richmond, destroy or severely damage the Army of the Potomac, and do both without expending more lives than was absolutely necessary.[9]

During the first three weeks of June, Lee met with his leading generals and got information from J.E.B. Stuart, who made his famous ride around McClellan's Army on June 12–15, and formulated a plan of action. The plan was simple enough when looking at the situation on a map. Lee knew that Porter was isolated on the north bank of the rain-swollen Chickahominy and was the only force protecting McClellan's supply and communication line to the White House on the Pamunkey River. Given McClellan's lethargy, Lee gambled that he could leave a small, well-entrenched garrison force in front of Richmond while he threw the rest of the Confederates around Richmond and Jackson's Valley Army at Porter who would be overwhelmed and destroyed or forced to retreat as fast as he possibly could. Such a threat to McClellan's communications could not be ignored and he would have to defend it. When the Army of the Potomac left its entrenchments to defend its communication and supply line, it would be exposed, strung out, and ripe for destruction.[10]

Since its stinging defeat and retreat at Hanover Court House, the 18th North Carolina had settled into a new campsite on the Brooke Turnpike north of Richmond at a Chickahominy River crossing called Half Sink. While there they drilled daily and performed picket duty along the banks of the river. Federal soldiers on the other side of the river were doing much the same thing and there was not a great deal of belligerence with informal truces occasionally taking place when the pickets would meet and fraternize and perhaps trade (so long as no officers were present to break up such officially forbidden meetings). For the three or so weeks Lee planned his destruction of McClellan's army, Stuart rode around it, and Jackson confounded multiple Unionist forces in the Valley. The eastern Carolinians, meanwhile, spent their time fighting another sort of blood-thirsty enemy, the mosquito. The heavy May rains and warm, humid weather combined to create ideal conditions for swarms of mosquitoes to torment the soldiers. One Tar Heel on picket duty that June wrote that "to our great regret [mosquitoes] assemble invariably at our [picket] post to entertain us for our term of 12 hours."[11]

The drill and picket routine ended, though, towards the end of the month. According to Lee's plan, Jackson's army would come down from the Valley in the early hours of June 26. When he crossed the Virginia Central, Jackson would alert Branch who was to inform his new division commander, A.P. Hill, that Jackson was on hand. Having performed that duty, Branch was to cross the Chickahominy at Half Sink and head his North Carolina brigade south and rejoin the rest of the Light Division, which was to clear the Meadow Bridge for Longstreet's and D.H. Hill's divisions. If all went as planned, 56,000 Rebels would pounce on 28,000 Yankees under Porter's command around Mechanicsville and destroy them or send them scurrying away, laying open McClellan's supply line. On June 24 the 18th North Carolina cooked its rations and put them in haversacks. They were told to travel light, to take only what they needed for combat on their backs along with one blanket. A.P. Hill's orders to his brigadiers read in part: "No wagons will be taken along except one for each Regt. and battery for ammunition.... Knapsacks will be left behind in camp with the sick. Artillery as well as Infantry, the men taking but one blanket...."[12]

But things did not go as planned on June 26. Expecting to hear something from Jackson early, Branch had the brigade up and prepared to cross the Chickahominy before daylight. In his official report, Branch noted: "It was stated that General Jackson would cross the [Virginia Central] railroad by 3 o'clock Thursday morning, and ... I was under arms and prepared to cross [the Chickahominy] at 4 A.M. of Thursday." Since there was nothing for the men to do but wait until orders came to head out, Colonel Cowan told his second in command, Tom Purdie, to have the men stack arms and rest under the trees. Purdie also had the company officers and NCOs understand that while the men were free to fall out and relax a bit, they were to be ready to fall in and march at a moment's notice. After several hours of sitting under the trees, smoking pipes, and talking about the possibility of getting some revenge for Hanover Court House later in the day, the 18th's men had their reverie broken as shouts of "Fall in!" rang through the area. They formed up in two ranks in front of their stacked muskets, took their arms, shouldered them, and marched out in column of fours, crossing the Chickahominy late that morning (and some six hours behind Lee's original schedule of events because Jackson's army was well short of its mark that day).[13]

Branch's brigade headed down the Old Cold Harbor Road to link up with the Light Division at the Meadow Bridge just northwest of the town of Mechanicsville. As the brigade moved towards Mechanicsville, they were slowed by cavalry pickets. The stiffest resistance came from elements of the 8th Illinois Cavalry near Atlee's Station, but the action was not serious; the Yankee troopers' job was simply so slow the Confederate columns up rather than defeat them. It worked. As Branch later wrote, the cavalry pickets resisted "our advance at every favorable point, but with no other effect than to retard, without checking, my march." At one point along the march, near where Old Cold Harbor Road is met by Shady Grove Church Road, the 18th North Carolina looked to its left and saw another large group of Confederates marching down a parallel road. These were General Richard Ewell's men from the Valley. The two groups of Confederates shouted and waved at one another, probably trading Rebel Yells as well.[14]

While General Branch did what was expected of him on June 26 in the sense that he had his men ready to move the instant he heard that Jackson had crossed the railroad, he failed in one important respect. As his report showed, he understood that Jackson was to have been in the vicinity much earlier than he actually was. This vital piece of information needed to be passed on to his commanding officer, A.P. Hill, so that Hill could let Lee know what was happening and how far off the original time frame the operation was. Unfortunately, Hill did not know that Jackson was late and not in position to jump on Porter's flank and rear as A.P. Hill, D.H. Hill, and James Longstreet attacked his front. All morning and into the afternoon A.P. Hill, who was to spearhead the attack on Porter's front, waited for word of Jackson's whereabouts. After hearing nothing and fearing that he was about to lose the opportunity to complete his assignment for the day, A.P. Hill attacked blindly the well-entrenched Federal position along Beaver Dam Creek one half-mile east of Mechanicsville. The result was a complete disaster for the Confederates. Fortunately because of the later start from Half Sink and the delays caused by Union cavalry, the 18th North Carolina was not on hand when the bloody mess that was the Battle of Mechanicsville opened. The regiment spent the day in reserve to exploit the breakthrough that never came. Though the regiment put Mechanicsville on its flag as a battle honor, the only danger it faced was from distant artillery fire, which cost the regiment three men wounded.[15]

The next morning Cowan and Purdie had the regiment up before dawn to renew the attack on the Federals. Lee intended to keep the pressure on Porter partly because doing so was still the best way to turn McClellan out of his entrenchments before Richmond and also because if he did not, McClellan, as Davis and others feared, might figure out that if there was a large force north of the Chickahominy there could not be too many in front of his massive army sitting in front of the Confederate capital. Armed with that intelligence it might occur to McClellan to attack the skeleton force in front of him. But, Lee reasoned, if he kept the pressure on north of the river, McClellan would not do anything rash or bold out of fear that his supply and communication line was in danger. But as the North Carolinians moved towards the Union works along Beaver Dam Creek, they were not met by enemy fire but they were met by the grisly scenes of the previous day's battle. Corpses lay strewn about in bunches and in the hot June sun were already beginning to bloat and turn black. One Tar Heel from the brigade recalled that the "Yankee dead had not been moved and the swarms of horse flies that arose from the dead carcasses rendered it necessary for each man to hold one hand over his mouth and nose." In some places Southern soldiers had been shot while wading in muddy, knee-deep water and remained rooted in the muck like macabre scarecrows.[16]

Hill's Light Division marched about two miles on the Old Cold Harbor Road and turned right at Walnut Grove Church onto the Telegraph Road. This was late morning, probably around eleven o'clock or so. After another couple of miles the 18th North Carolina passed Dr. William Gaines's gristmill before going about another mile reaching New Cold Harbor. There Hill's division had found Porter in another formidable position. Porter had arranged his force along an elevated area known to the locals as Turkey Hill. To get at him Lee's men would have to cross a sluggish, slow-moving stream, Boatswain's Swamp, as well as deal with the tangled morass of brush and trees. The Federals had laid out three lines of defense and at each one they had taken logs, fence rails, and knapsacks, anything that could possibly stop a bullet or ball, and established defensive works. To make things even more difficult for the Confederates, Porter also had seventeen batteries totaling nearly 100 guns he could use to tear into attackers.[17]

A.P. Hill opened the fight at Gaines's Mill. His brigades were, according to Lee's plans, to be supported by Longstreet while Jackson hit Porter on his right flank and threatened his rear; the same basic plan that was to have been executed at Mechanicsville. Again Lee's force north of the Chickahominy would overwhelm Porter's V Corps, which was outnumbered. But like at Mechanicsville the day before, things did not go quite as they were supposed to.

Maxcy Gregg's South Carolina brigade led the Light Division that morning, followed by Branch's North Carolinians. Neither brigade had seen action at Mechanicsville so they were out front on June 27. Gregg's South Carolinians attacked first at about two o'clock and were thrown back by the well-protected Federals. Branch ordered his brigade in next. The first ones to go in were the 7th and the 28th North Carolina and they got into a very hot fight. As those regiments were fighting, Colonel Cowan took the 18th and deployed it on the brigade's far right and advanced through very boggy undergrowth towards the Yankees behind Boatswain's Swamp at around two-thirty or three. As the 18th advanced against the Federals from the 9th Massachusetts and elements of the 14th New York and 62nd Pennsylvania, the terrain caused Cowan to continually shift to his right as he sought a less dense and boggy area to attack through. The result was, Colonel Cowan later reported, "I became separated from the remainder of the brigade, which had been formed on the left, and for a long time was wholly without assistance in my attempts upon the enemy's position." One New Yorker remembered: "We stood it and give it to them as fast as they could give it to us."

Between the tremendous amount of smoke from the artillery and musketry and the dense vegetation, Cowan had a limited view of what was going on around him; he knew only that his orders were to attack the enemy and keep trying to push him back until and unless he heard otherwise. Shouting to be heard over the din of the battle, Cowan and his officers ordered the 18th North Carolina forward into a steady stream of shot and shell. "Again and again was that position assailed," Cowan reported to Branch, "and again and again were we repulsed by vastly superior numbers." Pointing out that his Tar

Heels had done all they could under the circumstances, Cowan observed: "Regiment after regiment was sent in to the same attack shared the same fate, and it was not until late in the afternoon, when the continuous arrival of fresh troops [from Longstreet and Jackson] had given us something like an equality of forces, that any decided impression was made upon the enemy." Indeed, Hill's brigades opened one of the bloodiest battles of the Civil War and fought the first half of it largely unassisted and suffered heavily before Longstreet and Jackson arrived to turn the tide in the Confederates' favor at Gaines's Mill. A soldier who had been in the middle of it wrote afterward that all "the undergrowth of the very thick timbers were mowed in two ... by the iron and lead hailstorm which prevailed at that place." Over the ground where the 18th North Carolina and others had fought, "the pools of blood [were] so very thickly scattered about that a person could scarcely set his feet clear of them." Cowan related the fierceness of the fight to Branch a few days later when he reported that his "loss in killed and wounded was 68. Nothing but the thickness of the woods saved us from total destruction in our first unassisted efforts upon the enemy's works." Coming on top of the losses suffered at Hanover Court House, the regiment's numbers were dropping precipitously.

Cowan was very proud of how his regiment performed at Gaines's Mill. This was a truly bloody fight, like Hanover Court House, and like at Hanover Court House his men were roughly handled by a larger force fighting from the defensive position. The enemy commander, General Porter, had observed admiringly in his report that Hill's and Longstreet's men came

> dashing across the intervening plain, floundering in the swamps, and struggling against the tangled brushwood, brigade after brigade seemed almost to melt away before the concentrated fire of our artillery and infantry; yet others pressed on, followed by supports as dashing and brave as their predecessors, despite the heavy losses and the disheartening effect of having to clamber over many of their disabled and dead, and to meet their surviving comrades rushing back in great disorder from the deadly contest.

But despite the terrible terrain and the odds against them that Porter mentioned, Cowan's regiment behaved increasingly like a veteran regiment. The fire "was such that we were exposed to a heavy fire from the flank as well as from the front," a situation that caused many inexperienced regiments to panic and flee, but Cowan said his men never did. They were compelled to fall back several times under the galling fire but they stayed in ranks and obeyed their officers when ordered to re-form "with the promptness, if not the precision, of drill." Once again the 18th North Carolina had been given an incredibly difficult job to do and once again the regiment gave a good account of itself.[18]

Battlefield of Gaines's Mill where the 18th fought and distinguished itself in heavy and confused fighting on June 27, 1862. Library of Congress.

The next day, June 28, provided the regiment with a day free from marching and fighting but it was a mixed blessing. On the positive side, the Yankees had left behind all sorts of wonderful things in their retreat across the Chickahominy. Berry Benson of the 1st South Carolina wrote: "Knapsacks were captured by the thousands and rifled, while the whole Confed. army refitted itself with blankets, rubber clothes, tentflies, haversacks, and canteens." In those thousands of haversacks the North Carolinians found beef, hardtack, and coffee, which they promptly transferred to their own haversacks. Conversely, being the victors and holding the field meant that it was the Southerners' job to deal with the battle's aftermath. Hours were spent recovering the wounded and taking them to the surgeons and pulling out the dead for burial. A Texas soldier said he "never had a clear conception of the horrors of war until that night and the morning. Friends and foes all together.... Oh the awful scene witnessed on the battle field. May I never see any more such in life." The men of the 18th North Carolina had, of course, seen the carnage of battle when they marched through Mechanicsville the previous day but that was minor compared to Gaines's Mill where Porter lost nearly 4,000 killed and wounded and the Confederates lost nearly 8,000 killed and wounded. Confederate dead were treated with more care and tended to get at least a cursory burial while the thousands of Federal dead were not always so fortunate. One Southern soldier said that many Yankees were not buried while "a great many they throughed in the River and creeks when convenient." So much for the glory and romance of war.[19]

Thus far, Lee's plans for destroying McClellan's army had not materialized for a variety of reasons. He had, however, scared the Young Napoleon half to death and had McClellan rushing for the safety of Harrison's Landing on the James River. McClellan preferred to call his subsequent moves a "change of base" rather than a retreat, but he was fleeing from the Rebels all the same. Richmond was far safer than it had been just a few days earlier but that was not Lee's ultimate objective, which was to decisively defeat the massive Army of the Potomac. That would not only diminish its fighting ability but also be an illustration of Confederate military strength and help demoralize the Northern population, moving it to seek an end to hostilities rather than contemplate more bloody, fruitless battles. In keeping with the goal of crippling McClellan's army, when Lee saw that the Union commander was heading for the James he decided he had one more opportunity to accomplish what he had not so far. His idea, again a sound one on paper and potentially devastating if properly and completely executed on all fronts, was to hit the Army of the Potomac as it was strung out on the move from the Chickahominy to the James. While some elements had already gotten to Malvern Hill, the bulk was still moving to that location. If Jackson could threaten the flank and rear (again) while Longstreet and Hill pitched into the marching Yankees they would be dealt a crippling and decisive defeat.

On June 29 the 18th North Carolina was on the move again to try to destroy the enemy. They crossed the Chickahominy at the New Bridge along with the rest of the Light Division and Longstreet's division. Their long march that day took them west along Nine Mile Road behind the forces manning the Richmond defenses, south across the Williamsburg and Charles City roads, then left onto the Darbytown Road. The Darbytown Road was the center road between the Charles City Road on the left and the River Road on the right and it, like the other two, fed into the Long Bridge Road near the little hamlet of Glendale. Since the Federals had to go through the Glendale area along the Long Bridge Road to their position on Malvern Hill on the James, Lee's plan called for them to be attacked at or around Glendale where they would be cut to pieces before they could reach the safety of the river and Union gun boats.

Unfortunately once again for Lee, the execution of his plan did not go well. After a long march in hot, muggy conditions the 18th North Carolina was in position along with Longstreet and the rest of A.P. Hill's Light Division but delays in other sectors had them waiting around through the early and middle afternoon hours. With the day slipping away from him, and with it the opportunity to thrash the enemy, Lee ordered Longstreet to attack at five o'clock. In the battle that was known as Glendale or Frayser's Farm (spelled in the *Official Records* and on the 18th's battle flag as Frazier's Farm), Branch's brigade anchored the right of the Confederate line and went into the fight on the right of Kemper's Virginia brigade of Longstreet's division. When the regiment got its assignment to attack a Union artillery position, Colonel Cowan reported: "Without a sign of faltering, shouting the battle-cry of 'Stonewall,' which they adopted of their own accord, they advanced across two open fields in the face of a perfect shower of grape and musketry...." Despite the heavy fire, Cowan proudly reported that the men "maintained themselves ... until the arrival of re-enforcements, when they joined in the general charge which won the batteries." William McLaurin remembered the same hot conditions, writing in 1901:

> Sweeping across an open field, the Eighteenth Regiment charged a battery in the yard of a farm house, strongly supported by infantry. They gave us a warm reception with grape, canister, and minie, and were greatly aided by those on their left who gave us a galling flank fire — so trying at all times — before becoming engaged with those on our right, who did not advance as quickly as we did. With a yell and a rush, everything was carried before us, and at a fearful cost in killed and wounded.[20]

Finally, the 18th North Carolina had tasted the thrill of battlefield victory, but it had come at a heavy price. The records are not entirely clear on the regiment's losses at Frayser's Farm, but Colonel Cowan put it at 150 killed and wounded making it the bloodiest the regiment had yet fought and would ultimately make it one of the costliest the unit experienced during the entire war. Unfortunately, though the men from the Cape Fear region were elated over their accomplishment at Frayser's Farm, in the greater scheme of things a great opportunity was lost. The battle's plan was not effectively executed, and there was plenty of blame to share among Generals Jackson, Longstreet, and Theophilus Holmes for the missed opportunity. Rather than all of the Confederates Lee had scheduled attacking the strung-out enemy as planned, the battle was fought ineffectively and piecemeal, allowing the Federals to slip through Lee's fingers to Malvern Hill and the relative safety that position afforded by its terrain and the Union gun boats. This was truly a lost opportunity. While it is impossible to say with certainty that Frayser's Farm, or any other battle for that matter, could have so affected the course of future events that the war may have ended differently, many did see the failure to crush a large contingent of McClellan's army at that battle as extremely significant. Of the few serious chances the South had of militarily forcing the United States to recognize Confederate independence, Porter Alexander, Lee's talented artillerist, said after the war that the "chance of June 30th '62 impresses me as the best of all." The South, he argued, "at this moment was about in its prime & had more men available than ever before or after. And think of the moral shock to the North of the destruction & capture of McClellan's entire army, & the immense material gain to us in guns, muskets, stores, &c."[21]

Frayser's Farm was the last battle of the Seven Days the 18th North Carolina participated in directly. That was not because Lee had abandoned his hope of hurting McClellan's army while there was still a chance, no matter how long the odds. To that end the Rebel forces moved to attack the Federals atop Malvern Hill on June 30. A.P. Hill's depleted division was held in reserve to exploit any successes or holes opened during the bloody frontal assaults made by other units. None came and Malvern Hill was a bloody mess for the Southern side. Though the 18th did not fight in it, the regiment did lose several members to the intense artillery barrage from the Union side, especially the long range shots from Northern gun boats. Twenty-four-year-old Lazarus Tyson of Company B was killed in the shelling at Malvern Hill and James Dunham of Company K was mortally wounded. Company D's John Biggs was also hit in the elbow but survived his wound. These losses may explain why the regiment was permitted to put Malvern Hill on its flag as a battle honor despite not playing a direct role in the fighting on the hill itself.[22]

During the six or so weeks that ended on June 30, 1862, at Malvern Hill, the officers and men of the 18th North Carolina had undergone a significant transformation. The unit went from being a totally green outfit knowing nothing of life in a combat infantry regiment to one that had seen long marches on muddy roads in torrential rain storms and under a blazing sun. They had also earned the right to call themselves members of a fighting regiment, having fought in three very hard battles and helped drive the enemy from the capital. As proof of just how hot the fighting had been, the 18th North Carolina lost over half its numbers during the Seven Days Battles — thirty-seven killed and 187 wounded in addition to a number of captured. Colonel Cowan was impressed with his men, reporting that during the previous two weeks,

> it appeared to me that the men fought throughout the whole army as if each individual was thoroughly impressed with the belief that it was necessary that we should be victorious in the field before Richmond. Amid this army of heroes I have no reason to be dissatisfied with my regiment. Whether on the march, in the field, exposed to fatigue and privations, in midst of danger and in the face of death, they were cheerful and obedient,

prompt and daring. No order was given that they did not cheerfully and faithfully attempt to execute.

Cowan was proud of his whole regiment, and with good reason, but he was especially proud of the work performed by those he leaned on and relied on most heavily: his subordinate officers. They all "did their full duty," Cowan said, but in the heat of battle he leaned particularly heavily on his second-in-command. For that reason, he said, "I desire to make special mention of my lieutenant-colonel, Thomas J. Purdie. He was everywhere in the thickest of the fight, cool and courageous, encouraging the men and directing them in their duty. His services were invaluable." Company captains also played an important role and Cowan saluted Captains Savage, Barry, McLaurin, Gore, and Byrne by name in his report, pointing out that "all were conspicuous in the discharge of their duties, and all wounded on the field, the last three very seriously, Captain Byrne having lost an arm."[23]

The regiment's brigade commander was also pleased with his men's performance over the previous few weeks. In a somewhat over-the-top style so common to mid-nineteenth century speakers, especially politicians, Branch addressed his Tar Heels:

> While making this bloody but brilliant record for your brigade, you have been, as soldiers of freedom should always be, modest, uncomplaining and regardful of what is due to others. Your ranks have been thinned by the casualties of war, but be not discouraged. In a few days they will be filled by recruits, and yours will be the proud task of teaching them to maintain the reputation you have achieved.

Branch also singled out several officers for "special commendation" that included both Cowan and Purdie of the 18th North Carolina. The regiment was indeed making a name for itself but the experiences were perhaps not what they thought they would have been when they joined, before they had seen the smoke of battle and seen what battle produced. One brigade member said that he had managed the marching and fighting well enough at the time, "but after all the excitement & everything was over my whole system seemed to have given way. I was right sick for a few days." Captain Joseph Saunders of the 33rd North Carolina said after the Seven Days: "I have plenty of military glory to last me for life without getting into any more fights." A soldier in the 28th North Carolina who had missed the fighting while on sick leave thought that Branch's survivors were a good deal more subdued after their experiences. Rather than playing cards and "swearing every word they [spoke]" he noticed that the men were more civil to one another and he saw a lot more Bible reading going on even among those he could never recall seeing with one before Hanover Court House, Gaines's Mill, and Frayser's Farm.[24]

If the regiment could be happy with its recent performance, the ultimate goal of Southern independence was still not achieved. In fact, it seemed no closer than it had when the late June fighting began. Thus Lee went back to the drawing board to devise a new plan to destroy George McClellan's Army of the Potomac. But in the meantime, a new threat developed just to the north of Richmond in the formation of a new Union force, the Army of Virginia, under General John Pope. While Lee worked on a plan to crush McClellan, Pope would have to be dealt with and the 18th North Carolina would form part of the force sent to do that.

Chapter 4

Stonewall Salutes the 18th: The Battle of Cedar Mountain

In the warm hazy days following the Battle of Malvern Hill, which ended the Seven Days Battles, Colonel Robert Cowan and Lieutenant-Colonel Thomas Purdie had the relative peace and quiet to reflect on how quickly and dramatically life had changed. For nearly the entire first year of service the war had been quiet, routine, and even a bit boring. If they or other members of the regiment had entertained any ideas about military life being glamorous or romantic, the last eight weeks' experiences seemed to dispel them. The regiment was camped after Malvern Hill in the area around Charles City Court House and settled back into the routine of camp life, though on alert to fall in at a moment's notice. McClellan had been pushed away from Richmond but he still lurked about, and his large army still posed a very real threat. But for the time being there was little excitement and a short time to rest and recuperate a bit from the marching and fighting of the previous few weeks. There was, however, one incident that broke the camp routine. While still camped around Charles City Court House, McLaurin recalled that "a musket fell from a stack of guns and was discharged, wounding Lieutenant George W. Huggens, Company I, in the foot. He was asleep. It was a rude awakening, and from it he goes limping through life."[1]

While the regiment's officers and men had the luxury of musing over the past few weeks and of being primarily concerned with continuing to train for future battles, other higher-ranking officers did not have that same luxury. The Confederate high command recognized that saving the capital had been a glorious thing but that the military situation in Virginia remained quite dangerous. McClellan and his huge Army of the Potomac remained within twenty miles of Richmond and showed no signs of going anywhere. Indeed, McClellan did want to launch another attack on the Confederate capital, but typical of the Young Napoleon he said he could not consider such a move without about another 100,000 re-enforcements. Not only was the Army of the Potomac in striking distance, but Lee also learned that General Ambrose Burnside's force in North Carolina had been ordered to Virginia and landed at Fort Monroe in July.

McClellan's large and apparently growing force east of the capital was not the only problem that Lee and the Confederate capital faced at that point. Other sizeable Federal forces were all over Virginia. John C. Frémont commanded a force in the Shenandoah Valley; Nathaniel Banks had one just north of Culpeper Court House in central Virginia; and Irvin McDowell had a corps in the Fredericksburg area. Individually these three commands were little more than distractions compared to the threat posed by the Army of the Potomac, but as the Seven Days Battles were ending Union officials moved to better organize those independent groups into a new army to cooperate more efficiently with McClellan to destroy Lee's army, take the Confederate capital, and bring the war to a successful close. This new Army of Virginia under the command of General John Pope was a potentially nasty development for the Confederate high command, since it would be in a position to do one of several things that could spell disaster for the Southern cause. Once the commands were united they could work with the Army of the Potomac and attack Richmond simultaneously and trap the capital in a classic pincer. Or, the Army of Virginia could move on the important town of Gordonsville where the Orange and Alexandria and Virginia Central railroads came together. If Pope took Gordonsville he could cut off food supplies for Lee's army (as well as for the growing population of Richmond) by severing the east-west running Virginia Central from the Shenandoah Valley.[2]

The man commanding the Army of Virginia certainly came in roaring about all the terrible things he intended to do to the Rebels. John Pope is correctly remembered as a swaggering braggart, but his egotism could have been and would have been more easily forgiven had he backed up his braggadocio with positive results. The first thing Pope did when he got to Virginia from the western theater of operations, where things had gone quite well for the Federals to that point, was to alienate the vast majority of the officers and soldiers he now commanded. He introduced himself to his new army with the following:

> Let us understand each other. I have come to you from the West, where we have always seen the backs of our enemies; from an army whose business it has been to seek the adversary and to beat him when he was found; whose policy has been attack and not defense.

He also hinted that eastern troops and officers were timid, thinking of digging in and holding positions instead of taking the fight to the enemy. He condescendingly assured his new army that he thought they had it in them to be good soldiers and officers; they just lacked proper, aggressive leadership. Well, John Pope had arrived and he would turn them from skulking failures into manly warriors. One can well imagine the heated and resentful conversations in tents and around Union campfires the evening the great general's message was read.[3]

Pope not only irritated his own army, he managed to also thoroughly enrage Confederate leaders, especially Virginians, with his proclamations and general orders in his theater of operations. In the summer of 1862 the war still tended to be fought (at least among the organized armies and in official circles) with the idea of restricting as much as possible the destructiveness of war to uniformed combatants. Civilians and their property were still seen as officially off limits unless there was some compelling reason to view them otherwise. During the second half of the war and in the decades and centuries that followed whatever old fashioned concepts of "humane" and "civilized" warfare that existed disappeared. But in mid–1862 many still believed in such ideas, and when Pope announced that civilian property could be confiscated without payment, that civilians could be forced to leave their homes if they refused to take the oath of allegiance to the United States and executed if they returned, and that irregular or guerrilla soldiers could be summarily executed rather than treated as prisoners of war, Virginians were apoplectic. Jackson's mapmaker, Jed Hotchkiss, captured the feelings of many in the Old Dominion when he wrote to his family after reading about Pope's orders: "We are all very much incensed at Pope's atrocious orders and hope the day of retribution may soon come to him & his vile crew." Another Virginia soldier wrote, "Of all the things in the world I hate, it is fighting, but it would afford me the greatest pleasure to thrash that contemptible scoundrel, but we will pay him up for it yet."[4]

As a Virginian, General Lee was also angered by Pope's orders. Pope appears to have been the only Federal officer, in fact, for whom Lee ever expressed obvious personal dislike, referring to Pope as a "miscreant." And after the war his artillery chief, Porter Alexander, said Pope had never been respected by those who actually knew him and that he certainly lived up to his reputation when given important command. Of Pope, Alexander wrote that his reputation,

> in army circles, as I happened to know them, was that of a blatherskite, & shortly before he was promoted to the command of his new army (June 27th) over the heads of many prominent & distinguished major generals in the East — like McDowell, Franklin, Porter, Sumner, &c. — he had telegraphed some very sensational & absurd yarns about what he had accomplished with some cavalry out about Corinth, Miss. The old army officers now among the Confederates used to smile to think how Pope had managed to impose himself upon Mr. Lincoln & how bitterly many of the old officers, who knew Pope & who were overslaughed, would necessarily feel about it.

But Lee could not immediately concentrate on dealing with Pope, whose intentions remained unknown, with McClellan menacing Richmond in considerable force. But neither could he totally ignore Pope. Vital rail connections, especially to the Valley, had to be protected and with Jackson in Richmond those rail lines were extremely vulnerable. Lee learned on July 12 that Union forces had occupied Culpeper Court House, which was less than thirty miles from Gordonsville. The move seemed to indicate that the Federals were moving to cut Lee and Richmond off from the Valley, something he could not allow to happen. Already outnumbered by the Army of the Potomac, Lee was understandably reluctant to further weaken himself by sending a sizable force away from Richmond to protect his supply line to the west but at the same time he had little choice. The next day, July 13, Lee ordered Jackson to take his division along with Richard Ewell's from Richmond and head for Louisa Court House (and to Gordonsville if possible) to get a better grasp of what the Army of Virginia was up to, to help protect vital rail lines, and perhaps seize an opportunity if one presented itself to hit Pope and disrupt Union plans in central Virginia.[5]

Jackson's and Ewell's divisions completed a difficult trip, thanks to a shortage of cars and damaged rails, and arrived at Louisa Court House by July 18. Since the Federals had neglected to move to Gordonsville by that time, Jackson took advantage and occupied the town. For the next week or so, this small segment of the Army of Northern Virginia (about 11,000) continued to drill, something Jackson insisted upon, and guard the railroad while information was collected about the enemy. Jackson also sought ways to hit the Army of Virginia but with his small force being vastly outnumbered by Pope he did not see how it would be possible; at least he did not see how it would be possible without some significant reinforcement from the Richmond area. Jackson wrote to Lee about the problem and asked his commander for more men, but Lee remained reluctant to further weaken the Army of Northern Virginia with McClellan still so close and still getting stronger according to the latest intelligence.

Then, during the third week of July, Lee's view of the matter changed. His communications with Jackson got decidedly more aggressive regarding Pope. The messages from Richmond to Jackson were more positive; Jackson was not only to keep an eye on Pope and strike a blow if possible, he was to boldly and positively look for the chance to hit the Army of Virginia. On July 23 Lee told Jackson that he could have more troops soon if that would encourage Stonewall to find a way to strike Pope's force. A few days later on July 27 Lee's instructions to Jackson were even more aggressive: "I want Pope to be suppressed."[6]

The reasons for Lee's change of heart can only be guessed at. It is certainly plausible that the anger at Pope's policies and announcements played a role. Lee was a human being and no doubt harbored the same desires to give General Pope a bloody nose as other Virginians, despite his often being portrayed as above human motivations and failings. In fact, his communications with Jackson suggest that Pope's "ungentlemanly" orders were on his mind. On July 23 he expressed anger over Army of Virginia's scouts being "sent out for plunder, provisions, and devastation." In this same order, not coincidentally, Lee told Jackson: "I am ... ready to re-enforce you as soon as that prospect is available." Four days later Lee told Jackson to "suppress" Pope at least in part because the Union general's inhumane orders "if the newspapers report them correctly, cannot be permitted...." But while personal motives were no doubt present, they were not the only ones. It seems entirely likely that what Lee had in mind during that third week of July was having Jackson damage and disrupt Pope's army quickly enough to remove it as an immediate threat and allow the Army of Northern Virginia to be restored to full strength to deal exclusively with McClellan.[7]

The 18th North Carolina's men and officers knew little if any of these issues, at least not in any sort of detail. They knew the enemy was close by and that at any moment the long roll could sound calling them out to form up and march to battle. This was, after all, the height of the campaigning season. But for the first couple of weeks following Malvern Hill, the activity was mainly the routine of picket duty and drill. One change, though, was the form that drill took in Branch's brigade. Previously the five Tar Heel regiments had drilled independently of one another rather than as a single unit. Part of that may have been because mastering company and regimental drill could be difficult enough for green soldiers and inexperienced officers. But brigade drill, complicated as it was for all involved, was necessary for success, and perhaps even survival, on the battlefield. If the five regiments could work together efficiently and effectively as a single unit then Branch's brigade would pack a much more powerful punch. Brigade drill was more difficult to master, but having been in battle the officers and soldiers were well aware of its importance and so dedicated themselves to putting in the long, tedious hours learning it in the warm, humid conditions of Virginia in July. The 18th did not know it, but they were going to realize the advantages of brigade drill in battle in a very short time.[8]

At the time Lee was contemplating sending Jackson reinforcements, two of his best generals, James Longstreet and A.P. Hill, were at each other's throats. The situation was particularly problematic because Hill was under Longstreet's immediate command. Disagreement and hard feelings had developed over the reporting of Frayser's Farm. Both men felt they had been disparaged by the other and if the situation around their nation's capital had not been so dire the whole episode would have been comical. At one point Longstreet had Hill arrested while Hill challenged Longstreet to a duel. Fortunately the duel never took place but it was more than obvious these men would not be able to get along with one another and function well as a team. So, when Lee decided during the third week of July to reinforce Jackson's command at Gordonsville the choice was all but made for him by the falling out between "Old Pete" and "Little Powell"; the fast moving, hard-hitting Light Division would join Stonewall and the effort to "suppress" Pope. The 18th North Carolina was off to become part of another famous Confederate machine, Jackson's "foot cavalry."9

The 18th North Carolina boarded trains and headed for Gordonsville on July 27 and arrived there on the following day. For the next few days the brigade's routine was not appreciably different from what it had been in Richmond. They drilled and they performed guard and picket duty like everyone else. Like other officers serving under Jackson, those in the 18th had no idea what exactly he and his men were to expect from the move. Jackson was a notoriously secretive individual, a characteristic that often infuriated and frustrated those who served under him. About the only thing one could be reasonably sure of was that an order to strike camp, fall in, and move out could come at any moment. Therefore Lieutenant-Colonel Purdie, who had been standing in for Colonel Cowan who was ill and possibly wounded (the records are hazy) since the Seven Days Battles ended, made sure his officers and men

When A.P. Hill's division was assigned to Jackson's command after the Seven Days Battles, the 18th became part of Jackson's 'foot cavalry,' earning Jackson's respect at Cedar Mountain in August 1862. Library of Congress.

were prepared to march when the inevitable order came down the chain of command. It would come shortly.

Pope had determined to cut the Virginia Central Railroad connecting Richmond to the Shenandoah Valley. It was something Lee had feared all along and it also made perfectly logical tactical and strategic sense to cut the Army of Northern Virginia's major supply and communications line. If the plan was sound enough, the execution left much to be desired. Pope's army was still badly divided. Franz Sigel (after John C. Frémont got in a snit and resigned over serving under Pope, whom he outranked) commanded what amounted to the right wing of the Army of Virginia near Sperryville in the lower part of the Shenandoah Valley. The center of the army, Banks' corps, was at Culpeper Court House. Pope's left, McDowell's corps, was currently just outside Fredericksburg. Put simply, Pope had an army that outnumbered Jackson's newly reinforced command by about a two-to-one margin but it was so divided at the beginning of August that his advantage existed only on paper. Rather than wait for his full force to assemble, on August 5 Pope ordered Banks' corps forward (south) as part of his goal to control the Virginia Central by taking either Gordonsville or Charlottesville.[10]

While that was going on, Jackson's view of Pope's disposition and strength became clearer. From his cavalry as well as from local civilian spies he learned that part of Pope's command was isolated near Culpeper. With Hill's large division on hand, Jackson had a numerical advantage over the vulnerable Yankee division just north of him. When word came that the Federal force was moving south, Jackson must have figured that God had chosen to bless him with an opportunity to accomplish everything Lee wanted. If he moved quickly Jackson had the chance to pounce on this portion of the Army of Virginia, and maybe even destroy it, throwing the Army of Virginia into complete disarray and neutralizing, at least temporarily, the Union threat to Richmond from that direction. He would also be taking the opportunity to "suppress" the despised General Pope. And, best of all, if done properly it could be accomplished within the next few days and permit Jackson to reunite with the Army of Northern Virginia in plenty of time to help defend the capital should McClellan suddenly (and uncharacteristically) become energetic. On August 6 Jackson told his generals to prepare their commands to move out.

In typical Jackson fashion, that was about all he had to say on the matter. Where the army was going exactly and what its target would be was known only to Jackson. Purdie, after meeting with Colonel Cowan, went to his company captains and told them what little he knew. They were definitely going to be moving the next day, and knowing Jackson's reputation for early starts he told them to immediately cook any rations they had and to get what rest they could because they would very likely be up and several miles away by sunrise. During the warm, muggy evening of August 6, 1862, the regiment cooked rations and checked and double checked their arms and accoutrements. The atmosphere in the camp was suddenly transformed; the routine camp life of the last week or so ended as they prepared to seek out the enemy and hopefully strike a blow that would bring them one step closer to their ultimate goal of independence. There was an excitement but also a nervousness about the camp because these men, while wanting to defeat their foe, had also seen the horrors of combat. If they were ignorant of where Jackson was going to take them before the sun rose the following day, they knew well the horrors of the battlefield that likely awaited them. Few slept that night.[11]

In the inky pre-dawn darkness orders to "Fall in" were heard throughout the 18th North Carolina's camp. Cowan and Purdie had already risen and had their gear loaded onto their horses. The men quickly rose and put on only what they needed for marching — haversack; canteen; accoutrement belt, which held the cartridge box, cap box, and bayonet; and blanket roll. Hill's Light Division was indeed traveling light and it was a good thing they were this morning. The heat and humidity had been horribly oppressive ever since August began; all during the previous week the coolest day had been eighty-eight degrees. As the men fell in and prepared to march they could already tell that it was going to be a hot and difficult trek before they bedded down for the evening. Even these men who had lived in the South all their lives commented how warm and muggy the first day's march was. By seven A.M. the thermometer was already in the mid-eighties and climbing steadily. "By 2:00 P.M.," one historian has noted, "the mercury had reached 98. There were no measurable breezes." One soldier in the Rebel column said the weather was "so hot men faint[ed] and die[d] on the march." A member of the Light Division recalled that because of the steamy conditions, "straggling was deplorable, although hardly anything else was to be expected in such heat as we had."

Making the march from Gordonsville even worse was the huge amount of dust thousands of men, horses, and wagons kicked up on the dry dirt roads. With no breeze and no rain the dust clouds of each army could be seen for miles and made things miserable for the soldiers as the dust found and stuck to their sweaty skin and caked their throats. "Though it is seldom mentioned, and but little thought of, outside of army circles," one Southerner wrote while recalling the day's march towards Orange Court House, "one of the greatest discomforts of the soldier's life, and one of the severest tests of his physical endurance, is, undoubtedly, the great dust-clouds that hang over and envelop a moving army on a dry, hot day. It has to be seen and experienced to be thoroughly understood." From the Federal side, General George Gordon said, "Clouds of dust hung over us, there was not a breath of air, the road was like a furnace...." Under these trying conditions Colonel Purdie could do little more than ride along his regiment's line and offer encouragement to those on foot and remind company officers to do what they could to keep their groups together and moving to reduce straggling. The 18th North Carolina had done some hard marching under difficult circumstances during the previous weeks but nothing they had done to that point remotely compared to the stress and strains of traveling in such stifling, furnace-like conditions. The experience was another step in the process of becoming hardened veterans, though one they would have just as soon skipped.[12]

That evening the exhausted and sweat-soaked column unslung their bedrolls and collapsed at Orange Court House. Jackson gave orders for his divisions to be up and on the road at dawn; he intended to be moving fast and be near and hopefully occupying Culpeper Court House by the end of the next day. Such was not to be, however. Originally Jackson had told his division commanders, Ewell, Hill, and Winder (in that order) to march out the next morning at first light. But for reasons historians still do not understand, because Jackson never explained it verbally or in writing, those orders were changed. The lead division, Ewell's, was now to take a north-easterly route to Liberty Mills, cross the Rapidan River on the Madison Road, and rejoin the main column at Barnett's Ford. This may have been done to ease congestion on the Orange-Culpeper Road or it may have been done to deceive Pope. Either way, the change would not have been an issue had Jackson informed Hill and Winder of the change in plans, which he did not do.

The next morning, August 8, Branch's brigade, along with the rest of the Light Division awoke before dawn, rolled up their blankets, slung them over their shoulders, and fell in. Hill had made sure his men were in place and ready to fall in behind Ewell's division as it passed his own. The problem, of course, was that Hill did not know that Ewell's men had already left Orange by another route. Purdie and his men waited, along with an increasingly impatient Hill, for Ewell's column to march past. Finally, as the sun was coming over the horizon a Confederate column, presumably Ewell's, was seen coming down the road. In reality the column belonged to Jackson's old division under General Winder. Hill did not immediately realize that; he had no idea Jackson had changed the orders so he naturally assumed the men he saw coming from and headed in the appointed direction belonged to Ewell. When about half the column had passed in front of the Light Division, Hill realized that it was Winder, who was supposed to follow his own division that day, and decided to just let Winder's division pass and fall in behind it. It was not what Jackson had ordered, but Hill figured it would do more damage and cause more disruption to halt Winder and try to sort the mess out than to just wait and bring up the rear. Purdie could only tell his company commanders to wait a little longer. Given that the day promised to be every bit as torrid as the previous ones, Purdie may have also told the company captains to allow the men to stack arms and sit down along the roadside until it was time for them to take their place in the marching column.

And the wait continued for much longer than anyone thought. Having seen that something was amiss, Jackson had gone back to the Orange camp site to see what was going on. What he saw was the Light Division along the side of the road, which infuriated him. Hill was supposed to be on the road, in front of Winder, not passively standing on the sideline. Orders had been disobeyed and as a result Jackson was losing valuable time — at least that was Jackson's view of the situation. Why, Stonewall fumed, had Hill willfully disobeyed orders to move at first light ahead of General Winder and link up with General Ewell at Barnett's Ford?!

Perhaps wondering if he was ever going to serve under someone he could work with, Hill tried to explain to Jackson that he had no idea Ewell had moved out earlier by a different route. He had assumed that Winder's division was Ewell's and when he discovered the error he thought it best to simply fall in behind Winder and bring up the rear rather than further disrupt and delay the march. All of this was perfectly reasonable but Jackson was not impressed. Rather, he was livid at what he saw as Hill's indifference and disobedience and determined that he would salvage the situation personally. Looking back down the road Jackson saw a group from Winder's division marching along. Spurring his horse towards it, Jackson ordered the group to quickly move up and close the gap with the rest of Winder's column so that Hill and the Light Division could hurry and get on the road. While Stonewall thought he was acting to get Hill on the road sooner he was actually delaying the Light Division even further. Jackson had ordered the van of Winder's supply wagon train to close up, which meant that Hill's men would now have to wait while the long line of slow-moving wagons passed before filing into the marching column.

Purdie likely knew little of the details as to why the regiment continued to wait around as the sun climbed ever higher driving the temperature with it. He may or may not have gleaned that something had gone wrong and that sparks had flown between Jackson and Hill. Then again, by this point in his career he was no stranger to the "hurry up and wait" nature of military life. Purdie probably told his company commanders to have the men just sit and wait until it was clear to fall in. The men of eastern North Carolina waited most of the day, as it turned out, because further complicating the situation was the fact that Ewell and Winder had reached the rendezvous point at Barnett's Ford at the same time, causing a massive traffic jam that brought both columns to a grinding halt. By the time it unraveled it was late afternoon.

When Purdie mounted his horse and had the men fall in column of fours to finally start marching it was nearly sundown. So little progress was made that day by the Light Division that when the Tar Heels of Branch's brigade laid out their ground cloths and blanket rolls that muggy evening they were within eyesight of where they had begun the day.[13]

Jackson was in a foul mood over the lack of progress made on August 8, though as several historians have correctly noted, he did not seem to ever consider that the problems were due to his lack of communication and obsessive secretiveness. But while Jackson's men and officers had little idea where they were headed or what Jackson's plans were, all had the sense that action was imminent. One admiring Tennessee soldier in the Light Division wrote home: "Jackson must be going to attack. He is so quiet and quick no one can tell what he is going to do. He is the man for me." Hill, the object of Jackson's unwarranted wrath over the botched march was determined to show his commander that he and his division were an even match for the "foot cavalry" veterans. Being several miles behind Ewell's lead brigade Hill gave orders for his force to be up earlier than usual and marching to close the gap. Purdie and the 18th North Carolina were thus awake, packed up, and on the march well before dawn on August 9, 1862. General Branch had ordered his brigade up at 1:00 A.M. and "immediately put his North Carolinians under arms, and before long the tired men moved forward sluggishly." Even at that early hour it was obvious the day's march would be another stifling one, one made worse by the fact that being so far back in the column of march ensured they would eat the most dust.[14]

The march was indeed one of the hottest and most miserable the men ever experienced. Jackson was determined to move quickly up the Orange-Culpeper Road to strike the isolated Federal force in front of him leading him to push his divisions hard. By 7:00 A.M. the temperature was already in the low eighties with no breeze or clouds to relieve the sweaty, dust-encrusted column. All was hazy, hot, and humid. An artillerist noted that "we travelled fast as we could under a sun that must have been one hundred degrees in the shade." Another Confederate marching that day recalled: "Oh how hot the weather was. [A] great many fell on the road with exhaustion, some died with sun stroke." In his report to Lee, Jackson mentioned that August 9 had been "oppressively hot; several men had sun-strokes." Purdie's job of encouraging the men and minimizing straggling was especially difficult because they had been on the road the longest. By mid-morning the 18th North Carolina had already been on the road marching at a brisk pace for over six hours. Fortunately there were streams nearby on the route like Crooked Run where water details could be sent out to fill canteens fairly quickly and then return to the still-marching column bringing a measure of relief to dust-choked throats.[15]

If anyone had any ideas about Jackson easing the pace at all because of the extreme conditions they quickly understood that was out of the question. At some point that morning Jackson received confirmation of who commanded the section of the Army of the Potomac he was after — Nathaniel Banks. Banks had been one of the Federal commanders Jackson had defeated during his famous Valley Campaign, and Stonewall did not hold his opponent in very high regard. In fact, for such a rigidly religious individual, Jackson is reported to have permitted himself to indulge in the sin of pride upon hearing who his adversary was. According to one of his staff officers, Jackson was heard to say, "Banks is in our front and he is generally willing to fight, and, he generally gets whipped." Jackson apparently now had visions of totally embarrassing (again) a Federal opponent and he was anxious, too anxious perhaps, to get at an ill-led Yankee force and destroy it.[16]

A few miles ahead of the brigade, the head of Jackson's column came to a fork in the road at Major's School House and took the right-hand fork onto the Culpeper Road, the same road Banks' command was marching south/southwest on. All that morning each side's cavalry had been running into each other; by the early afternoon Jackson was certain Banks was immediately in front of him and he meant to take him. Initial contact was made around one o'clock that afternoon by lead elements of Ewell's division commanded by General Jubal Early. Though Jackson's full force was strung out behind him for miles he began deploying for battle. He intended to use Cedar Mountain (known locally as Slaughter's Mountain) to anchor his right and set artillery there and to the left of the mountain. Ewell's division would cover the front between Cedar Mountain and the Culpeper Road. Winder's division, following Ewell's was to come up and deploy on the left of the Confederate battle front, on the left (north) side of the Culpeper Road. If all went according to plan, and with Banks commanding, Jackson certainly saw no reason everything should not go according to plan: his artillery on the right would take out the opposing artillery and soften the infantry; Ewell's division would attack on the right and roll up the Federal left flank; the Light Division would come and exploit Ewell's success and complete Banks' inevitable destruction.[17]

The 18th North Carolina, several miles behind the Confederate van, had no idea that the day was about to get very exciting or that these men from eastern Carolina were going to play a significant role in defeating Banks (and saving Jackson's command). At about three-thirty in the hazy afternoon cannon fire could be heard from the direction of Cedar Mountain to the regiment's front and right. Given the extreme conditions most of the men probably joked how they hoped it was thunder and the promise of a cooling storm. Some may have thought it was merely some shots to disperse Yankee cavalry trying to penetrate their screen to discern their movements. But the fire did not cease after a few scattering rounds; it increased in intensity and the rate of fire signaled to the men and officers who had a few battles under their belts that the two armies had found each other here in the shadow of Cedar Mountain. Suddenly couriers and staff officers were seen racing up and down the column with orders and communications for division and brigade commanders. Colonel Cowan and Lieutenant-Colonel Purdie rode along the column and with an increased urgency told the men to "close up" and had company officers round up the stragglers not completely incapacitated by the heat. The atmosphere in the ranks had changed; the enemy was close by and a mood of anxious nervousness fell over the officers and men of the 18th North Carolina.[18]

The artillery duel lasted for about ninety minutes, ending at about five o'clock. Generals Early and William Taliaferro (pronounced Tolliver) deployed their brigades along the high ground overlooking a cornfield on the right (south) side of the Culpeper Road. At that time only General James Garnett's brigade along with the 10th Virginia was on the left side of the Culpeper Road, and about half of those regiments were facing to their right across the Culpeper Road rather than the front. Jackson seemed to be fixated on the right side of his line and had not sent out cavalry for intelligence about what may or may not be in front of his left. Thus, only the 10th Virginia, 1st Virginia Battalion, and 42nd Virginia were facing that direction. When Jackson ordered the attack at around 5:45, only the right-hand side of the road was properly deployed; on the left there was a single brigade on his left flank because Winder and the Light Division were still a considerable distance to the rear and not on hand. Jackson apparently had decided he would simply insert units into the battle as they arrived; after all, that is what he had done at Port Republic and it had worked there. This was not the Valley and Banks did not have any intention of sitting still while Jackson manhandled his force.[19]

The problem was that Banks had no intention of sitting there while Jackson whipped him again. In fact, he had the same plan as Jackson did for the battle — turn the enemy's left. To that end Banks had ordered General Samuel W. Crawford's brigade (3rd WI, 46th PA, 28th NY, 5th CT) to the right. The plan was for Crawford's brigade to attack across the wheat field in their front and roll up the Confederate left. The Union commander probably had no idea how sound that plan was. Jackson had paid virtually no attention to his left and would have no idea until it was in the process of being turned and was fighting for its life. The best historian of the battle, Robert Krick, has noted: "An outmanned and outgunned Federal force, attacking from a weaker position, was about to pounce upon Jackson's patchwork quilt of a line and shiver it from end to end."[20]

While Federal General Christopher Auger battled Generals Early and

Taliaferro on the Confederate right all hell was about to erupt on Jackson's left. As ordered, Crawford's Federals emerged from the woods, bayonets gleaming in the shimmering sun and in line of battle ready to attack across the wheat field in front of them. With flags flying and drums beating the Northern soldiers cheered as they launched their assault on the Rebel left. The march across the wheat field was open and therefore deadly, but at the same time the Union men had the numerical advantage. The 10th Virginia, sent to extend the Confederate left, was still arriving and deploying as the Yankees attacked and only half of Garnett's regiments, the 1st Virginia Battalion and 42nd Virginia, were facing the attack when it came. The Stonewall Brigade was on the way but was just beginning to arrive on the right when Crawford's men came crashing through the wheat field.

As Crawford's men got across the wheat field and to the tree line where the Virginians had been placed, an awful fight ensued. The 28th New York and 5th Connecticut were able to get around the 1st Virginia Battalion and by all accounts that unit fled the field without putting up much of a fight to protect the left side of the line. Their flight effectively put the burden of holding back the Yankee assault on the shoulders of the 42nd Virginia alone. Unlike the 1st Virginia Battalion, the Forty-second stood its ground and fought desperately against the New Yorkers and Connecticut men, buying precious time for the Stonewall Brigade and Light Division to get up and into the battle. "The close-in combat on the ground defended by the Forty-second Virginia was unsurpassed for ferocity by any other engagement during the war. A Connecticut soldier described the fray as 'such a hand to hand conflict with bayonet and gunbutt as was equaled by only a few contests of the war.' Neither side was anywhere near out of ammunition, but there was no opportunity to load weapons." According to a Southerner, "The Confederates were giving ground and fighting with clubbed guns, stones, and anything they could get." This was war at its most vicious, its most animalistic. The 42nd Virginia could boast that it did all that could be expected of it and more of any single regiment under those circumstances, but it could not hope to hold off the surging Yankees alone and it was ultimately forced to fall back. Meanwhile the Stonewall Brigade was in the process of arriving to seal the Confederate left but they were a bit to the left of Garnett and did not link up with it at that point. If Banks threw in reinforcements on his right, and he was intending to do just that, Jackson's left would be in extreme danger of being turned and his line completely rolled up — exactly what he had planned to do to Banks.

While the 42nd Virginia was fighting bitterly for its life, the men of the Light Division could hear the sounds of a fierce battle going on. Officers were racing up and down the column, getting the brigades to close up and quicken the pace; the battle hinged on their ability to get into the fight. The 18th had been up and marching since two o'clock that morning and had been marching in sweltering heat and choking dust for over twelve hours. Now their officers, including Thomas Purdie, were shouting orders for all to close up and step up the pace. Branch's North Carolinians, who were second in the Light Division's marching order that day, double-quicked up the Orange-Culpeper Road, turned right at Major's School House onto the Culpeper Road, and headed for the sound of battle.

At 6:00, barely an hour after the battle started, Jackson's left was in considerable danger. Garnett's brigade on the left side of the Culpeper Road was collapsing, thanks in no small part to half of it facing to the right and across the road where Jackson planned for the fighting and the victory to take place. The Stonewall Brigade was arriving to extend and anchor the extreme left of Jackson's line. What was needed, and quickly, was for Hill to have his men enter the maelstrom between the Stonewall Brigade and the Culpeper Road where Garnett was getting pounded and driven. If the gap on the left made by Crawford's Federals was not stabilized by the Confederates, Banks stood an excellent chance of getting some revenge on Jackson.

The Light Division's lead brigade was sent to the right of the Culpeper Road while the rest of the division was sent into the tree line on the left where Garnett's brigade had been. Branch's North Carolina brigade was second in the marching column and drew the job of sealing the breach Crawford had created. The officers of the 18th North Carolina ordered the men to unsling their bedrolls and stack them by the road; they were going into the fight with only what they needed for combat. Purdie dismounted, leaving his horse with the 18th's bedrolls where they would be looked after by non-combatant personnel like cooks and teamsters. They then quickly ordered the regiment into a two-rank battle line. During the Battle of Cedar Mountain the 18th formed the extreme left of the brigade with the 33rd North Carolina on its immediate right followed by the 28th and 37th North Carolina. The Seventh had been pulled out as a reserve and took no active part in the battle.[21]

Despite the critical situation just in front of him, the politician in General Branch could not help taking an opportunity to inspire his men with fiery words about duty and driving Yankee hordes. This was not, obviously, the place for speeches and Stonewall himself rode up to Branch and told him so, telling him to hush and get his men moving, which he did. The Tar Heels moved forward, Purdie leading from the front, sword drawn. Some accounts have Branch's men marching towards the woods where Garnett's men had fallen back chanting "Stonewall Jackson! Stonewall Jackson!" Whether they chanted Jackson's name or not, they definitely threw up a loud yell as they moved towards the scene of battle, something all regiments did as much to steel themselves for the dangerous job ahead as to intimidate the enemy. One of the men in the brigade wrote that they "raised a shout [with] which they are accustomed to go into battle." About a mile to the right of the North Carolinians, a Louisiana soldier remembered hearing them let out a "victorious hurrah" that he could hear above the din of the desperate fight.

Purdie led the regiment about 200 yards when he saw Confederate soldiers running at him in complete disorder. This proved to be elements of the 27th Virginia and probably parts of the 10th Virginia as well. These soldiers had arrived on the scene as Crawford's Federal brigade poured through the wheat field and got pushed backward by the charging Yankees. They were not to be stopped and Purdie turned and ordered his men to open ranks and let the fleeing soldiers through. This, of course, caused a good bit of confusion and probably a lot of jeering in the North Carolinians' ranks, but the regiment's officers quickly restored order and continued forward towards the woods and wheat field beyond. With the right of the brigade resting on the left of the Culpeper Road, Branch's regiments marched forward to the spot Garnett had occupied and where the Federals were threatening to roll up the Rebel left.

Branch's brigade entered the woods where barely thirty minutes earlier the 42nd Virginia had fought so desperately to buy Jackson time for Hill and the Light Division to come to the rescue. As the 18th North Carolina arrived on the scene screaming at the top of their lungs, the macabre scene before them was horrifying. Through the dense smoke could be seen the dead and wounded from both sides littering the ground along with broken muskets, canteens, and all sorts of other equipment. However, given the close quarters combat that had taken place there the scene was particularly grisly. But while the Federals had been able to turn part of Jackson's left they were in some disorder and not well prepared to deal with a fresh brigade ready to fight. The Tar Heels pitched into the decimated and disorganized Federals and this time the Confederates had the manpower advantage. Shouting encouragement from just behind the right side of his regiment's line, Thomas Purdie ordered his men to pour in as hot a fire as they could as quickly as they could into the Northerners in the woods. The pressure proved too great for what remained of Crawford's brigade and he ordered it back across the wheat field. In his report Jackson wrote that "Branch's brigade, ... met the Federal forces, flushed with their temporary triumph, and drove them back with terrible slaughter through the woods." The North Carolinians cheered wildly, elated over their rather quick and easy victory over their enemy.[22]

But they did not realize that the day's fighting was not over yet. As Crawford pulled the survivors back across the wheat field another Federal regiment, the 10th Maine, was entering it. The Union regiment was supposed to have gone forward with the rest of the brigade in the initial attack, but its orders did not arrive in time. When the Maine men attacked they did so by themselves against the arriving Light Division. As the Unionists moved across the wheat field, they ran into the 18th North Carolina as well as elements of Archer's brigade, which had arrived and formed on the regiment's left. Archer's men and the 18th North Carolina badly mauled the lone Maine regiment. One of the survivors remembered that so many men were getting hit and knocked down by Rebel musketry that "it looked as if we had a crowd of howling dervishes dancing and kicking around in our ranks." The 10th Maine's position was doomed and those who could sensibly retreated when they got the chance.[23]

As the 18th helped decimate the 10th Maine they heard what sounded like the roll of thunder. The sound was not thunder or artillery, but the steady beat of charging cavalry coming on obliquely from the right front. It was now 6:45, about forty minutes after they had arrived to help save Jackson's left flank, and the 1st Pennsylvania Cavalry, numbering 164 horses under the command of Major Richard Falls ran off the Culpeper Road and into the wheat field's southern end. As spectacular and romantic as mounted warriors shouting for all they were worth and charging with drawn sabers may have been, they were no match for massed muskets. Even the old smoothbores many of the Tar Heels were carrying that fired buck and ball cartridges could seriously damage a charging mass of horsemen before they could get close enough to use sabers or pistols with any effectiveness. One Confederate admired the doomed troopers who galloped onto the field with sabers drawn, recalling that the earth was "fairly trembling beneath the tread of their magnificent horses." Magnificent or not they were about to be shot to pieces. As they charged the field they rode diagonally across the front of Branch's and Taliaferro's (whose Virginians had largely rallied and rejoined the fight) brigades presenting vulnerable targets. Jackson reported that "the Federal cavalry charged upon Taliaferro's brigade with impetuous valor, but were met with such determined resistance by Taliaferro's brigade in its front, and by so galling a fire from Branch's brigade in flank, that it was forced rapidly from the field with loss and in disorder." One of the Confederates pouring in that "galling fire" recalled that one of the horses he saw shot "turned a summerset and threw his rider as if he had been shot from a cannon. The last I saw of him he was about fifteen feet above his saddle." Hill would write that in the charge the Pennsylvanians "had many saddles emptied and fled in utter confusion." This pointless charge lasted little more than ten minutes as horses and riders were slaughtered by hundreds of muskets firing controlled volleys at well under 200 yards.[24]

The Federals were clearly reeling now as Jackson threw in his full force and exploited his numerical advantage over Banks. A small brigade of Indiana and Massachusetts troops along with part of the 3rd Wisconsin entered the northern part of the wheat field about 7:00 P.M. but Branch's men would not be needed there; the bulk of the Stonewall Brigade was in that part of the field along with Archer's and Pender's brigades to quickly push those Federals back where they had come from. Purdie led the regiment from the tree line forward through the wheat field itself. After moving seventy-five yards Branch halted the brigade to re-form. As it did, the 18th North Carolina's color bearer ran forward, flag in hand, to the crest of the nearest hill and defiantly planted the standard, standing "as steady as if on parade." For the second time in less than an hour the famous Stonewall make an appearance in front of the regiment; but this time it was not to admonish the brigade commander to shut up and get his men in the fight. Jackson rode silently along the brigade front and then halted in front of the color bearer. After staring at the flag and the men for several seconds, Jackson tipped his battered cap. This simple, silent gesture of appreciation for a job well done sent a thrill throughout the regiment, and the entire line shook with thunderous cheers. "It was a grand sight," one Tar Heel remembered, "Stonewall Jackson the Great, baring his sun-crowned head in our presence."[25]

At the end of the day, how is the 18th North Carolina's role in the victory at Cedar Mountain to be assessed? To hear its brigade commander tell it, Branch and his brigade saved the day for old Stonewall single handed, snatching victory from the jaws of certain defeat. As he marched his brigade to the scene of the fighting, Branch claimed, "We met the celebrated Stonewall Brigade, utterly routed and fleeing as fast at they could run." After allowing the Virginians to pass through their ranks, the Tar Heels poured in a murderous fire that drove the Yankees back through the wheat, saving the left flank and securing the victory. At least that was how Branch preferred to have the battle understood. This version of events is repeated by the 18th North Carolina's William McLaurin in Walter Clark's *Histories of the Several Regiments and Battalions from North Carolina*.[26]

The reality was a little different. Robert Krick has most accurately described Branch's men's contribution: "Stripped of hyperbole, the performance of [Branch's] brigade was solid and workmanlike, but his sole unaided achievement was clearing the woods to the edge of the wheat field." Also, Branch's boast that his brigade stood fast when the famous Stonewall Brigade thought the fighting was too hot was pure fabrication. One regiment of the Stonewall Brigade, the 27th Virginia, did flee through the North Carolina ranks before rallying and returning to the battle but that was all Branch saw. The famous Virginia brigade stood its ground and anchored Jackson's left at Cedar Mountain and lived up to its well-deserved reputation as one of the finest in Lee's army. Branch had been in the service long enough to have known that he had not simply mistaken one regiment for an entire brigade; so why the gross exaggeration? Possibly the politician in the man recognized the opportunity to enhance his own reputation and postwar political career by claiming that he had been the one most responsible for saving Jackson's left and winning the battle for him. He knew that casting himself as the potential "Hero of Cedar Mountain" would be worth a lot of votes after independence was secured. Americans do, after all, love their war heroes. State pride as well as the long-standing (and not always friendly) rivalry between North Carolina and Virginia may have been a factor as well. Like other North Carolinians, he probably felt that the Virginians got a disproportionate share of the glory and admiration while others, especially North Carolinians, never seemed to get any recognition. So, portraying the battle as one where the Tar Heels of the Old North State had stood their ground and saved the day after the cavaliers of the Old Dominion had unceremoniously skedaddled made the story all the more satisfying.[27]

Thus the 18th North Carolina did not exactly charge in and save the day all by themselves, but worked well and effectively with the Stonewall Brigade as well as William Dorsey Pender's North Carolina brigade and James J. Archer's brigade of Tennesseans and Alabamians to help stabilize Jackson's left flank and defeat Banks' smaller Union force. But that should not diminish what they did accomplish. The 18th North Carolina had been up and marching for over fifteen hours when they entered the battle. Like the rest of Hill's Light Division, the regiment had pushed themselves to their physical limits under sweltering and debilitating conditions to arrive on the scene in time to help turn the tide of battle. And while the 18th's section of the battle did not match the intensity or ferocity of other parts, these men from eastern North Carolina accepted and accomplished all of their assignments in "solid and workmanlike" fashion. They had earned the tip of Stonewall Jackson's cap.

Chapter 5

Battling the "Miscreant" Pope: Second Manassas and Chantilly/Ox Hill

The victory at Cedar Mountain was certainly a morale boost for the South but was not enough to make Richmond safe or the situation facing Lee significantly less dangerous. Though Lee could not have known it at the time, the battle had altered John Pope's attitude towards the war in the East. Before Cedar Mountain Pope was full of bluster and had deeply insulted many of his subordinates by suggesting that they had been too timid. Now that he was on the scene, the Rebels would be harassed and crushed. Cedar Mountain did not put a complete halt to Pope's brashness, but as John Hennessy has pointed out, Pope's correspondence with officials in Washington got noticeably more cautious and subdued about just what he could accomplish.[1]

During the second week of August, Lee got reliable reports that McClellan was evacuating the peninsula. That was good in the sense that it meant Richmond was safe from that direction for the moment, but it likely meant that the Army of the Potomac was on its way to join forces with Pope. If that happened the Army of Northern Virginia would face an almost impossible situation. The danger of being completely overrun and destroyed and Richmond taken was a very real possibility once the two Federal armies in Virginia came together. It was clear to Lee that he had to act and act quickly to accomplish something significant before McClellan could arrive.

Lee decided that Pope must be crushed or at the very least driven out of Central Virginia. There were a couple of reasons that Lee came to that conclusion. One was purely military; he had to eliminate a major enemy force before that force got larger. Having disposed of Pope, Lee planned to force McClellan react to him by heading from Virginia altogether for a foray into

Maryland. Typical of Lee's methods, he had no intention of sitting back and reacting to McClellan and his large force; that gave his opponent the advantage. Whenever he was able to do so, Lee seized the initiative and forced his opponents to deal with him on his, not their, terms.

Lee's other motive for going after the Army of Virginia was somewhat personal. Lee is often portrayed as a figure who was always calm and collected. It is difficult for many people to imagine him getting angry or having the desire to strike at an opponent specifically to hurt him, to punish him. Many still believe the myth that the "marble man" was so free of malice towards the Yankees that he never called them "the enemy" but always referred to them as "those people." The truth is that Lee was human and he could get extremely angry, so much so, in fact, that those who ever saw it never wished to again. And Lee was angry at Pope. Pope, to Lee, was nothing more than a vandal who had brought pain and suffering to his beloved state and who threatened to make war on civilians, and Lee sought to make Pope pay for his transgressions.

By August 13 Lee had decided that the time had come to hit Pope's army and hit it hard. With McClellan moving away from Richmond and taking his army back up the Chesapeake Bay towards Alexandria, the capital was relatively safe and the Army of Virginia was on its own for at least the next week or so, possibly longer with McClellan in charge. On that day Lee sent orders to Longstreet to get ten brigades aboard trains headed for Gordonsville and Jackson's wing of the Army of Northern Virginia. Lee's plan was to leave a skeleton garrison to guard Richmond and unite his wings for an attack on Pope while the opportunity presented itself. After taking two days to arrange for the capital's defense Lee was on the way to Gordonsville himself to meet with his two principal lieutenants and direct the campaign to drive "that miscreant Pope" out of the state.[2]

When Lee got to Gordonsville and sat down with Longstreet and Jackson, Longstreet suggested moving to the northwest around Pope's right flank but Lee rejected that plan. At that point the Army of Virginia was in a "V" between two rivers, the Rapidan, which was at Pope's front, and the Rappahannock at his back. Lee preferred to have his wings cross the Rapidan at Racoon and Somerville fords and attack the numerically disadvantaged Army of Virginia's left. In that scenario Pope faced a very serious problem because not only would he be facing a larger enemy, Confederate cavalry under Fitzhugh Lee was to have raced to the rear of Pope's army and destroyed the bridge at Rappahannock Station, Pope's only means of escape across the Rappahannock. His obvious escape route gone, Pope would have to fight on Lee's terms on unfavorable ground or figure a way out of the area quickly before Lee could jump on him. Lee doubted Pope could pull off the sort of maneuvering and fighting that would be necessary to save his army in such dire straits. Lee intended for the operation to be executed in two days, on August 17.[3]

Unfortunately for Lee, his plans to thrash Pope were destined to be thwarted by a combination of factors. A major one was that Fitz Lee's cavalry, which had a critical role to play in the plans, was behind schedule and was not ready to perform its role on the seventeenth. Longstreet also complained that his supply wagons were still too far to the rear and that they needed to be closer before attacking, which severely irritated Stonewall Jackson, who could not imagine passing up a fight because of supply wagons' locations. Another was an unexpected change in Pope's attitude. Pope had come to Virginia blustering about taking the fight to the Rebels so Lee did not particularly mind having to wait a couple of days for his cavalry to be in place and properly rested or for Longstreet's supply wagons to be on hand; Pope was surely not going to go anywhere. But Pope was not quite as confident as he had been before Cedar Mountain. Jackson's strike at him there had worried him because he had not expected it at all. After that, Pope seemed to get very concerned about getting caught by surprise by the Confederates, especially Jackson. As John Hennessy has noted, Pope's correspondence with Henry Halleck during the third week of August shows Pope to be fearful of an attack on his left. So when one of Pope's aides showed him copies of Lee's plans, captured from one of Stuart's cavalrymen on August 18, it served to confirm his worst fears that he was about to be attacked on his left by Jackson's and Longstreet's superior numbers. With that bit of important information, Pope ordered his army to prepare to evacuate the area the next day. As Lee climbed nearby Clark Mountain with Longstreet to observe Pope's camps, he was surprised to see the Army of Virginia moving away and across the Rappahannock. "General," he said turning to Longstreet, "we little thought that the enemy would turn his back upon us this early in the campaign."[4]

During these few days of relative inactivity, the 18th North Carolina remained in a state of restless inactivity. Clearly they were going to seek out and engage the Federals who were just across the river, but when? To that question nobody in the regiment had an answer, so the men and officers did their best to carry on with some semblance of a routine. The regiment drilled and took its turns at picket duty and broke the monotony and tension of waiting for the order to "Fall in!" with card games, letter writing, and any other diversion they could think of. Unfortunately, though, part of the routine in Jackson's foot cavalry was the enforcement of rigid discipline. Jackson was famous for insisting in the sort of iron devotion to duty that he possessed, and when officers and men were found wanting the punishments for failing were often severe. Since the army was not moving anyway, Jackson took the opportunity to make an example of three deserters. The poor wretches probably would have had no chance of Jackson taking pity on them under normal circumstances, but he was in a bit of a foul mood brought on by what he judged to be warrantless delays in getting after John Pope's army. The dissenters had no chance whatsoever. Desertion was to be punished by death and on August 19 the three condemned soldiers were executed by firing squad in front of the entire command. When it was over the men of the 18th and the other members of the Light Division were compelled to march past the bodies so that they would be duly impressed with the gravity and finality with which Stonewall Jackson dealt with those who failed to do their duty.

The executions of the nineteenth had cast a pall over the regiment but fortunately they would not have the time to sit around and dwell on them. Lee had no intention of letting John Pope give him the slip and orders went out to the two wings to be up and moving at dawn on the following morning, August 20. This was welcome news to Jackson who was up at two o'clock. He had been angry over the delays and he did not wish to miss any time getting moving that morning. General Branch had received his orders to have his North Carolinians up and ready to move out by dawn and he made sure that all of his regimental commanders understood that their men were to have their rations cooked and to be ready to march at first light. Lieutenant-Colonel Thomas Purdie was still in command of the regiment because Colonel Cowan remained unable to return to duty. Purdie was up and dressed before dawn and as he packed his gear on his horse he made sure that his company captains understood that the men were to be up and formed by dawn. Just before dawn, at probably around four or four-thirty that morning, Jackson rode through A.P. Hill's command and was furious. With the exception of the 18th North Carolina and the other regiments in Branch's brigade, the Light Division was still milling around cooking and eating breakfast. There is no record of how Purdie felt at that moment, but the 18th's commander must have been consumed with an equal measure of pride that his regiment had been one of the few that met Jackson's expectations and sheer unadulterated mix of joy and relief that came from knowing that Old Jack may be apoplectic but that someone else was responsible.[5]

Very soon the rest of Jackson's wing fell into line and began marching in pursuit of Pope's army. In the early morning between five and six o'clock the leading column reached the banks of the Rapidan River at Somerville Ford where it was to cross. Many remembered the crossing as welcome relief. August had been a horribly hot and sticky month. The men and officers had endured long marches where they were thoroughly parched and dust coated. August 20 promised to be no different than most of those other near-tropical days so the chance to romp across a cool river was welcome relief indeed. One of Jackson's soldiers recalled: "The water was pretty deep but very pleasant to our warm bodies." With muskets and cartridge boxes held out above the water, the men of the 18th eagerly plunged into the Rapidan's refreshing waters, splashing about like schoolboys in no particular hurry to get to the other side, which promised only the resumption of hot, dusty marching. There was work to be done, however, and having seen Jackson's wrath a couple of hours earlier and having no wish to see it again, Colonel Purdie gently but firmly encouraged his regiment to keep moving.[6]

Crossing the Rapidan proved to be the only pleasant part of the August 20 march. One Confederate recounted: "No water could be had along the road, and the dust had so completely covered us that it was only by the voice that we could recognize each other." Stonewall wanted, as usual, to be moving quickly. He was already irritated at what he perceived as Pope's being allowed to slip away. He had no intention of missing the next opportunity. Colonel Purdie rode along his column, making sure his men stayed reasonably on pace despite the heat and the dust. Straggling was inevitable under such conditions but Purdie hoped to keep the problem to a minimum.[7]

The regiment was fortunate that during the hot march they passed through two towns, Stevensburg and Culpeper. To the citizens of these places the sight of Confederate flags and faces was a major relief, the reviled Army of Virginia having been lurking about for so long. The people, mostly women (at least that was who the soldiers seemed to remember most), poured out of their homes offering the men and officers any and all relief they had. They were "greeted by the females with every demonstration of joy" one former member of Jackson's foot cavalry remembered. "The ladies rushed out of their homes," another recalled, "and showered us with flowers, singing, and praising and thanking God for their deliverance from the enemy." Biscuits, cornbread, water, iced lemonade, and other welcome items were freely given by the inhabitants of Stevensburg and Culpeper and were gratefully accepted by the soldiers. Such lavish expressions of joy and especially gratitude as the ladies of these towns exhibited helped remind the men of the 18th North Carolina why they were fighting this war. For a short time the march was a little more endurable. At the end of the day the regiment bivouacked between Brandy Station and Stevensburg.[8]

While Lee was chasing Pope and hoping to attack him before he could be massively reinforced by McClellan, Pope was doing a pretty good job of avoiding that situation. The Confederates were on the south bank of the Rappahannock, but Pope was well aware of them and had posted artillery and part of Irvin McDowell's corps on the opposite bank, making the opportunity for a quick crossing and attack virtually impossible. Believing Pope's right to be most vulnerable, Lee had his wings sidle around to the left in an effort to get into position to attack Pope's right flank near Sulphur Springs. During the two days of August 21 and 22, the 18th moved northwest as part of the attempt to get around the Army of Virginia's right. There was not a lot of action for the regiment but it was not without its dangers. Federal and Confederate artillery dueled regularly, posing significant danger to the men in the ranks who could do nothing to defend themselves from the incoming projectiles. By the end of the day on August 22 the regiment and the rest of Jackson's wing had reached the Sulphur Springs area where they made camp in the midst of a torrential thunderstorm. The men must have figured they could not win when it came to the weather situation. If they were not eating pounds of dust and getting baked by the sun, they were getting thoroughly drenched by pounding summer storms. Then again, such has always been the lot of the infantryman.

For the regiment the following day (August 23) was uneventful. While they faced the Federals and their artillery across the river they did little more than wait for something to do or somewhere to march. August 24 was a different matter. The day opened with both sides hammering each other with their artillery. Jackson's staff officer, Henry Kyd Douglas, remembered it as "the noisiest artillery duel I ever witnessed." But Lee was still no closer to being able to decisively attack Pope. This was a full week past his original attack date and even with McClellan moving in his usual sloth-like way time was becoming an increasingly large problem. In fact, elements of the Army of the Potomac were already arriving from Fredericksburg and Alexandria and reinforcements were also moving in from western Virginia. As happened on more than one occasion during the war, Lee would have to create plans that were bold to the point of reckless if he wanted to seize and maintain control of the situation. Fortunately for him he had a man with him who relished such plans in Stonewall Jackson.

Lee decided to do something that was, to say the least, extremely risky. The standard practice and belief in military circles was that one never split an army in the close proximity of the enemy, but Lee felt that under the circumstances he really had very little in the way of viable alternatives if he was going to keep the Federals off balance. Jackson would take his wing, which contained about 24,000 men, completely around Pope's right and fall on his supply line, the Orange and Alexandria Railroad. In order for Jackson to have the time he needed, Longstreet's wing would remain in Pope's front and make enough noise to hold his attention. When the Confederates cut his supply line, Pope would be forced to respond to that serious problem and fall back in that direction. This plan also had Pope moving his army away from elements of the Army of the Potomac, which was another benefit. As the Army of Virginia moved to deal with the threat in its rear, Longstreet would rush to link up with Jackson and together they would destroy Pope's army before other Federal units could arrive to save it.[9]

This was the sort of boldness that Jackson loved and believed in. He was often at his best when given such assignments. Jackson plucked an officer from Fauquier County, Captain James K. Boswell, to plot out the best route around Pope. For the next couple of days Boswell would be the left wing's guide. With his knowledge of the local terrain and roads, Captain Boswell charted a course westward through the hamlet of Amissville and had Jackson's column cross the Rappahannock at Hinson's Mill. From there they would proceed north through the towns of Orleans and Salem after which the column would turn right and head southeastward through Thoroughfare Gap straight into Gainesville, the Orange and Alexandria Railroad and Pope's rear. The 18th was about to participate in one of the most famous and hard marches of the entire Civil War. That evening as the men camped near the town of Jeffersonton, they were ordered to cook what rations they had — they were to have been issued a full three days' worth but many of Jackson's men, including men of the 18th North Carolina, did not get their full issue — and be ready to move at dawn.[10]

As per Jackson's wishes, Colonel Purdie awakened the 18th North Carolina at 3:00 A.M. The regiment was going to be marching quickly and as unencumbered as possible. The men were issued sixty rounds of ammunition and all knapsacks and other unnecessary gear was sent to the rear. Orders for the day came down the chain of command and Purdie told all of his company officers: "No straggling: every man must keep his place in ranks: in crossing streams officers are to see that no delay is occasioned by removing shoes or clothing." With that, Branch's North Carolinians fell in with the rest of A.P. Hill's Light Division behind Ewell's division, which led Jackson's column that morning. The regiment marched hard all day, passing through Amissville and across the Rappahannock at Hinson's Mill Ford to just beyond the town of Salem, a route that covered twenty-five miles. Even Jackson had to admit that the marching on August 25 was a "severe day's march." As the day came to a close and the tired men of the 18th North Carolina neared the little town of Salem, they looked up to see their commanding general standing upon a nearby rock watching the column pass. The sight of Stonewall caused the men to break out into cheers; but Jackson, ever concerned about alerting the enemy to his actions, made it known he did not want any unnecessary noise. His men complied and as the 18th North Carolina passed, they, like thousands of others, lifted their hats in silent tribute. Stonewall was a man rarely given to emotional statements, but as his regiments passed before him brimming with enough enthusiasm after a hard day's march to have to be quieted down at the sight of their commander, he was heard to utter: "Who could not conquer with troops such as these?"[11]

The men and officers of the 18th North Carolina did not get much sleep after their long march. They entered Salem at between 11:00 P.M. and midnight and orders were again to be up before dawn. The men fell out along the road and collapsed for what must have seemed to most of them no more than a few minutes when the non-commissioned officers came through waking them up, telling them to roll their blankets, take arms, and fall in. From Salem the column headed to the northwest before turning right and heading for Thoroughfare Gap and John Pope's supply and communication lines.

The day's march would be just as difficult as the previous day's one had been only the men were a bit less rested. A Light Division veteran remembered that day well, saying: "There was no mood for speech, nor breath to spare if there had been, only the shuffling tramp of the marching feet, the steady rumbling of wheels, the creak and rattle and clank of harness and accoutrements, with an occasional order ... 'Close up! Close up, men!'" Many former Confederates remembered too that this forced march was performed by men who were, after a heavy summer of campaigning, not in good material condition. "Many were barefoot," one recounted, "many more without a decent garment to their backs, more still ill with diarrhea and dysentery, and all half-famished." Certainly a lot of the Tar Heels in Branch's brigade were hungry. All were to have been issued three days' rations but a number of accounts indicate that many soldiers did not get all their rations. So the men from Eastern North Carolina had to scrounge what they could along the way and hope it calmed the worst of their hunger pangs. One old member of Jackson's command recounted that all he had had on the entire march was "a handful of parched corn and three or four small, sour green apples." Another related: "I paid an old woman twenty-five cents for a mouldy, half-done hoecake that lay on the floor in the corner of her house, and when I scraped off the edges I was envied by my comrades." Even allowing for some exaggeration, the regiment was underfed and many were shoeless. Despite the hardships of August 26, the officers of the regiment, men like Tom Purdie, kept the soldiers moving at a rapid pace. At four o'clock that afternoon the head of Jackson's column reached Gainesville and the Orange and Alexandria Railroad.[12]

The arrival at Gainesville marked another major test placed before the officers and men of the 18th North Carolina, one they passed with flying colors. The march had covered a remarkable distance, just over fifty miles, in two days. Few feats of marching matched it over the course of the entire war. The weather was hot, humid, and horribly dusty, sapping the men's strength and stamina with every step. To make matters worse, many were performing this incredible marching exhibition on empty or near-empty stomachs. In one of Colonel Purdie's few surviving letters, he wrote home on the twenty-fourth: "We are having a hard time just now — moving day and night, & are looking for a hard battle every day & almost every hour. There has been a continual shelling going on for the last four days & the enemy is now just across the river in force & shelling our battery near a bridge we put up yesterday." Another member of the brigade remembered: "Every man was pressed to the utmost of his walking capacity." As the regiment had ever since it arrived in Virginia as a green regiment in May, it met the challenges placed before it and overcame them.[13]

On the evening of August 26 Jackson had his force move to the south to Bristoe Station. He thought that Manassas Junction was probably well defended and in sturdy earthworks. Since he was not interested in bringing on a major battle until Longstreet joined him (and since Lee had also told him to avoid such a situation), he took his wing to a point about five miles below the junction. During the night the Confederates destroyed several trains, alerting the Federals to the presence of rebels in the vicinity. Meanwhile Jackson also sent a brigade under Isaac Trimble to scout the area around Manassas Junction. Much to his surprise, Trimble discovered the important point to be only lightly defended and he took it with little difficulty. The best historian of the battle of Second Manassas, John Hennessy, has noted: "Trimble's capture of Manassas Junction culminated two of Stonewall Jackson's most successful days." His men had marched fifty miles, wrecked two trains, and captured several hundred Federals, eight cannon, and stores beyond their wildest fantasy. More important than the captures, however, was the rupture of Pope's supply line."[14]

The Federals were now aware of some sort of Confederate activity around Manassas Junction, but nobody at the time thought anything more than a body of cavalry was around. Nobody had any idea that half of Lee's army under Stonewall Jackson was actually behind Pope's Army of Virginia. Since a mere cavalry raiding party was all that was at the depot, a very green unit of New Yorkers went to scatter the horsemen. The Second New York Heavy Artillery — under the command of Colonel Gustav Waagner — was a garrison unit that had thus far been confined to the defenses of Washington. They had been transformed into an infantry unit and this morning they marched out in splendid style complete with artillery to reclaim the area. Jackson had a brigade watching the eastern approaches to the junction, and as the 2nd New York came into range the artillery began to fire during the early morning hours. Hearing the cannon fire Jackson thought it best to make sure that sufficient force was available to deal with the threat from Washington so he sent the Light Division to reinforce the eastern works. The 18th North Carolina was held out of this mission to guard the captured provisions at the railroad junction. With Waagner commanding barely 1,000 green garrison troops and with the Confederate position reinforced to some 9,000 veterans complete with artillery by nine A.M., the result was predictable. After a few volleys and artillery rounds, Waagner realized he was in way over his head. There was a whole lot more than a few raiders at Manassas Junction, and he had his men break off their engagement and start back where they had come from. After hurrying the New Yorkers along, the regiment and the rest of the brigade headed back to the railroad depot.[15]

Upon arrival at the rail yard the 18th North Carolina eagerly participated in one of the most famous incidents of the war. Having secured the area, Jackson's wing had rail car after rail car of eatables for the taking. There was more food there than the lean Rebels had seen in weeks and more than they could ever hope to eat and carry off. They were allowed to take all they could consume and carry before the rest was destroyed to keep the provisions from the enemy. One member of the brigade fondly remembered the unparalleled feasting that Branch's Tar Heels enjoyed on August 27. "It was more than funny," he recalled, "to see the ragged, rough, dirty fellows, who had been living on roasted corn and green apples for days, now drinking Rhine wine, eating lobster salad, potted tongue, cream biscuit, pound cake, canned fruits, and the like; and filling his pockets and haversacks with ground coffee, toothbrushes, condensed milk, [and] silk handkerchiefs." One of the brigade's surgeons recalled: "The depot was an immense building, filled with unlimited supplies of flour, crackers, bacon, molasses, sugar, coffee, whiskey, clothing, harness for wagons and artillery, fixed ammunition for small arms and for cannon. We tarried here all day, got out whatever we needed that we could carry for rations...."[16]

Not long after filling their stomachs and haversacks at the Federals' expense, what was left at Manassas Junction was put to the torch. As the flames grew and the air was filled with the scent of surplus bacon sizzling in their railroad cars, the 18th fell in and prepared to march. It was near midnight and Jackson wanted to leave the area for a safer one nearby. Now that the Yankees knew there was far more than a small body of cavalry on a raid they would be heading to the area in force. Jackson had no intention of getting trapped by Pope or any other Unionist force with Longstreet's wing still on the march. As A.P. Hill's division moved out there was a miscommunication somewhere and the division crossed Bull Run and marched in the direction of Centreville some ten miles away. That night the 18th North Carolina camped at Centreville, cooked rations, and grabbed a few hours sleep. At 10:00 the next morning (August 28th) the regiment fell in and headed back towards Jackson's command near Manassas. No doubt there was some grumbling in the regiment about marching back and forth over the same roads, but these men were getting used to army life; as often as not this included performing tasks that seem calculated to do little more than make the poor infantryman's life just a little less comfortable. This march away from Manassas and then back to Manassas the very next day seemed just such a situation.[17]

The 18th North Carolina reached the rest of Jackson's command near Groveton about mid-day on the 28th and was posted on the far left of Jackson's line. Hill's division had the vitally important job of anchoring Jackson's left flank. This was critical because if the Federals got around the Confederate left (as almost happened at Cedar Mountain) and got control of the fords over Catharpin Run at Sudley Springs and Sudley Mill, Jackson's route of retreat, should he need it, would be closed off to him. Then, unless he did some brilliant maneuvering and desperate fighting, his wing — one half of the Army of Northern Virginia — would be destroyed. Even if he did manage to wiggle out of that worst case scenario, his force would be severely damaged and of little use to Lee until the damage could be repaired with fresh replacements. General Branch deployed his North Carolinians to the left and rear of Maxcy Gregg's South Carolina brigade, forming the extreme left of Jackson's line, just across and west of the Groveton-Sudley Road.

On the previous day there had been a vicious Union attack at the Brawner farm on Jackson's right that the Confederates repulsed. The men of the 18th no doubt heard the fight and wondered if they would get into it but they remained where they were on the left because of the importance of holding Jackson's left. But Pope wanted to take another run at Jackson. At this point in the battle Pope was operating under the mistaken impression (some would say delusion) that he had Jackson's force on the ropes. General Pope convinced himself that Jackson was trying to retreat and could be trapped; his strong desire to, as he put it, "bag" Jackson and his whole command seemed to blind him to the reality of the situation. Whether Pope was permitting his desire to best the mighty Stonewall Jackson and bask in the praise such a feat would no doubt bring to a man famous for his concern about his reputation is a matter of conjecture. But whatever his motivations, he was utterly mistaken about what was transpiring on the field. Consequently, Pope thought all he had to do was find the weak spot in Jackson's line and exploit it.[18]

On the morning of August 29 one of Pope's corps commanders, General Franz Sigel, planned to attack Jackson's line at the center and (Federal) right. Sigel ordered General Carl Schurz to take his division to the Federal right and attack there to create an opening in the Rebel line. Schurz's division attacked at eight A.M. and began a long bloody day of fighting. The bulk of Sigel's effort for the next five hours occurred to the 18th North Carolina's right. They heard the terrible fighting between Sigel's Yankees and the South Carolinians of their own division. Maxcy Gregg's 1st and 12th South Carolina and other elements of the Light Division fought stubbornly for hours to help keep the Federals from breaking through Jackson's position, holding on desperately while Longstreet and the rest of the Army of Northern Virginia marched to the area.

All morning and into the early afternoon, the 18th North Carolina and the rest of Branch's brigade remained witnesses to the battle on their right and were not actively involved in the battle beyond the occasional artillery round coming into their sector. They remained guarding the far left and the vital fords. The relative inactivity on the regiment's front was not by design, though. Sigel had fully intended for there to be serious action on that part of the field that morning. It had come to Sigel's attention that there was a real possibility of getting around the Confederate left flank. If the Federals could crack the Rebel left they could pour into the rear of Jackson's position and roll up his command. General Phil Kearney, in fact, was supposed to attempt just such a maneuver. Kearney had arrived on the scene at about ten that morning, but when he got there he did virtually nothing. Had Kearney moved as he was supposed to have done, Branch's brigade would have borne the brunt of the attack. But while the 18th and the rest of the brigade were deployed in readiness for anything coming from their front, nothing significant happened. Ever since, General Kearney has been criticized for his unwillingness to move against Jackson's left that morning. In the end, by the time Kearney did, Longstreet had arrived and any chance Pope had of "bagging" Jackson was gone.[19]

Not that Pope grasped that reality at the time. He still thought Jackson was isolated and vulnerable. He had no idea (because he had not bothered to find out) that by 1:00 P.M. Longstreet had arrived to link up with and extend Jackson's right. Pope still thought Jackson's right was "in the air" and could be turned. Given what he perceived to be the situation, Pope decided to make an attack on Jackson's center and center-left one more time. But this attack was to be merely a strong diversion; Pope wanted to hold Jackson's attention in his front while a crushing hammer blow was delivered to his "exposed" right flank by the divisions of Fitz John Porter and Irvin McDowell.

Earlier fighting in the center had taken its toll on the Confederates; in Hill's division, Thomas's Georgians and Gregg's South Carolinians had endured several hot hours of very heavy fighting. Each time the Federals came on they were beaten back, but by late afternoon these units were dangerously low on ammunition and energy and they had lost nearly one-third of their strength. The only fresh brigades Hill had were Archer's and Branch's. Hill ordered Archer to relieve Pender's North Carolinians, which had also seen action during the day's attacks, and Hill probably should have pulled Gregg's men back and replaced them with Branch's unbloodied regiments. But he left the South Carolinians where they were. Branch's Tar Heels shifted to their right and deployed behind Gregg to provide support should the Yankees attack again and where they could provide support for Crenshaw's and Braxton's batteries should they need it.

While the late afternoon attack that got underway about 5:00 was intended to be a diversion, it became the largest Federal assault of the day. Kearney launched his attack with eight regiments numbering around 2,700 men. When the Unionists crashed into the Confederate line they hit it hard, striking Gregg's South Carolina regiments again. These men were close to their breaking point. As one officer remembered, "Our feet were worn and weary, and our arms were nerveless. Our ears were deadened with the continuous roar of the battle, and our eyes were dimmed with the smoke." Another said shortly after the Federal attack began the Rebels found themselves in "a semicircle of flame and smoke." With such pressure after hours of fighting, the South Carolinians needed reinforcing if the Federals were to be held at bay one more time.

At this point Branch's brigade entered the Battle of Second Manassas. Seeing the situation Gregg's men were facing, Branch ordered the 37th North Carolina into the fight to help shore up Gregg's position. Quickly realizing that one regiment was not going to be enough, he went back and personally brought the 7th North Carolina up and into the battle against the oncoming Federals. Despite the addition of two fresh regiments, the Yankees continued to make steady, and bloody, progress, reaching 300 yards into the Confederate position. Hoping nothing significant developed on the far left, Branch threw his whole brigade into the fight to keep the enemy from breaking through. Thus the three remaining regiments entered an extremely hot part of the field.

Receiving orders from Branch to come up into the fight, Colonel Purdie ordered his regiment forward. The 18th moved behind and to the right of Gregg's position to go to the aid of Archer's brigade, which was engaged in a nasty fight in a wooded area with a brigade of Pennsylvanians. Struggling to be heard over the noise of the battle, Purdie directed the regiment into the battle and soon had the men firing into the Yankees as they could load their muskets. Given the wooded terrain and the smoke from thousands of guns, the soldiers could barely make out their targets so they continued to pour in volley after volley in the direction they were receiving fire and hoped they were doing some damage. They were. Though it must have seemed much longer to those engaged in the fight, within forty-five minutes the Federal attack began to lose steam as A.P. Hill fed in brigades where they were needed. The 18th North Carolina played a significant role in halting the Unionist tide. Firing among Branch's men was fast and furious; when it was over he reported that only twenty-four rounds of ammunition could be found in his entire brigade. This stout firing blunted the Federal attack and when Jubal Early's untouched Virginia brigade came up, it was able to completely turn the Yankees around and send them back where they had come from. Once again Pope's attempt to take the Confederates and become the hero he so wished to become was foiled. And once again, the 18th North Carolina had stepped onto the battlefield and given a solid account of itself. According to John Hennessy, the North Carolinians "served distinctively that afternoon as Hill's emergency response team."[20]

With the Federal attack repulsed, Jackson's line was again stabilized, but the enemy was still in the area. For the rest of the evening, from around six until midnight, the 18th remained in position, occasionally trading shots until darkness fell completely over the field. Night attacks were rare in the Civil War but not unknown, so the regiment remained on alert, listening for any alarm coming from the skirmishers out front. Nothing happened during the evening, but there was some minor skirmishing along the regiment's front as the sun came over the horizon the next day. The regiment was already low on ammunition and after trading shots with some Yankee skirmishers they ran completely out and were relieved by Early's Virginians. After the skirmishing that morning, one veteran wrote, "Our brigade went to the rear and obtained a day's rations of crackers and meat, and each man was furnished with 100 rounds of ammunition. We then moved towards our left and remained in position all day, unengaged, though all the time within range of the enemy's guns." Back to their original position on Jackson's left the regiment did not see further action at Second Manassas outside of some artillery fire that did no real damage to the 18th North Carolina.[21]

By the end of the day's fighting on August 30, Lee had won a dazzling tactical victory over Pope's Army of Virginia and had it running back towards the safety of Washington, specifically the safety of the fortifications at Centreville. Though the victory was clear and while citizens of the Confederacy were thrilled, especially those of Central Virginia who had special reason to revel in Pope's misery, Lee remained unsatisfied. As was the case during the Seven Days Battles, the purpose was not simply to drive the enemy away or merely inflict a tactical defeat; the point was to destroy the enemy force. A defeated but intact Federal army lived to fight another day and Lee fully understood that the South had a limited number of days to work with if independence was to be achieved. Therefore Lee wanted to try one more time to hit Pope before McClellan arrived in full force so he called on Jackson one more time to see if his "foot cavalry" could do that.

At the moment Pope's army was in the relative safety of the Centreville defenses. Lee wanted one of two things to happen regarding Pope: he wanted to either bring him out of those defenses to fight on Lee's terms or he wanted to maneuver him out of Centreville and back to Washington by threatening his flanks. Annihilating Pope would be satisfying certainly, but forcing the Federals even farther away from his army was positive as well. That left his way clear to head northwest and cross the Potomac into Maryland and possibly beyond. Taking the war in the East out of Virginia and onto Northern soil had been part of Lee's strategic thinking since he took Johnston's place after Seven Pines. The events that immediately followed Second Manassas, but have been only lightly addressed, were part of Lee's overall strategic blueprint.

The basic plan was simple enough and virtually identical to what the Army of Northern Virginia had done the previous week. Jackson's divisions would cross Bull Run and march down the Little River Turnpike in the direction of Germantown (sometimes spelled Jermantown) and Fairfax Court House. This route took Jackson around Pope's right flank and if he could reach Germantown, this body of Confederates would not only have gotten around Pope's flank but would be in his rear. The strong defenses at Pope's Centreville position would be useless at that point with the Rebels between Pope and Washington. Pope would have to come out and fight on the Southerners' terms or retreat quickly. Either way Lee got something he wanted.

The 18th moved out on August 31 and for the next two days it made very slow progress on the Little River Turnpike. The "foot cavalry" did not have that nickname for nothing, but a number of factors combined to keep Jackson's marching average to a mere ten miles per day on August 31 and September 1, 1862. Most obviously these men were just worn out. They had been pushed to the limits of human endurance over the last week having marched fifty miles in two days (the 18th North Carolina had added an additional twenty with its marching to and from Centreville on the 29th and 30th) and fought one of the war's largest battles. Mother Nature also played a role. Late summer rains struck and for the last two days of August and into the first days of September heavy thunderstorms turned the turnpike into a bog that made marching for exhausted men even more difficult. Jackson was also concerned about the possibility of running into the Federals so he set a slower pace that was designed more to keep his divisions together than to make time. A Georgia veteran remembered that the column kept "a very slow advance with skirmishers out 200 yards to the right" because Jackson was concerned about a possible attack from that direction while on the move, a situation that would be very difficult to get out of without getting seriously injured. This was precisely the sort of damaging blow Lee had intended to inflict on the Army of the Potomac at Frayser's Farm.[22]

As it turned out Jackson was right to be concerned about being hit on his right on September 1. The Federals were aware of Jackson's column heading down the Little River Turnpike for Germantown, and preparations were made to strengthen the line there to keep Jackson from getting beyond the town and between Pope and Washington. To further slow down Jackson's wing, Union divisions under General Isaac Stevens and David Birney were sent in the direction of the Little River Turnpike via Ox Road to attack Stonewall and buy more time to strengthen the Germantown line. Throughout the early afternoon Stevens' Federals, the two small divisions of the IX Corps, moved to intercept Jackson near Ox Hill, which was near the little town of Chantilly. The Northerners took a narrow wagon path from the Warrenton Turnpike that paralleled Ox Road. As they crossed Rocky Run and emerged from the tree line near an unfinished railroad cut (an extension of the same cut that Jackson's men had used so effectively in the recent fight around Manassas) they could see a Confederate skirmish line deployed near a farmhouse known locally as the Reid House. Behind the skirmish line were two fields: the one on the left (the western side) was a mature corn field while the one on the right was an open field. Both were surrounded by split rail fences. On the opposite side of the fences a sizeable force of Confederates was seen with possibly, probably, many more in the woods to their rear.[23]

General Stevens knew his job was to hold Jackson's attention and slow him down so between three-thirty and four he sent out two companies of the 79th New York as skirmishers to drive the Confederates away from their position around the Reid House. Once the Rebels retreated, Stevens intended to attack the Confederates on the opposite side of the fields. When the New Yorkers formed their line and moved out, firing between the skirmishers escalated in the increasing gloom and misting rain, but the Unionists successfully forced the Southern skirmishers back. This allowed Stevens to move his divisions out of the woods and deploy them to attack the Confederate position. Stevens formed his force on the eastern side of the Reid House to attack across the open field and hopefully blow through the enemy line there.

Colonel Purdie and the 18th North Carolina were on hand to witness the arrival of the Federals on Jackson's right. Branch's North Carolina brigade had been posted, along with Field's brigade between the tree line and the rail fences at the northern end of the fields — these were the Confederates General Stevens saw when he came down the wagon path and emerged from the woods south of the Reid House. The 18th North Carolina helped to form the extreme right of the Confederate line, as it did at Frayser's Farm, which was an important and precarious position. There was no natural feature to anchor the right flank, so Branch's North Carolinians were the anchor. If the Yankees managed to get around them they could roll up the Rebel line and severely damage a major part of Jackson's army. As Jackson became aware of a major Federal force on his right and deployed his divisions to meet it, the 18th North Carolina would share the vital job with the other Tar Heels in Branch's brigade, once again, of defending one of the wing's vulnerable flanks.

At four-thirty the Federals came at the Southern line with flags unfurled determined to take a measure of revenge for their most recent defeat. The skies had gotten much darker, and the earlier misty rain gave way to a thunderstorm of impressive power. According to a Massachusetts soldier, "The roar of musketry and the roar of cannon left all of us unmoved, but the crash of thunder and the vividness of the lightning, whose blinding flashes seemed to be in our very midst, caused uneasiness and disturbance among some of the bravest men." A New York officer commented: "Suddenly the sky opened and we were deluged with one of the worst thunder storms I ever saw." Another Federal officer remembered what he referred to as "Heaven's artillery" being mixed "with the roar of the cannon," and that the former's power was more than a match for that of the batteries that were hard at work that afternoon.

Initially there was not a lot of action on the 18th North Carolina's front. The Federals had attacked across the open field to their left where Hays' and Gregg's brigades manned the position just behind the fence line. There was danger, though, in the form of Union artillery, which was firing away to help soften the Rebel position for the oncoming Federals. Colonel Purdie walked the rear of his regiment's line and ordered the men to lie down to avoid the artillery fire. As one historian of the fight has remarked, such an order was probably unnecessary because the soldiers had most likely already hit the ground to gain a little added security from being hit by incoming shells and cannon balls. For the moment the regiment lay in the pouring rain and tried to keep the inside of their musket barrels and their powder from getting soaked. The heavy fighting was off to the left but it was probably only a matter of time before they would get the order to rise up and join the fray. By this point, having been in several battles, even the dimmest private in the ranks understood that flanks were frequent targets. And since they were the flank, they would surely be fighting more than the elements shortly.[24]

They were correct. As the fighting intensified between 4:30 and 5:00, the Federals extended their front increasingly to their left towards the Confederate right. The 50th Pennsylvania and the 6th New Hampshire moved through the corn field towards Branch's and the entire Confederate line's right flank. General Branch understood that if the New Hampshire men got around him that could be it for the whole line. With Yankees plowing in from the right and from the front, Jackson's position would be in deep trouble. Lacking any sort of natural feature to anchor his brigade, Branch ordered Colonel Purdie to take the 18th North Carolina from its current position in the brigade's center, move to the extreme right, and hold the Federals back. Shouting to be heard above the driving rain and thunder, Purdie called the regiment to attention and pulled them out of line with the other regiments of the brigade and moved them to the right and deployed them at an angle to it. The eastern Carolinians were now the right flank's anchor. Their job was to meet and stop (refuse) a Unionist attack on the right.[25]

The Pennsylvanians and New Hampshire men faltered under Branch's fire and were pulled back, and the 101st New York and 4th Maine took their places. As the Unionists got within firing distance, the New York commander shouted out: "Give it to them, boys." The excited, and unorthodox, order began a fierce fight on that part of the field. General Lane said in his report that from then on the 18th received "a deadly fire" from two directions and, given their position, had to take it for the rest of the battle "unsupported." The regiment fired as quickly as it could into the New Yorkers in front of them and at the Maine men trying to get around their right. Visibility was low thanks to the driving rain, but the soldiers on each side fired for all they were worth, aiming at their enemy's muzzle flashes. At one point General Hill grew concerned that his men may have trouble holding on because of wet ammunition. Hill sent a courier to Jackson, who replied that he understood Hill's concerns but that the enemy's powder was no drier. If it came to it, there was always the bayonet.[26]

The 18th North Carolina continued to hold its ground, falling back a couple of times before pushing back towards the corn field. The regiment again fought well, keeping two regiments at bay until the battle began to slacken at just after 6:00 when the Federals pulled back. This fight at Ox Hill is like many of the smaller actions that took place during the Civil War in that it has generally been forgotten and seems small and inconsequential to all except those who fought in it. This one is probably best remembered for the death of the popular Union General Phil Kearney. But as James H. Lane wrote a few weeks later, Ox Hill was "regarded by this brigade as one of our severest." The elements were certainly a factor and were mentioned prominently in all the post-battle reports. Jackson, who generally only mentioned the difficulties imposed by Mother Nature when they were extreme, said the men performed well as a "cold and drenching thunder-shower swept over the field ... striking directly into the faces of our troops." A.P. Hill noted: "This battle commenced under the most unfavorable circumstances — a heavy, blinding rain-storm directly in the faces of my men." The 18th North Carolina also contended with fire from multiple fronts making a bad situation worse.

But, again, the regiment held its own and performed the job assigned to it in solid fashion. Ox Hill represented the end of the Second Manassas Campaign and another chapter in the history of the 18th North Carolina Regiment. Describing of his and his men's experiences since June, Branch wrote home:

> Since I wrote you last we have been almost constantly in the enemy's rear.... We have performed the most remarkable marches recorded in history. If we had not the actual experience it would not be credited that human nature could endure what we have endured. Fighting all day and marching all night — not for one day only, but for a whole week. The little sleep we have had has been generally on the battle field surrounded by the dead and wounded. Some

of the soundest sleep I have ever had has been on the naked ground without cover and the rain pouring down in torrents.

Even allowing for Branch's tendency towards flowery hyperbole, his letter to his wife does reasonably capture the experiences and dangers his command endured through the summer of 1862. Such experiences were to be repeated, and soon, as Lee realized his desire to take the Army of Northern Virginia into Maryland that September.[27]

Chapter 6

More Hard Marching: The Maryland Campaign

The firing had barely stopped at Ox Hill when plans were finalized between Robert E. Lee and Jefferson Davis for yet another strike at the enemy. What was on Lee's mind, though, was something far bolder than just looking for a place to defeat a major Union army. He wanted to put in motion a plan that he had had for some time of taking the fight to the enemy, to lead the Army of Northern Virginia outside the borders of the Confederacy and, as he told a reporter after the war, "give battle." While the weather still permitted Lee wanted to take his army northwestward into Maryland and, if everything went well, into Pennsylvania.

An officer who had known Lee before the war assured a fellow officer when Lee came to command the Army of Northern Virginia that all those sniping at him and calling him the "King of Spades" and "Granny Lee" would be proven wrong. That officer explained that Lee was nothing if not daring: "His very name could be audacity!" he exclaimed. The Maryland campaign proved that. But Lee was not merely giving in to what many have described as his natural tendency to gamble and take big risks. Lee was a gambler and — unlike his more timid opponent, George B. McClellan — was an aggressive military commander willing to assume risks, but he did not do so foolishly. All gamblers take risks but good ones only do so when the chances for success are highest and the potential payoffs warrant them. Lee felt that September 1862 was an excellent time to take a bold chance.

Some have suggested that the Maryland campaign was mainly to relieve Federal pressure on the Virginia countryside and to live off the enemy in his lands for a while. Virginia had indeed suffered a great deal and much of the state had been picked clean and torn up by the opposing armies. And being a Virginian, one who had in fact lost his beloved home, Arlington, to the

Federals, forever as it turned out, Lee was doubtless sensitive to the devastation that had come to his home state. But Lee and Davis had much grander hopes and goals for the campaign. Both men understood the importance of continued popular support for the war effort, something that was a major factor in both sections. If the Confederates were capable of launching a massive raid into enemy territory, sustain themselves there for an extended period of time, and inflict a stinging defeat on a major Union army, Northern public morale would be dealt a severe blow. With the Yankee public already restive and agitated after being very roughly handled all summer, doing more of the same in Union-controlled areas like Maryland (and Kentucky) would cause many to question either the Lincoln administration's ability to prosecute the war or if the war was even winnable if Southern armies could come into Northern areas and slap Union forces around. Military victories in places like Maryland and perhaps Pennsylvania could, Lee and Davis hoped, induce such an atmosphere in the North and force a power change in Washington. With the Republicans out of power, officials in Richmond understood that the possibility of negotiating an end to the war with Confederate independence as the centerpiece of the negotiations was more likely. With mid-term elections just around the corner, it was imperative to take the opportunity to further deflate and demoralize the Northern voting public right then.

The possibility of getting foreign recognition was also part of the equation, though not so much on Lee's part. Lee preferred to rely only on the tools he actually had rather than having to rely on things that may or may not come to pass. He certainly did not oppose trying to get England and other significant European powers involved to help the South achieve its goal, but he always thought that the Confederacy should do what it could by itself to win the war rather than banking on foreign pressure or intervention that may never materialize. However, foreign recognition and aid for the outmanned and outgunned Confederates would be extremely helpful, but England, France, and others would not support a losing cause so getting the sort of overt recognition and aid they needed required sustained battlefield successes. In fact, as word was getting to Europe of the Army of the Potomac's retrograde record during the Seven Days, Jackson's victory at Cedar Mountain, and especially Pope's whipping at Second Manassas, England was leaning very heavily towards stepping in to negotiate an end to the war with Confederate independence as the central talking point. The South, it appeared, was making a powerful bid and was proving itself in the field, so it was time for Europe to step in. The decision among Europe's top nations to step in could be sealed, and Southern independence realized by the end of the year perhaps, with victories beyond Confederate borders. Thus, while Lee did not like to let himself dwell too long on diplomacy and outside aid, he was not unaware of how the upcoming campaign could go a long way to securing foreign recognition, a major step towards independence for the South.

Lee also felt that the time was right militarily. He fully appreciated how tired and decimated his army was in early September 1862 but he still thought he held an edge over his opponent. He wrote Davis on September 3: "We cannot afford to be idle, and though weaker than our opponents in men and military equipments, must endeavor to harass, if we cannot destroy them." He reiterated the point in his later report of the campaign:

> The best course appeared to be the transfer of the army into Maryland. Although not properly equipped for invasion, lacking much of the material of war, ... the troops poorly provided with clothing, and thousands of them destitute of shoes, it was yet believed to be strong enough to detain the enemy upon the northern frontier until the approach of winter should render his advance into Virginia difficult, if not impracticable.

The Army of Northern Virginia was in need of rest and re-provisioning to be sure, but Lee knew he had an army of veterans whose morale was at a high point, which counted for a lot. He also knew that his enemy's armies were in some disarray around Washington, which he felt gave him an additional edge. Furthermore, the Federal forces around Washington were refilling their ranks with new, green troops. That, Lee thought, was also an edge for his veterans; when he thought of his veteran regiments going against green brigades he liked his chances. But they would not be untried and unsteady for long, so the time to strike was now.[1]

With Colonel Cowan still out of commission, Lieutenant-Colonel Thomas Purdie continued to lead the regiment and received orders to have the 18th North Carolina prepared to move on September 3, 1862. The regiment, like the rest of Jackson's command, was worn out. Over the previous three weeks they had made two fatiguing marches and fought in two battles. One of Jackson's "foot cavalry" wrote: "I tell you a soldier in Jackson's Army has got not time to write.... If he can only address his wife he is satisfied to close and return to bed immediately." One Tar Heel who did not appreciate the trade-off of hard marching for victories said at the time that "Stonewall gets the good out of his men too soon. He marches them so hard that they are nearly broke down before they get to the battle field." The 18th North Carolina had barely finished a sharp fight at Ox Hill when the company officers came through the camp near Chantilly ordering the men to fall in. By this time these Confederates from the Cape Fear were getting used to packing up their gear and getting on the road quickly. Where they were headed nobody knew, but they speculated, and probably boasted, that wherever they were headed on September 3 and 4 they would find the Yankees and teach them another lesson.[2]

Their immediate destination was the picturesque old town of Leesburg, which was near several places to ford the Potomac into Maryland. Getting from Chantilly to Leesburg was hard on many of the Confederates because of the lack of shoes Lee had mentioned in his reports. The previous months' marching and fighting and been hard on shoes and clothing and for many both were about given out. Orders were clear about preventing straggling, but Purdie and his officers had a good bit of difficulty keeping all the men in the ranks and marching because of the shoe situation. It was also difficult to tell which soldiers were legitimately having trouble keeping up and which ones were just skulking. But straggling in Branch's brigade was a problem, as it was for others. Numbers for the 18th North Carolina are not recorded, but in the 33rd North Carolina seventy-nine members were reported absent without leave and the 37th North Carolina reported eighty-two. One of the brigade's soldiers commented on the regiments not being at full strength because of straggling and other non-combat causes in a hometown newspaper; he complained, "If we can get in our stragglers and sick ones at home, which, bye the bye, is AN ARMY WITHIN ITSELF, we will have nothing to fear. All we have to fear is from straggling and absenteeism from the ranks on frivolous pretenses."³

Many were also making the march on empty or near-empty stomachs. One of the most famous descriptions of Lee's men during the Maryland campaign, which was penned a few days after they actually entered Maryland, referred to the Southern army as a "most ragged, lean, and hungry set of wolves." A Leesburg resident recalled later: "When I say that they were hungry, I convey no impression of the gaunt starvation that looked from their cavernous eyes. All day they crowded to the doors of our houses," asking for any food that could be spared. Many of the Leesburg ladies were only too happy to help the men fighting for their independence. "Everything that wears crinoline or a pretty face is out," one Southern correspondent recorded, "and such shouts and wavings of handkerchiefs and hurrahs by the overjoyed gender never emanated from human lips...." Many of the residents, one North Carolina soldier said, were "giving bread, honey & fruit pies & throwing open their spring houses" to the Rebels. An elderly lady, who lived along the army's line of march, came rushing out of her house with tears streaming down her face; she threw up her arms as the men went by, saying: "The Lord bless your dirty ragged souls."

Provisionally speaking, as these brief descriptions point out, this was a low point for Lee's army, but many accounts also have the soldiers' spirits being high regardless; they felt they had the enemy on the ropes and were perhaps within a battle or two of achieving their goal. As one angry Marylander put it, "this horde of ragamuffins" was maddeningly cheerful, most sporting "the broad grin all the time...." Another described Jackson's long column, which took several hours to pass, as dirty and "bronzed by exposure — marked by hardship & suffering — badly clad from want — yet with a look of firm, patient, and cheerful endurance and unflinching courage and determination. They looked to me not made of flesh and blood but stone and iron." Writing to his sister, one from Lee's army wrote: "We all have such confidence in the ability of our General, the valor of our men and the justness of our cause as it makes very little to us which way we go, so we can do our duty to our country."[4]

On Thursday, September 4, the first elements of the Army of Northern Virginia began crossing the Potomac near Leesburg at White's Ford. The 18th North Carolina crossed there the following day with the rest of A.P. Hill's Light Division. There were some North Carolina soldiers who were reluctant to cross the Potomac into Maryland. Their reluctance did not reflect a lack of courage or willingness to fight. Rather, they felt, they had volunteered to defend the South generally and North Carolina specifically from what they viewed as Northern invaders. To leave the Confederacy's borders and "invade" the North was, from their way of thinking, an illegitimate course of action for the same reasons it was wrong for the United States to "invade" the South. Such concerns seem to have been confined to some of the regiments from the western part of the state and despite their qualms about the legitimacy of "invasion" most ultimately crossed and fought bravely in the upcoming battles. There is no evidence that there was any concern in the 18th North Carolina about taking the fight to the enemy. Support for secession had been most pronounced in the southeastern counties where the regiment was born. Colonel Cowan had given numerous pro-secession speeches in early 1861 and Tom Purdie had run in early 1861 as Bladen County's pro-secession candidate for the state convention to consider that decision. Like most other Confederates, those in the 18th North Carolina seemed to view the idea of visiting a little destruction and pain on the North, especially given the increasingly hard policies the Lincoln administration was adopting, as a perfectly legitimate means to their end. Thus on September 5, 1862, the regiment crossed the Potomac, which on that clear sunny day, seemed to one Rebel "to sparkle with the brilliancy of a sea of silver studded with diamonds set in dancing beds of burnished gold.... The scene was one of grand & magnificent interest." Upon reaching the other side they could hear the many regimental bands striking up the tune "Maryland, My Maryland" as well as thousands of confident Confederates engaged in "yipping the Rebel yell" as they splashed into Unionist territory.[5]

Having made it into Maryland on September 5, the 18th North Carolina marched to the outskirts of Frederick the following day where they bivouacked and rested for a few days until orders came directing the next phase. Expectations had been that Maryland, because it was a slaveholding state, would view the Army of Northern Virginia as a friendly force and hopefully provide much-needed recruits for its depleted ranks. The 18th North Carolina, for example, was below half strength after the summer's battles, as were numerous units in Lee's army. The Rebels were to be disappointed on that front; they were in western Maryland where slaveholders were far fewer and where Unionism was decidedly higher and in the majority. A few Marylanders did join Lee's army but the records indicate that none of them became members of the 18th North Carolina.[6]

When Lee marched his army to Frederick, he had expected that the Union garrisons at Martinsburg and Harpers Ferry would be evacuated in response to his move. And that was precisely what McClellan wanted to do. That would have been standard operating procedure because those smaller forces were in danger of being flanked by a significantly larger force. Lee needed those Yankees out of the area in order to keep open his supply and communication line to the Shenandoah Valley. Lee guessed correctly that cautious McClellan wanted to do exactly what the book said to do in that situation, but he was thwarted by General Henry Halleck, who had succeeded McClellan as head of all Union armies in March and he refused to evacuate either Martinsburg or Harpers Ferry. So, on September 9, Lee decided, to split his army, sending Jackson to force the evacuation of Martinsburg and Harpers Ferry. The decision was extremely dangerous, and Longstreet did not like it for that very reason. They were operating in, if not totally hostile, then unfriendly, territory with the Army of the Potomac heading in their general direction. Lee brushed aside the concerns believing that between McClellan's demonstrated unwillingness to move above a snail's pace and the protection that South Mountain provided, Jackson could perform his task and rejoin the army by September 12, which was probably days before the Army of the Potomac would be close enough to be any sort of threat.[7]

With the plans made Jackson sent out orders to the divisions under his command to be ready to move first thing the next morning, September 10. In his report Jackson said,

> My command left the vicinity of Frederick City on the 10th, and, passing rapidly through Middletown, Boonsborough, and Williamsport, recrossed the Potomac into Virginia, at Light's Ford on the 11th. General [A.P.] Hill moved with his division on the turnpike direct from Williamsport to Martinsburg.

Typical of the experiences under Jackson, the 18th North Carolina was on the march by 4:00 that morning and it would be a long, tiring one. The original plan had Jackson's men heading northwest from Frederick to Boonsboro and turning south to take the most direct route through the town of Sharpsburg to get to Harpers Ferry and the Yankee garrison there. But when the column reached Boonsboro, scouts alerted Jackson that the Martinsburg force had not evacuated as expected. These 2,500 Yankees had to be moved and Jackson had more than enough men to do the job. The problem was that it would add an additional sixty miles to the march and it would also seriously threaten Lee's plan to have his army reunited by September 12. But McClellan would be slow; surely he would not pose a serious problem so another day or so should not make too much of a difference. Thus the column continued northwest to Williamsport where it crossed back into Virginia above Martinsburg, with bands playing "Carry Me Back to Ole Virginny."[8]

The 18th was near the front of Jackson's column that closed on Martinsburg with overwhelming numerical superiority over the tiny garrison. Elements of Branch's brigade were sent forward as skirmishers on September 11 and had little trouble with the enemy soldiers who had formed a skirmish line of their own to delay Jackson a little just to give the Federals more time to evacuate the town. There was some shooting outside the town and the 18th North Carolina had a couple of men wounded in the encounter but nothing terribly serious. The Federals had no intention of foolishly staying and putting up a serious fight and they evacuated the town the same day.[9]

After organizing some of the captured items at Martinsburg, the march continued towards Harpers Ferry roughly twelve miles southeastward. The Federals at Harpers Ferry were in a very tight spot. They were effectively trapped in the town, which sits at the bottom of an area dominated by three sets of heights: Loudoun, Maryland, and Bolivar. Confederate forces were already in the process of occupying two of those heights by September 12. General Lafayette McLaws was atop Maryland Heights while another division commanded by General John Walker secured Loudoun Heights for the Confederates. The only high ground the Unionists had was Bolivar Heights at the rear of the town. It was this group that the 18th North Carolina and the rest of the Light Division were marching towards. By sundown on September 12, the 18th was camped within two miles of those Federals.

Jackson's plan for taking Harpers Ferry on September 14 (two full days after the army was supposed to be reunited) called for a massive artillery barrage at dawn from all three positions followed by an attack by Hill's men. The 18th North Carolina's job in the taking of Harpers Ferry had them going with the rest of Branch's brigade and Maxcy Gregg's South Carolinians around the Federal flank under cover of darkness on the night of September 13. When the next morning's barrage ended, that would be the signal for the infantry assault. The Federals' position was doomed as Hill hit them from the front and Branch and Gregg hit them in the flank and rear. Jackson and Hill both recorded in their post-battle reports that "Branch and Gregg ... gained the positions indicated for them, and day break found them in rear of the enemy's line of defense." Through the night the regiment waited for dawn and for their chance to strike at the enemy. At dawn the Confederate artillery opened up on the Federals on Bolivar Heights and beat them into submission fairly quickly. A member of the 125th New York recalled:

> Our regiment was napping and lounging around ... when suddenly ... a shell came whizzing into our midst — we saw our helplessness; we were at their mercy; to remain was to be slaughtered, so we ran like hounds to get under the cover of a hillside.... I tell you, it is dreadful to be a mark for artillery, bad enough for any but especially for raw troops [as most there were]; it demoralizes them — it rouses one's courage to be able to fight [back], but to sit still and calmly be cut in two is too much to ask.

At nine the Federals surrendered without need of the infantry assault and once again Harpers Ferry changed hands.[10]

Jackson's men, being the closest to the town, descended on it ahead of the other Confederates who had been on Loudoun and Maryland Heights.

Harpers Ferry. The 18th North Carolina helped take the town during the Sharpsburg Campaign in September 1862. From here the regiment participated in A.P. Hill's famous lightning march to strengthen Lee's crumbling right flank at Sharpsburg on September 17, 1862. Library of Congress.

To the "horde of ragamuffins" Harpers Ferry offered a bonanza. It may not have been the cornucopia of all things good that the Manassas Depot had provided the previous month, but for hungry, shoeless Rebels in threadbare clothes Harpers Ferry offered them everything so many of them needed. Not only did the 18th North Carolina get to fill their haversacks and put on new shoes, they got to upgrade their weaponry. Thousands of rifled muskets were stored at Harpers Ferry and surrendered by the Federals; when the regiment hit the town "up-to-date Springfield rifles replaced our smooth-bores." Not surprisingly, spirits in the regiment were high on September 14. The men were well fed for the first time in weeks, shoes and other clothing were issued to those in need, and the regiment got itself outfitted with state-of-the-art rifles. The 18th North Carolina, in helping to capture some 11,000 Yankees, had also played a direct role in the largest capture of U.S. soldiers in history prior to World War II.[11]

Meanwhile, McClellan was got uncharacteristically aggressive and closed in on Lee while Jackson's command took Harpers Ferry. Something extraordinary had to have happened to make McClellan move and something had; he had gotten a copy of Lee's Order 191, which told the Federal commander that Lee had his army strung out all over western Maryland and northwestern Virginia making him vulnerable. An Indiana corporal had stumbled upon a bundle of cigars near his camping site on September 13 and thought he was lucky indeed to have found some precious tobacco lost by some careless Reb. When he unwrapped the cigars, though, he saw that they were wrapped in what appeared to be official orders. They looked genuine and he knew they could be very important so he began the process of taking the orders up the chain of command until the orders wound up at the headquarters tent of the commanding general himself. McClellan understood the good fortune that had befallen him and he exclaimed, "Now I know what to do!" He contacted Washington at midnight of September 13 and reported:

> I have the whole rebel force in front of me, but am confident, and no time shall be lost. I have a difficult task to perform, but with God's blessing will accomplish it. I think Lee has made a gross mistake, and that he will be severely punished for it.... I have all the plans of the rebels, and will catch them in their own trap if my men are equal to the emergency. I now feel that I can count on them as of old.... Will send you trophies.[12]

This was precisely the sort of situation that Longstreet had worried about when Lee announced four days earlier that he would break every standard military dictum and split his army with a larger enemy force within striking distance. McClellan moved towards South Mountain with an eye towards going through Crampton's and Turner's gaps to get to Lee's weakened and vulnerable army. As historian Stephen Sears has noted, the only reason

McClellan was moving with anything approaching decisiveness was that he knew he had a significant numerical advantage over Lee. With Jackson's and part of Longstreet's commands some seventeen miles away at Harpers Ferry, McClellan had an actual advantage of about four-to-one. Of course he tended to vastly inflate Confederate numbers so he only thought he held a two-to-one edge, but for the first time (in his mind) he was stronger numerically than his opponent. So he moved and in savage fighting along South Mountain on September 14 the Southern survivors had to pull back to the area around Sharpsburg. Things looked extremely dangerous for the Confederates in Maryland.[13]

Given the precarious situation Lee could have considered that the most prudent course would be to continue heading back towards Virginia and reunite his army. He could not bring himself to do that, though. Perhaps it was the sound tactical decision to back away under the circumstances but Lee felt strongly that the Maryland campaign should not be abandoned with only Harpers Ferry and its stores taken. From his perspective, to have done so would have been nearly as bad as a battlefield defeat. This was the best chance to boost Southern morale and crush the North's, to undermine Republican control of Washington, and to perhaps even gain that elusive prize of foreign recognition. With so much riding on this campaign, he could not bring himself to abandon it without taking a serious shot at achieving what he had entered Maryland for in the first place. Gambling that McClellan had not suddenly morphed into an aggressive fighter who would follow up his success at South Mountain, Lee determined that he would make a stand around Sharpsburg with Longstreet's divisions and send for Jackson to bring his up as quickly as possible. As it turned out, Lee had correctly gauged his opposite number and McClellan did indeed waste September 15 and 16 meticulously preparing his attack on the Army of Northern Virginia.[14]

Most of the Confederates at Harpers Ferry left the town on September 16 for Sharpsburg. But the job of gathering, cataloguing, and packing up the captured items still had to be completed. The massive number of Union prisoners had to be documented and paroled as well. This job was left to A.P. Hill's division, which was to finish the work as quickly as possible and get on the road to join the rest of Jackson's force at Sharpsburg. The 18th North Carolina was thus busily engaged in helping to finish this job before falling in and marching for Sharpsburg.

The next day, the bloodiest single day in American military history erupted in front of Stonewall Jackson's command on the Confederate left above Sharpsburg with furious artillery fire. In the early morning hours of September 17, Colonel Purdie collected his officers and told them to rouse the regiment and have them fall in immediately; there was an urgency in his voice that let them know that the men were about to be moving somewhere quickly. Purdie's insistence on getting the men up and ready to march combined with what was first thought to be distant thunder. But the day dawned clear and sunny, causing veterans to tell new replacements who had recently joined over the previous couple of weeks, to get ready for their first real day in the Light Division; that was not thunder they were hearing, it was the booming of Yankee cannons. The veterans of the summer battles knew before the day was out that their green replacements would see their first serious engagement.

The 18th North Carolina hurriedly packed up their gear into blanket rolls, fell into line, and was on the move at the double quick by 7:30. The regiment's veterans had made rapid marches before and were somewhat used to them. The new recruits, however, were getting a rough indoctrination to infantry life. The march from Boonsboro had been long but the pace was considerably slower than this one and they had been given breaks every hour. Normally Jackson's marching routine was to give the men a ten-minute break for every hour of marching. Today speed outweighed all other considerations as Hill had to get the Light Division to the front as fast as he possibly could. He would probably lose some of them to the brutal pace but that could not be helped. To help bolster his soldiers he was seen riding along the column shouting out words of encouragement. The fact that Hill was wearing his soon-to-be-famous red flannel shirt told the veterans that he was definitely shoving them along to get them into a fight with the Federals somewhere up the road.[15]

There was a bloody fight going on up ahead, one that the men and officers of the 18th North Carolina could hear ever more clearly as Hill shoved them mercilessly forward. Veterans were likely flashing back to the march that culminated in the battle at Manassas or, more likely, to the terrible forced march to Cedar Mountain. While they splashed across the Potomac at Boteler's Ford near Shepherdstown at about 2:30, Lee was doing his best to hang on as furious fighting took place on his left and center where places like the "Sunken Road," "Dunker Church," and "Mumma's Farm" were entering the bloody annals of the Civil War. All morning Lee steadily and effectively shifted troops from his right, which enjoyed a good defensive position, to other parts of the field that were under attack. It left his right flank thinly protected but the Federal IX Corps on the other side the Rohrbach Bridge, which spanned Antietam Creek, had fortunately not posed a threat to that part of the field.

That, McClellan later argued, was not supposed to have been the situation at all. Claims were made after the battle that the IX Corps was to have engaged the enemy during the morning rather than sitting idle until the early afternoon hours. Whatever the merits of the arguments, the Unionists on the east bank of Antietam Creek indeed did nothing while the battle raged on their right. When the Yankees did move to cross the creek at the Rohrbach Bridge (soon to become famous as "Burnside's Bridge") the Confederates on the other side, Georgians under Robert Toombs, had taken advantage of the high ground and dug in. The Northerners had the unpleasant and very dangerous job of crossing a very narrow bridge, which caused a natural bottleneck of massed troops (targets), where the approaches to it were totally exposed for several hundred yards to Rebel riflemen firing down on them from the relative protection of their rifle pits. For most of the morning and into the early afternoon the outnumbered Georgians were able to keep the Yankees from crossing and threatening Lee's right flank. But by 2:00 their ammunition ran very low and they were no longer able to sustain their effective fire. Sensing their opportunity the Federal division under the command of General Samuel Sturgis rushed across the bridge in force and secured a position on the Confederate side of the creek.

Having gotten across the bridge, though, the Federal surge stalled. Sturgis's command was also low on ammunition, and no other Union divisions were prepared to immediately follow up Sturgis's attack and continue to pressure Lee's right flank. General Orlando Wilcox's division reached the Rohrbach Bridge around 2:00 but it was another hour before he got his men across, followed by General Isaac Rodman's division to relieve Sturgis and allow his men to replenish their cartridge boxes. If the Federals on Lee's right flank were not exactly advancing like a well-oiled machine, they were advancing nonetheless as the afternoon wore on and that was a serious problem for Lee. The right flank was very thinly defended and while General David R. Jones had done all he could with his division on that flank, he and his men, many of whom were completely out of ammunition, were facing increasingly heavy pressure between three and four in the afternoon. In fact the flank was showing signs of completely falling apart as elements of Willcox's division began to close in.

As the tide was turning in the IX Corps's favor on the Confederate right, one of Lee's aides spotted a column of soldiers kicking up a huge dust cloud as they rapidly advanced from the direction of Harpers Ferry. Initially they were thought to spell disaster as the soldiers appeared to be wearing blue (and many of the soldiers were wearing parts of Yankee uniforms that they took at Harpers Ferry to replace their worn-out Confederate uniforms), but then the aide reported seeing Confederate flags flying amidst the column. "It is A.P. Hill from Harpers Ferry," a relieved Lee told his aide. The right was about to get some much needed support. As a tired Georgian remembered, "They were in good condition and cheered General Lee as they hurried on. The old general's worried look left him as he noticed the enthusiasm of Hill's Division." Reaching the scene Hill did not take any time halting and sorting out the division but threw his men into the fighting as they arrived on the scene. Hill ordered Brockenbrough and Pender to secure the right while he directed Archer, Gregg, and Branch to pitch in to help Rodman's division of New Yorkers and New Englanders from Connecticut and Rhode Island. While the other regiments of Branch's brigade followed him into the attack, the 18th North Carolina was held in reserve, an unenviable position since they would not be able to shoot at the enemy while bullets and shell fragments raked the ranks. While the regiment was "not actively engaged" at Sharpsburg, they still lost eight men killed and fourteen wounded. One, James Burchett of Company I, had barely become a member before being killed, having joined the regiment while it paroled prisoners and packed things up at Harpers Ferry just two days earlier. The Light Division's arrival could not have come at a better time and by four-thirty the Federals were falling back and recrossing Antietam Creek.

The brigade had losses, of course, in its successful attack but the most significant loss was its commander. Sharpsburg/Antietam was a battle where numerous high-ranking officers were killed or wounded and like those others, General Branch went down, shot through the head, as he led the brigade in the attack to throw the Yankees back to other side of the bridge. In his report of the fight, Hill wrote: "The Confederacy has to mourn the loss of a gallant soldier and accomplished gentleman, who fell in battle at the head of his brigade — Brig. Gen. L.O'B. Branch, of North Carolina." Lee, too, expressed regret at losing Branch, saying that in the attack, "the brave and lamented Brig. Gen. L.O'B. Branch was killed, gallantly leading his brigade."

But it was his men who would miss him the most. Branch had been their commander from the beginning of the war. Losing him was, for many, like losing a father. Branch had suffered all the pains and dangers his men had and set an example of leading from the front. He never missed an opportunity to compliment and encourage his soldiers and for all these reasons he was highly regarded and deeply mourned by his men when he died. A member of the 33rd North Carolina said the brigade "almost idolized him. He died as a soldier would wish to die, facing the enemy, in the discharge of his duty." Command of the brigade went to Colonel James H. Lane of the 28th North Carolina, a position that became permanent in the following weeks and it would be known for the rest of the war as Lane's Brigade.[16]

That evening the 18th North Carolina slept on its arms, expecting to see the enemy again the next day. But while Lee held his army defiantly in front of the Union general and dared him to attack his undermanned position, McClellan chose not to do so. During the night of September 18 the Army of Northern Virginia began retreating from Sharpsburg. The 18th North Carolina formed part of the rear guard protecting the rest of the army and it was while performing this duty that it saw the hottest fighting of the Maryland campaign.

With most of the army safely across the Potomac near Shepherdstown,

Virginia (now West Virginia), the 18th North Carolina crossed over at 10:00 A.M. on September 19. Early the next morning it appeared that Federals from the Fifth Corps intended to pursue Lee and, as Jackson later reported, "the enemy appeared in considerable force on the northern side of the Potomac, and commenced planting heavy batteries on its heights." With artillery in place (Hill estimated as many as seventy guns were on the ridge on the opposite side of the river), the Unionists began coming across in force. At six-thirty A.P. Hill took his division back towards Shepherdstown to neutralize the threat to the army's rear. Arriving on the scene, Hill's division moved to push the enemy back under heavy artillery fire from the other side of the river. The 18th's adjutant remembered that the artillery coming in from the Maryland side of the river "had our range accurately, and their shells plowed through the Eighteenth several times."

Despite the galling fire the regiment continued forward. "This advance," Hill reported, "was made in the face of the most tremendous fire of artillery I ever saw, and too much praise cannot be awarded my regiments for their steady, unwavering step. It was as if each man felt that the fate of the army was centered in himself." The 18th pushed forward and "raised a yell and poured a deadly volley into the enemy, who fled precipitously and in great confusion to the river. Advancing at a double-quick, we soon gained the bank of the river, and continued our destructive fire upon those who were attempting to regain the Maryland shore at the old dam just above the ferry." Hill echoed that report, saying that as soon as his men got the upper hand in the fighting at Shepherdstown there "commenced the most terrible slaughter that this war has yet witnessed. The broad surface of the Potomac was blue with the floating bodies of our foe. But few escaped to tell the tale." Such, he added, "was a wholesome lesson to the enemy, and taught them to know that it may be dangerous sometimes to press a retreating enemy." Indeed, Federal losses at Shepherdstown vary from between seventy and just over ninety killed and over 130 wounded. Losses in the 18th North Carolina were slightly higher in this action than those suffered at Sharpsburg with most of the damage being done by artillery. Many of the casualties were new recruits. One, K.B. Harris of Company F, was a mere boy of eighteen who had been in Confederate service one month to the day when he was killed at Shepherdstown.[17]

The Battle of Shepherdstown brought the Maryland campaign to a close. While most did their full duty, some stood out more than others; in his post-campaign report, Lane added:

> Lieutenant-Colonel Purdie, who bravely commanded the Eighteenth in most of these engagements, desires that special mention should be made of Capt. John D. Barry, of Company I, for his coolness and gallantry and devotion to duty.

Barry was quickly making a reputation for himself for bravery. Conspicuously leading his company out front, he had been wounded in the head at Frayser's Farm and had returned to duty quickly. Unfortunately the Army of Northern Virginia had not achieved any of the goals Lee had set for it when it began. Their division commander was nevertheless proud of it and all the regiments he commanded. After the Maryland Campaign A.P. Hill proudly addressed his Light Division:

> You have done well and I am pleased with you. You have fought in every battle from Mechanicsville to Shepherdstown, and no man can yet say that the Light Division was ever broken. You held the left at Manassas against overwhelming numbers and saved the army. You saved the day at Sharpsburg and Shepherdstown. You were selected to face a storm of round shot, shell, and grape such as I have never before seen. I am proud to say that your services are appreciated by our general, and that you have a reputation in this army which it should be the object of every officer and private to sustain.

If Hill gilded the lily a bit there was much truth in it and the 18th North Carolina had certainly shown itself to be as good a regiment as there was to be found in the Army of Northern Virginia. They had been bloodied in May at Hanover Court House and fought well at Gaines's Mill and Frayser's Farm. They had made grueling marches in the Second Manassas and Maryland campaigns. And they had played significant roles in helping to save the army's flanks at Cedar Mountain and Sharpsburg. Though not actively engaged in the famous fight at Sharpsburg, they showed once again at Shepherdstown that they were as capable as any of punishing the enemy.[18]

Chapter 7

A Difficult Way to End a Year: Fall and Winter of 1862

With the Maryland campaign finished, the regiment camped for a few days near Martinsburg, Virginia, before heading for the lower (northern) end of the Shenandoah Valley. The 18th North Carolina, or what remained of it, established camp at Bunker Hill about ten miles north of Winchester in late September. The regiment remained in the lower Valley until late November, when it marched out for Fredericksburg.

The regiment at this point was in very poor material condition despite the bounty Harpers Ferry had provided for many. The summer of 1862 had seen a lot of hard marching, hot fighting, as well as constant exposure to the elements. One member of the Light Division described it as "badly broken down" and one of Lane's men said that the brigade members after the Maryland campaign "were sun-burnt, gaunt, ragged, scarcely at all shod ... an emaciated, limping, filthy mass." "It is difficult to describe the condition of the troops at this time," one of A.P. Hill's men recalled, "so great and various was their wretchedness." The biggest deficiency was shoes, which was true not only for the 18th North Carolina but the whole army. In late October Thomas Purdie wrote home to encourage the people back in his home county to send shoes as well as other clothing items to the soldiers. "Our men, the old members of the regt., are suffering very much for shoes & clothing & I wish ... to remind the folks in the country & get them to do something for the Bladen men." He went on to say: "I imagine there are now a dozen or more Bladen men bare foot." Purdie was a man of considerable financial means in his own right, the 1860 census indicated that he owned over forty slaves, and he tried to use his own money to buy his men some shoes. "It is very severe to march over these rough rocky roads bare foot in cold weather," and as his men's leader he tried to do all he could, even using his own money, to get his men shoes. This concern for his men likely explains why, when so many of the regiment's original officers were defeated in the regiment's April elections, Purdie not only survived the purge but was promoted.[1]

The regiment needed to replenish its ranks as well as improve the men's material conditions. Lee's Army of Northern Virginia had been severely depleted between the Seven Days and Sharpsburg with its numbers dipping to some 30,000. The Light Division and the 18th North Carolina were certainly no exceptions. The regiment had lost half its numbers since leaving North Carolina in the spring and was in serious need of repopulation. Regimental numbers had been improving in the late summer through conscription or the threat of it. Between the end of July and mid–September, the 18th North Carolina, like other regiments in the brigade, received new recruits to help replace those lost in the summer fighting.[2]

The attempt to build the 18th's strength back up through the Conscription Act proved to be a mixed blessing and only marginally successful. On the one hand, some of the new members of the regiment entered and became valuable additions to the unit. Hackaliah Hoffman, for example, joined the regiment in the middle of August and stood fast in the ranks and was wounded three times. Joseph Hawn also joined the regiment in mid–August and earned a promotion to corporal in January 1864 before being captured at the Wilderness and enduring the war's final year between two Union prisons, Point Lookout, Maryland, and Elmira, New York.

Others, however, were not so willing to serve the cause with the same selflessness. Some conscripted soldiers never actually reported for duty and some who did took the opportunity to desert relatively quickly. John Shook of Company A, for example, came to the regiment in August and deserted three months later at Fredericksburg. Richmond officials gave him (and all others) the chance to avoid punishment and return to duty in early 1863, and Shook went back to the 18th only to desert again after Chancellorsville. That was his last chance and he was caught and shot for desertion on November 5, 1863. While desertion among the new recruits and conscripts was not the norm, it does seem to have been exceptionally high compared to other regiments. During the fall and early winter of 1862, nearly 10 percent of the 18th North Carolina's new additions deserted compared to 2.5 percent in the 7th North Carolina and 4.7 percent in the 37th North Carolina. It is impossible to determine accurately exactly why the rate was so much higher in the 18th North Carolina, but one modern scholar of the brigade has suggested that one factor may have been where the new arrivals came from. Most of the replacements came from the state's western counties like Catawba, Iredell, and Rutherford counties; a good number of men joined up in Wilkes and Caldwell counties. It is possible that some of these western Carolinians bore some resentment at not being placed with companies made up of people from their home counties as others were. William Rufus Barlow of Caldwell County was one who, though he never deserted, did express some irritation at being assigned to Company B of the 18th North Carolina. Upset, he wrote to his wife in late August from Camp Lee in Richmond: "We don't get to go to the regiment we wanted to go to. We have been assigned to the 18th regiment, Branch's Brigade." He preferred serving in the 26th North Carolina where some of the other Caldwell County boys went and where he apparently had relatives. So there may be something to this theory since the 7th and 37th both drew far more new members from their home counties than did the 18th.[3]

A far greater problem, though, was that many of these new members died in a fairly short amount of time. This was not terribly uncommon unfortunately. Disease stalked military camps throughout the Civil War and for every soldier who died on the battlefield two died of disease. Those newest to military life were also the ones most often afflicted because they often came from rural areas where they had not been exposed to a variety of communicable diseases. Static military camps were notoriously unhygienic, and when combined with bad food and questionable water supplies it was inevitable that green recruits would succumb to disease; it was just a matter of how many. New recruit William Barlow, who never had much good to say about military life, told his wife in late October that there was "a good deal of sickness in camp now and a good many deaths. They say the smallpox is right at us, in the same brigade, and the measles and the mumps. I look to have the mumps every week." Between August and December 1862 the 18th North Carolina lost just over 130 soldiers to disease. And after the most common killers, diarrhea and dysentery, Barlow was right that measles was a big killer of new members, being second on the surgeon's list of killers for October 1862. Most of the deaths, about 90 or nearly 68 percent, were among the new members. Despite the losses to disease, as the summer months gave way to cooler fall weather, the 18th North Carolina was able to build its numbers back up through conscription, recruiting, and the return of those who had been sick or wounded during the summer.[4]

During the fall of 1862 there were several changes that affected the regiment. In early November the Confederate Congress approved a proposal to divide the Army of Northern Virginia into two corps with James Longstreet getting a slightly larger First Corps and Stonewall Jackson becoming commander of the new Second Corps. Both men, in turn, received promotion to lieutenant-general. A.P. Hill's Light Division remained a vital part of Jackson's corps and Branch's old brigade remained part of that hard-hitting division. Command of the brigade had unofficially fallen to James H. Lane after General

Branch was killed at Sharpsburg. That fall his promotion to brigadier general was approved and he became the official commander of the brigade; he would lead it for the rest of the war except for a brief period in 1864 when he was out with a wound. In the 18th North Carolina there were also changes in the upper ranks. At some point towards the end of the Seven Days Battles, Colonel Robert H. Cowan turned over command of the regiment to Thomas Purdie, his second-in-command. It is not entirely clear whether Cowan was wounded or suffering from a severe illness; the records seem to indicate both. Lieutenant-Colonel Purdie had led the 18th North Carolina through much of the summer and early fall while Cowan was convalescing. On November 1, 1862, Cowan resigned from the service because of "congestion of the liver and chronic diarrhea," and ten days later Thomas Purdie was promoted to colonel of the regiment. Purdie does not appear to have particularly wanted the job, though he had been doing it quite well up to that point. In a letter from late October he says that Cowan "speaks of resigning & if he does I feel like doing the same for I have no desire to command a regt." Ultimately he determined that he had been given a job to do and he would do his duty. A Columbus County attorney, Major Forney George, became the regiment's second-in-command and the young twenty-two-year-old captain of Company I, John Decatur Barry, an officer Colonel Purdie very much respected and who had proven his leadership ability and his personal bravery on several fields, was promoted to major.[5]

During the fall of 1862 the regiment did not see much in the way of action while camped in the Bunker Hill area. A good bit of the reason for that was that McClellan had decided to go as slowly as possible in following up his victory over Lee at Sharpsburg. This, of course, drove Lincoln and others in the administration to distraction. Lee's army was in about as bad a shape as it was possible to be in but still McClellan inched forward in pursuit. General-in-Chief Henry Halleck railed: "There is an immobility here that exceeds all that any man can conceive of. It requires the lever of Archimedes to move this inert mass." Lincoln tried one last time to be cordial with McClellan, asking him if he did not "remember my speaking to you of what I called your over-cautiousness?" Still McClellan complained that he could do no more than he already had given the army's condition. He said his army's horses — so necessary to move supplies — were in such dilapidated shape that they were just too tired for a vigorous pursuit of Lee's army. At that point Lincoln had about had it with his general, responding, "Will you pardon me for asking what the horses of your army have done since the battle of Antietam that fatigues anything?" With General McClellan moving so slowly (he did not cross the Potomac until October 26), the men of the 18th North Carolina were able to have a relatively easy fall season keeping an eye on the Army of the Potomac's flank. The most activity the eastern Tar Heels had was destroying a twenty-mile segment of the strategic Baltimore and Ohio Railroad between Berryville and Harpers Ferry towards the end of October, a job that took them about a week.[6]

The relative quiet in the lower Shenandoah Valley that had been the norm for Jackson's men from late September through early November led most to assume that they would start building winter quarters and wait for the spring campaigning season. That was, after all, the general schedule for fighting wars at that time. The winter months made the movement of large forces difficult at best as roads, especially in Virginia, alternatively froze and thawed creating knee-deep mud, making them all but unusable. Generally winter meant drill, picket duty, and a general monotony until spring came and the roads dried, making movement again possible. But the Lincoln administration was in deep political trouble in the second half of 1862 and demanded a positive military victory in the Virginia theater before the year was out to keep the Copperheads (the segment of the Democratic Party who viewed the war as either unwinnable or too costly in terms of blood and treasure and who thus favored negotiating an end to it) from gaining any more momentum. It had become too obvious that McClellan would never provide that victory and he was sacked on November 7 in favor of General Ambrose Burnside in hopes of getting something positive going before the new year dawned; there would be no going into winter quarters just yet.

The order firing McClellan was delivered by General Cartharinus P. Buckingham and came with a second message for General Burnside. In it the Army of the Potomac's new commander was made aware that he was expected to succeed where his predecessor had so often failed. Burnside was not permitted to meander about and permit the rebellion to continue by allowing what many perceived as the Confederacy's principal army to continue to exist. "Immediately on assuming command of the Army of the Potomac," Burnside's orders read, "you will report the position of your troops, and what you propose doing with them." The new commander did not have the luxury of easing into his new position. Rather, he was expected to take command and come up with something positive to do right away as opposed to waiting for the spring campaigning season.[7]

Looking back, the choice of Ambrose Burnside to turn the military fortunes around in Virginia, and with them the Republicans' political fortunes, seems a very questionable choice. Even Burnside thought the choice was a huge mistake. Certainly he felt very awkward taking over for his friend who had bailed him out financially before the war. He was also well aware of how popular McClellan was among most of the officers and men of the army and that any replacement would be viewed negatively. Being thrust into the position and told to do something grand, and to do it now, was certainly daunting. But mostly Burnside doubted his own ability for this level of command. At the time, though, Burnside had been carving out a solid reputation in North Carolina as a general who accomplished things and he was persuaded to take the job that was given to him by the administration. Besides, Burnside knew too that if he refused the job, command of the Army of the Potomac would go to Joseph Hooker, a choice Burnside felt was even worse.[8]

Since Secretary of War Edwin Stanton had been more than clear that Burnside was expected to do something, he fleshed out a plan that he had been working on to present to McClellan that fall. On November 9 Burnside informed the War Department that he had a plan. Rather than organize the Army of the Potomac for an attack on Lee's forces while they were strung out between the Shenandoah Valley and Culpeper Court House, something Lincoln probably expected and desired given his conviction that it was the destruction of the South's military forces that would most quickly end the rebellion, he would feint towards the upper Rappahannock as if he were intending to attack Culpeper or Gordonsville. That, he explained, would focus Lee's attention on that area while Burnside quickly stole a march on him and headed for Fredericksburg. Once there, Burnside expected to use the city as the base from which he would move on Richmond and bring the war to a successful close or at the very least, bring that goal a giant step closer.

Neither Lincoln nor Stanton was thrilled with the idea of moving *away* from Lee's army; that was the objective as far as they were concerned. But Burnside, like McClellan before him, still viewed the taking of Richmond as the objective. In arguing for his plan he told the administration that the taking of the Confederate capital, "I think, should be the great object of the campaign" because, he believed, it would "tend more to cripple the rebel cause than almost any other military event." The loss of one of the Confederacy's major industrial centers, which Richmond undeniably was, as well as the emotional blow of having the capital taken and occupied by the enemy were significant benefits for the Union cause. So Burnside would move away from Lee's immediate front, get to Fredericksburg, cross the Rappahannock River, and make a dash for Richmond. Fredericksburg was closer to Richmond than his current location anyway, he argued, plus it offered more secure communication and supply lines by both rail and water since the Federals controlled the Chesapeake Bay. Worst case scenario, if the campaign was not able to accomplish everything for whatever reason, Fredericksburg was a much more secure base than the piedmont area in terms of supplies. The administration did not like it but it was the promise of something positive, which was better than nothing, so Lincoln told Burnside to proceed.[9]

On November 15 Burnside made good on the first part of his plan. The

Army of the Potomac made a strong show of force all along Lee's upper Rappahannock position where only Longstreet's corps faced them. The Confederates were significantly outnumbered but then the Federals did something that Lee found very strange. Instead of taking advantage of the situation, something he would have done, all along the Rappahannock line the Federals pulled up short. None of the Unionists who came to the river in such a menacing and provocative posture pressed their way across to hit the Confederates. Lee quickly determined that something was amiss. If Burnside was not coming directly at him in the piedmont, he must have something else in mind. The Confederate general concluded that the scenario that made the most sense was that Burnside was trying to get around his right, heading for Fredericksburg where he could interpose himself between Lee and Richmond. Lee could not allow that to happen so he sent warnings to Confederates in the Fredericksburg area to be aware that the Union army may be heading their way. He also had Longstreet's corps get moving east with the idea of blocking Burnside's southward move by establishing a defensive line along the North Anna River. Burnside had a head start, Lee figured, and would reach Fredericksburg and cross the Rappahannock before the Army of Northern Virginia could unite to block him there.[10]

With the Federals on the move the 18th North Carolina did not hang around their lower Valley camp for much longer. November 20 and 21 were spent cooking rations and preparing to march. At 2:30 A.M. on November 22 the regiment was up and marching south, up the Valley Turnpike, in column of fours. Though the regiment had built up its numbers and had some time to rest, many of the men were still in sub-par material condition. When they marched through Winchester the townspeople turned out to greet them and offer encouragement. One of the ladies of Winchester noted sadly, "They were very destitute, many without shoes, and all without overcoats or gloves, although the weather is freezing. Their poor hands looked so red and cold holding their muskets in the biting wind...." One of Jackson's soldiers recorded: "Many of the men are yet without shoes in some of the regiments, and it is almost piteous to see them painfully picking their way along through frost and ice." Marching through the often-windy Valley in late November could be miserable enough, but the 18th had to endure sleet and freezing rain that soaked them and their gear, and left a thin layer of ice. It also made carrying muskets with ice-cold barrels without gloves truly painful.[11]

Jackson's column continued south from Winchester to New Market. At New Market the foot cavalry turned eastward through the Luray Valley towards and through Fisher's Gap. The whole time the regiment battled rain, sleet, biting winds, and mountain roads made particularly treacherous because of the icy conditions. As they got through Fisher's Gap and got closer to

Madison Court House a lot of Jackson's men got a welcome surprise. A number of Blue Ridge citizens, who had a tradition of distilling their own liquor, saw in the column of very chilled and miserable soldiers a chance to make some money. All along the marching route around Madison and points west could be found stands and individuals selling homemade whiskey. This was a rare opportunity for soldiers who were traditionally forbidden from drink in the first place, but the miserable conditions they had put up with for the last week made these jars of clear liquid comfort all the more tempting. Attempts were made, of course, to enforce the rules against enlisted men drinking; this was Jackson's command after all and his religious convictions (some have said fanaticism) provided him with very little sympathy for cold men trying to ease their discomfort with alcohol. Not all Jackson's officers agreed with his views on the evils of demon rum. General Jubal Early was said to have filled his own canteen up with whiskey and enjoyed himself. One remembered that "old Jubal was merry and a-grinning," which did not sit well with his corps commander. But others felt as Early did and turned a blind eye as their miserable charges got a little forbidden alcohol. As one of the soldiers recalled, when they came through Fisher's Gap it "was a cool November afternoon, [but] the brandy warmed the boys up and made them hilarious." "Nearly everybody in the Louisiana brigade," a soldier recalled of that hard fighting group, "and many in other brigades, had taken a drink too many."[12]

The whiskey and brandy-induced merriment was welcome to many but it was a brief break from another of Jackson's famous marches. This one was not quite as fast as the pace of the one that ended at Manassas or as the one just a few weeks earlier from Harpers Ferry to Sharpsburg but it was tough pace nevertheless. The 18th North Carolina and the rest of the foot cavalry were averaging about twenty miles a day to get to the Fredericksburg area in time to unite the Army of Northern Virginia and deal with Burnside's threat. In the twelve days spent marching that began on November 22, the regiment marched 175 miles with only a brief couple of days' rest around Madison and Orange Court House. The Light Division got to Fredericksburg on December 3 and established camp at the Yerby farm about five miles south of the town itself. The march was over but conditions still left much to be desired. "Many of our soldiers are thinly clothed and without shoes and in addition to this," one of Hill's soldiers recorded, "very few of the infantry have tents. With this freezing weather their sufferings are indescribable." William Barlow from Company B echoed this in a December 4 letter to his wife: "We see hard times now. We don't get near enough to eat."[13]

Burnside had intended to beat Lee to Fredericksburg and cross the Rappahannock quickly. He had gotten to the Fredericksburg area first, but he had not been able to get across the river because the pontoons, the moveable floating bridges that he needed to get the Army of the Potomac across, were late arriving. Attempts to cross at more shallow fords north and south of the town were explored but Lee had put troops at all those likely crossing points. The plan for the quick strike on Richmond was beginning to fall apart on Burnside, who got together with his commanders and decided on December 9 that he would cross the river (now that the pontoon boats had finally arrived) and attack Lee's center on Marye's Heights above the city. Burnside reasoned that if Lee had posted Longstreet and Jackson to block him above and below Fredericksburg that the Army of Northern Virginia was weakest in the center; that was where he would hit Lee hardest. But first he had to get across the river.

On the south side of the river, Lee had had time to deploy the Army of Northern Virginia along a strong defensive line above and south of Fredericksburg. Longstreet's corps constituted the right side of the Confederate position, holding and digging in along Marye's Heights immediately behind the city and stretching southward another mile to where it joined with Jackson's corps, which constituted the right of the line and was deployed along Prospect Hill behind the Richmond, Fredericksburg, and Potomac Railroad south about a mile to Hamilton's Crossing. Jeb Stuart's cavalry and horse artillery anchored the right for Lee's army. On Jackson's section of the field the general decided to have his largest division, Hill's Light Division, out front. Lane's brigade was the furthest forward brigade, taking up a position just behind and along the railroad tracks aligned from left to right, 7th, 18th, 33rd, 28th, 37th North Carolina. James Archer's brigade of Georgians, Tennesseans, and Alabamians were on Lane's right, but there was a marshy area some 500 yards wide on the 37th North Carolina's right so Hill posted Archer on the other side of the low, wet area. That left a large gap between Lane and Archer, one that General Lane complained of to his commander to no avail. Hill did not think that the area was passable so the gap between the brigades did not, he reassured Lane, constitute a problem. To the left and rear of Lane was William Dorsey Pender's North Carolina brigade. About 600 yards to the rear of the forward brigades were Edward Thomas's Georgians behind Lane and Maxcy Gregg's South Carolinians to Thomas's right and who were also directly above the gap between Lane and Archer.[14]

On December 11, 1862, Burnside made his move to get across the river. His pontoons were in place but the Confederates made life miserable and precarious for anyone wearing blue that went close to the river. To protect the soldiers the Federal batteries on Stafford Heights rained a terrible shower of iron on the city of Fredericksburg, reducing much of that lovely city to rubble. Though most of the civilians had been safely evacuated, the destruction of private homes and property on such a scale marked a new phase in the Civil War where civilians would increasingly feel the hard hand of war if they continued to resist. Even with heavy artillery support the Federals found getting across the river and into Fredericksburg difficult and dangerous. General William Barksdale had sent his Mississippi brigade into the town to slow the Yankee crossing. Fighting from house to house and from behind fences and piles of rubble, the Mississippians made the Yankees pay a hard price for getting across the Rappahannock. The 18th North Carolina, posted a couple of miles from the city, was not involved in any of the action on December 11 but they did hear the cannons and musketry and understood that they were most likely going to be involved in at least one more battle before 1862 was out.[15]

On December 12 Colonel Purdie led the 18th North Carolina to its position behind the railroad tracks. The new position was not a comfortable one for a couple of reasons. Being the most forward brigade and with a huge gap on the right, there was a feeling of isolation. Plus their new position was essentially a cold, wet ditch. Typical of Virginia winters, the nights were very cold with temperatures falling below freezing. During the days the temperatures often got into the fifties, which may have helped the soldiers warm up a bit but it also turned their ditch into a muddy mess as the frosty ground thawed.

Colonel Purdie's men did not have a lot of time to grouse about their cold, wet, and exposed position. Burnside had determined that he would attack the following day, December 13. His basic plan for the battle called for his left "Grand Division" under Major General William Franklin to strike the Confederate right, Jackson's corps, while part of Burnside's right under Major General William Sumner held the left's attention. That would enable Burnside to hit the supposed weakened center behind Fredericksburg along Marye's Heights with the bulk of his force under Major General Joe Hooker. As the heavy fog began to lift, Lane's North Carolinians saw a large Federal force shaking out into a line of battle that covered 1,000 yards across its front with flags unfurled. These Yankees were veteran Pennsylvanians commanded by General George Gordon Meade and New Yorkers and New Englanders commanded by General John Gibbon. At 11:00 following Union artillery attacks on the Confederate batteries, the Unionists came on at a steady pace with a shout. One of Hill's men said, "It was a grand sight seeing them come in[to] position." Another said, "We could see their guns and bayonets glittering in the sun, oh! it looked awful and yet beautiful for it was the grandest sight I ever beheld."

The 18th North Carolina could see very little of the advance. Directly in front of them and just across the railroad track was a short knoll or rise that was topped by a battery and blocked their direct view of their front. They could hear the oncoming Yankees but they could not see them, a nerve-racking position to be in. The men gripped their muskets a little tighter as Purdie and his officers gave encouragement to them. For the first few hundred yards the Federals had an easy time of it. Aside from skirmishers they met little resistance. They were confident that the Confederate artillery had been taken out by the earlier Union barrage. What they had no way of knowing, however, was that Jackson had ordered his batteries to remain silent until the Yankees were within 200 yards of Lane and Archer. When they got in that close they were to hit the Northerners with everything they had. The cheering Yankees got to within 150 to 200 yards of the railroad track when suddenly Meade's and Gibbon's divisions were hit with a wall of shot and shell from the Rebel batteries on Prospect Hill. At such close range the Confederate guns cut large holes in the attacking Unionists with every shot. Meade's division, with Gibbon's division to his right and in front of Lane's brigade, had to fall back and fling themselves down into the muddy fields and roadbeds to avoid being cut to pieces by the Southern batteries.

This was not good for Burnside's plan. Meade, who had been given overall control of the attack on the Federal left because of his seniority and combat experience, had the job of striking and breaking through Jackson's corps and rolling up Lee's right flank so that the center attack by Hooker could smash through with relative ease. With Meade and Gibbon back to nearly where they began the attack, Federal guns opened up with renewed vigor on the Confederate position on Prospect Hill. This intense barrage put a terrible strain on the Confederates. Getting shot at by infantry was unpleasant enough, but intense artillery fire was more difficult to deal with psychologically. There was no defense and death was totally random and generally particularly gruesome. The 18th North Carolina lost several men to this artillery fire. The cannon atop the knoll to their front was a target and Union shells rained down on it, sometimes overshooting it and hitting the railroad ditch where Lane's brigade huddled and hoped to avoid the jagged iron whistling through their position, until it was forced to retreat from the position. Members of the 7th and 18th North Carolina helped to cover the artillery's withdrawal, taking several casualties in the process. After sixty to ninety minutes of shelling, the Union guns, which were more numerous and more amply supplied ammunition, got the better of the duel and the Confederate guns were effectively silenced.

At one A.M. Meade ordered his Pennsylvanians to rise again and move forward. Meade's force headed straight for Archer where they were met with heavy fire. With the volume of balls coming at them, Meade's men drifted a bit to their right, towards the marshy gap between Archer and Lane where nobody was posted and therefore where nobody was shooting at them. Theoretically Gregg's South Carolina brigade should have dealt with the Yankees approaching the gap and threatening to get around Archer's left. Gregg, however, did not think that any Federals would be coming from that direction so he had his brigade resting with arms stacked to help keep them from mistakenly firing into Confederate troops by accident. Even when soldiers began to appear through the gap, Gregg did not believe they were enemy soldiers. By the time he realized the mistake, he had been mortally wounded, and his surprised South Carolina brigade had been forced to flee. The gap that was not supposed to be penetrable by the enemy was being penetrated, and Archer's left, with Gregg's brigade unable to help, was in an extremely hot fight with the brigade also taking fire from two directions. Whenever units got into fights where they faced fire from multiple directions, they rarely held on; after about thirty minutes Archer's regiments began to crack from the front and flank fire as well as from the fact they were running low on ammunition. Though later than Burnside had wanted, Meade had pierced the Rebel line on Lane's right.

Had John Gibbon attacked with Meade rather than beginning his attack on Lane's front some thirty minutes later the situation on Hill's front could have been much worse than it was; and it was bad enough. With Gregg gone three Pennsylvania regiments—6th, 4th, and 8th Pennsylvania Reserves—came at Lane's right at a ninety degree angle from the front as Gibbon approached the railroad track with General Nelson Taylor's brigade followed by Colonel Peter Lyle's and Colonel Adrian Root's brigades. The firing on Lane's right became increasingly intense. The 37th North Carolina turned at a right angle to refuse the flank and fought for all it was worth while facing fire from the front and flank. The Thirty-seventh's colonel, William Barbour, was wounded and command passed to Major William Grove Morris who walked the line shouting to his men to load and fire as quickly as possible as the bullets flew all around him. One caught him in the ear and took away part of the lobe causing him to continue commanding despite being "bloody as a hog." The 37th North Carolina fought hard with help from the 28th and 33rd North Carolina. The 18th and the 7th North Carolina were blocked by the ridge in their front from firing at the Federals coming from that direction and could only offer oblique fire from their position on the brigade's left. They probably were also ordered to restrain their firing for a couple of very good reasons. For one thing, with the smoke of thousands of muskets obscuring their view, firing in the vague direction of the enemy's muzzle flashes was not terribly effective. For another, they would soon be in the thick of the fight and needed their ammunition.

After about forty-five minutes of hard fighting, the 37th and 28th North Carolina began to run low on ammunition. Lane reported that these regiments held their ground as long as they could and "fired away not only their own ammunition but that of their dead and wounded, which in some cases was handed to them by their officers." When this gave out the Unionists charged the railroad track and the Thirty-seventh and Twenty-eighth had to give way.

As the Yankees streamed in they met the 33rd and 18th North Carolina in bloody hand-to-hand fighting where there were reports of Confederate soldiers flinging their muskets with fixed bayonets at the Federals like spears. The Thirty-third, though, was also running out of ammunition and had to abandon the position along the railroad. As the regiment peeled away Colonel Purdie turned the 18th North Carolina to the right to meet the oncoming Yankees. Purdie shouted to his men to pour their fire into the enemy as fast as they could as he ran along his regiment's line. In the midst of the flying lead, Purdie, like so many other officers that day, was wounded. The records do not indicate where he was hit, only that the wound was "slight." There is no indication that he was forced or chose to leave the field because of it.

The Confederate right had been breached but reinforcements came to the scene in both Archer's and Lane's sectors. The first Rebels to reach Lane's area were fellow North Carolinians from Pender's brigade. Pender sent out a heavy skirmish line from elements of the 16th and 22nd North Carolina to slow down the Federal pursuit and buy Lane a few minutes to rally his brigade. Pender's Tar Heels did not reach the scene too soon and they, along with canister from Greenlee Davidson's and Joseph Latimer's guns, helped check Gibbon's Yankees on Hill's left. Lane was able to rally much of the 33rd, 18th, and 7th North Carolina in a stand of woods about 150 yards above the railroad. Purdie quickly re-formed his regiment and had them prepare to return to the fight. The Federals had gotten through their line but they were not to be allowed to remain there; they were to be driven back where they came from. As more Confederates were coming to the scene on their immediate right, Purdie encouraged his men by telling them they could not let it be said the Yankees drove them. They would retake their former position and send the Northerners back to the river.

The other Confederate reinforcements that had arrived on their right were Georgians from Edward Thomas's brigade coming to Lane's call for help on his front and flank. Thomas's fresh troops began shooting into Gibbon's Yankees and marching forward to drive them back towards Fredericksburg. While the 33rd North Carolina remained in the wood line, the 18th and 7th North Carolina joined the Georgians. One Union soldier looked up to see the Georgians and North Carolinians come "out of the woods like a band of wolves." A New Englander said, "As we drew back reluctantly, the rebels followed, in defiance of the batteries protecting our flanks, and swept us again with musketry, and their batteries caught us out in the open; shells burst close upon us, and solid shot plunged into our ranks and knocked men, bleeding and senseless, into the mud to die." Another described the deadly scene, saying "the rebs give it to us good and my comrades fell on all sides." One of Thomas's Georgians said the dead and wounded Yankees along the railroad were strewn "a little thicker than you ever saw pumpkins in a new ground." The Confederates descending on Gibbon's men were able to push them out of the railroad ditch and back across the field towards the Rappahannock. Some members of the 18th North Carolina were not content to simply retake their previous position and continued chasing the retreating Yankees for another 100 yards before running into their rear guard and returning to the railroad bank.

It was 2:30 in the afternoon, a mere ninety minutes after Meade and Gibbon had attacked and broken through Hill's line. The 18th North Carolina had once again been in a hard fight and lost thirteen killed and seventy-seven wounded. The brigade lost sixty-two killed and 257 wounded. William Barlow, who had been hit slightly at Sharpsburg, had just come through his first true test of battle and he was understandably a bit unnerved by the experience. He was amazed that he was not killed "while so many fell to rise no more." "You don't know what awful time it is in battle," he told his wife just four days later, "the cannon balls and bullets flying just as thick it looks like every man would be killed, but God can save a man's life in the midst of danger. I want your prayers in my behalf." The regiment had again proven that it was a fighting regiment. Though hit from the front and flank the regiment stubbornly held its ground as long as it could, and when Purdie pulled the 18th out of line they did so in an orderly fashion without panicking and actually rallied and rejoined the fight to help push the Yankees back and seal the breach in Jackson's line.[16]

Chapter 8

The Regiment Loses Its Colonel and Its Colors: The Bloody Battle of Chancellorsville

In the wake of the bloody debacle that was Fredericksburg and after the exercise in futility (those who experienced it firsthand would have called it stupidity) that came to be known infamously as the Mud March, General Ambrose Burnside lost the respect and support of most, if not all, of his officers and soldiers. The death toll from Fredericksburg and the Mud March were certainly key factors in Burnside's losing his army's faith, but in his short tenure as the Army of the Potomac's commanding general there were other serious problems. The men were not paid regularly, and food and other supplies were failing to get to the soldiers as efficiently as they should have. And he had the misfortune of following a general most in the army adored. Say what you will about McClellan's shortcomings as a commander, and the list is rather long, but in early 1863 the officers and soldiers could and did say that at least "Little Mac" never sent them on suicidal charges and they always got fed and paid regularly. In this atmosphere Burnside's days were numbered as the head of the army charged with defeating Robert E. Lee's Army of Northern Virginia.

Being the highly politicized nest of vipers the Army of the Potomac was, when Burnside failed at Fredericksburg, and that mightily, they did not hesitate to send agents to Washington to lobby for Burnside's removal. This was not only cowardly in the sense that it was done behind the commanding general's back, but it was also wholly inappropriate from a military perspective. That they justified their actions on grounds that they were merely trying to get a more competent person to lead the Army of the Potomac and thus hasten ultimate victory is no excuse.

8. The Regiment Loses Its Colonel and Its Colors

Burnside's subordinates' job was to do their duty to the best of their ability under his command, not jump at the first chance to undermine him in the vain hope of having McClellan restored to command of the army. In fact, that was what many earnestly hoped for, unrealistic as it was at that point given that Lincoln had washed his hands of the Young Napoleon. But this was the Army of the Potomac and playing politics was something that was part of the organization.

Burnside realized that he had been undermined by those under his command. Given his situation he went to Lincoln with a proposal to fix the problem, at least to Burnside's satisfaction. He told the president in late January that he could not continue to command effectively with so many subordinates who refused to respect his authority. Therefore, he said, those officers had to go. On the one hand Burnside had a point; his list was long and included far too many high-level commanders for him to expect that Lincoln would reassign all of them somewhere else just because Burnside asked him to. If that could not be arranged, Burnside wanted to resign. Lincoln thought it over for a day and then told Burnside that he was not going to get rid of all the backbiting officers but neither would he accept his resignation. Lincoln told Burnside he needed experienced generals so he sent the bewhiskered general west to the Army of the Ohio.

With Burnside out, Lincoln had to find yet another commander for the army that most in the nation were looking to put down the rebellion. That he chose General Joseph Hooker was no real surprise. He had posted a decent reputation as a competent field commander and he had friends and supporters in high political places, especially among the radical branch of the Republican Party. He had the support of most of the officers, and the soldiers seemed to also view him positively. He had even accidentally, due to a typographical error in a newspaper, gained the nickname of "Fighting Joe," which he actually hated. Hooker had also shamelessly angled for command of the army and been part of the group undermining Burnside. Lincoln was well aware of Hooker's political shenanigans and let him know up front that Hooker was being trusted with this important job in spite of them rather than because of them.

Hooker may have desperately wanted the job but in early 1863 he had inherited a desperate situation. The army was in a slump; they were — to use a term common to the period — demoralized. The Army of the Potomac was an unmotivated, surly group. Hooker's first job was to restore the men's confidence in their leaders and in themselves. He had to reenergize them as McClellan had reenergized them after First Manassas. And he did. During the first four months of 1863 the dispirited force that was the Army of the Potomac regained its pride. Hooker improved the food distribution and the quality, introducing more soft bread rations. The soldiers were paid regularly again.

Furloughs home were increased. Improvements were made in how the sick were treated, and the camps became healthier. To infuse the men with a sense of unit pride, corps badges, various shapes corresponding to a particular corps, were introduced and worn on the men's caps. During the weeks and months following Burnside's removal, the force across the Rappahannock from the 18th North Carolina became reinvigorated and looking forward to a chance at redemption in the spring for Fredericksburg.[1]

On the Confederate side of the river, Lee's army went into winter quarters and had good reason to feel very confident after Fredericksburg, though the 18th North Carolina and the rest of A.P. Hill's division probably did not feel quite as overconfident as the rest of the army. They had done the most difficult fighting at Fredericksburg and had seen how close the Federals had come to breaking through the Confederate lines. With the battle over and the Army of the Potomac getting reorganized, the regiment went into their winter quarters to await the spring campaigning season. Lane's Tar Heels were with the rest of the division at the far southern end of Jackson's line near Port Royal. There they "burrowed into the ground, added walls of logs and a fireplace, and from a ridgepole draped shelter tents for a roof." They also continued to strengthen their defensive works along the river bank. One wrote: "We have this country all fortified from Fredericksburg to Port Royal. I have helped to build them, and if I have to do any more fighting I would like to have some of the ditches to fight in on the Rappahannock: it is now the strongest position that [the] army has ever occupied."[2]

Despite the relative closeness of the two armies, life settled down into a fairly safe routine, though it was not always pleasant. One Southerner summed up life in winter quarters in late January 1863, describing it simply and amply as, "Picket, Picket, Picket. Mud, Mud, Mud. Rain, Rain, Rain." One Rebel told a family member that he "awoke before day nearly frozen; taking [his] blanket by the edge it would stand up like a plank, it was frozen so hard and stiff." Colonel Purdie wrote home in early February about the weather conditions, saying it "is very bad up here rain or snow every other day & a constant freeze & thaw which makes the roads almost unpassable." Normally during winter quarters the men were kept busy with drill and dress parades but Purdie related that during much of the early weeks of 1863 it was "so wet we can't drill." Regardless of the wet and cold conditions, picket duty was required and the regiment did its share along the Rappahannock that winter. As often happened during the Civil War (when officers were not present) those performing picket duty worked out truces where they agreed not to shoot at one another. These were also times where items were traded between the soldiers. Usually the Confederates would offer tobacco and cigars, some of the few items they had in abundance, in return for coffee and tea, which they rarely got. Officers forbade the practice and broke up such truces when they discovered them but the men on either side of the river that winter shared a bond; they were fellow soldiers who knew what it was to endure privations and risk their lives. Their common experiences and traumas gave them an appreciation for these respites from the horrors of war and they reached a mutual understanding that while fighting and dying on various battlefields was a duty they accepted, it would be a shame and a waste to die at some nameless picket post.[3]

During the early winter months of 1863, Lee's army was in a well-entrenched position and confident that they could deal with anything the Yankees could throw at them. After all, since Lee had assumed command of the Army of Northern Virginia the Unionists had been kept off balance and on the run pretty steadily since the early summer. Even Sharpsburg was viewed as a withdrawal on Lee's terms rather than as a defeat. And with replacements entering the service Lee's army grew to about 90,000 men. But at the same time the army suffered terribly from a lack of provisions, especially food. His men and horses, he wrote to the government in a plea for more effective provisioning, "have suffered much from scarcity of food & I fear they are destined to move. I am doubtful whether I shall be able to sustain my position...." To James Seddon, the secretary of war, he wrote: "I am more than unusually anxious about the supplies of the army, as it will be impossible to keep it together without food." "The Yankees say that we have a new gen'l in command of our army," a Georgian quipped, "& say his name is General Starvation & I think for once they are about right." The food and general supply situation was so bad that the Yankees even expressed some sympathy for their enemies across the Rappahannock. A member of the 140th PA recorded:

> The Rebs are getting hard up for grub and clothes. You can see them when they change pickets. The man on post peels off his coat and gives it to his relief and runs to his quarters. One of them told me they only had five or six coats to a company and those on duty use them. He also said lots of men in his camp were barefooted and there was no use going around stumping about it.

While many of Lee's veterans were increasingly used to making do on very little and kept a stoic, even cheerful, attitude toward their material conditions during the winter of 1863, not everyone did. "Just think of so many thousand men camped in the naked woods without any tents and some barefooted," one of Lee's discontented soldiers wrote, "some without blankets and living on a little beef and bread. Only God knows what will become of us. If this is independence I don't want it."[4]

In March Colonel Purdie and the other brigade officers requested a meeting with their brigade commander, General Lane. Lane had no idea what the purpose of the gathering was and hoped it was not a formal complaint about food or clothing because there was not a thing in the world he could do about the poor material conditions. When he got to the meeting he found his officers smiling. They had gotten together to show their appreciation and recognition of Lane's abilities in a tangible (and expensive) way, presenting General Lane with a sword, sash, saddle, and bridle. The grateful general thanked his subordinates, telling them that they "bear upon your persons honorable scars, silent witness of dangers you have encountered and bravely faced in defense of all that a freeman holds dear." Lane also had praise for the men in the ranks, telling them that the Old North State ought to "be proud of such gallant sons."[5]

The party for General Lane and the presentation of gifts was a pleasant diversion for the 18th North Carolina's colonel, but Tom Purdie was increasingly concerned about his regiment as the campaign season drew nearer. He had the same concerns other regimental commanders in Lee's army had about food and provisions, of course, but he was also worried about the regiment's leadership structure. Since the previous spring Purdie had grown with others as an officer. He had fought with and commanded officers who had gained battlefield experience and he relied on them in the thick of battle. But the men he would be leading into the summer campaigns were largely unknown quantities. In one of his few surviving letters, Purdie expressed great concern over the fact that "there is not a Capt that was elected at the reorganization [in April] — all dead wounded & resigned on acct of wounds." The loss of his lieutenant-colonel, Forney George, was particularly bothersome to Purdie. George had not been killed or wounded but he had submitted his resignation to serve in the state legislature. He was an experienced and brave officer who had been wounded at Cedar Mountain; Purdie had expected to lean on him as his right hand in the coming battles and he expressed the hope that his resignation would not be accepted, though he knew that it was a long shot. There is no record of Purdie going to George to plead with him to stay, but George did remain and help lead the regiment until his resignation was formally accepted and he was required to head to Raleigh. At least Purdie would have one experienced field officer, if only for a limited period, when the weather warmed and the roads dried.[6]

Colonel Purdie was not the only person thinking about the spring campaigning season. On the other side of the river, General Hooker was doing more than rebuilding his army's morale. He was also doing a lot to figure out how to destroy Robert E. Lee. The Confederates hoped Hooker would decide to come straight at them in their fortified positions and duplicate Marye's Heights. But "Mr. F.J. Hooker," as Lee derisively referred to his opposite number, had no intention of making the same mistakes that his predecessor had. Despite the nickname and despite the fears that many soldiers had that it indicated that Hooker was the sort of general that threw men at the enemy with little regard for their lives, he had no intention of engaging Lee in any battle on the Confederates' terms. So far in the war Hooker had seen the folly of frontal assaults firsthand and he was not going to rely on such tactics now that he was in command of the Army of the Potomac. He wanted to defeat Lee, punish him even, but he wanted to do it by maneuvering the Rebels out of their fortifications and forcing them to attack his army, forcing the Confederates to do the bloody work of assaulting Union troops on ground of Hooker's choosing. Hooker intended to destroy Lee by beating him at his own game, by seizing the initiative, outmaneuvering his opponent, and forcing him to fight when and where he wanted.

General Hooker believed through March and April that he was going to be able to do what no other Federal general had accomplished so far in the war against Lee's army. Unlike McClellan who had constantly inflated Southern numbers, Hooker had a much more realistic idea of Confederate strength. McClellan's old intelligence chief, Allen Pinkerton, went the way of the man who had brought him into the army and the new Bureau of Military Intelligence was reporting far more accurate information to Hooker. As a result Hooker did not shake from fear that he faced a numerically superior foe; he knew very well that he outnumbered the Army of Northern Virginia by a roughly two-to-one ratio. He also was well aware of the Southerners' food problems, his intelligence sources having told him that the "subsistence of the Southern Army ... seems to be nearing the point of failure." Hooker understood that he had several key advantages over Lee and he intended to use that information to strike a decisive blow as soon as the weather moderated in April. "My plans are perfect," he told his officers, "and when I start to carry them out, may God have mercy on General Lee, for I will have none."[7]

In retrospect such confident statements coming out of "Mr. F.J. Hooker" draw smiles and even a good bit of snickering because as events unfolded General Hooker wound up as yet another Yankee general that Lee defeated. But during the late winter and early spring of 1863, Hooker performed very well and had the advantage over Lee in just about every area. He had sent groups to several parts of the Rappahannock to keep Lee guessing as to just what his plans were; he had his signal corps plant the false idea that Hooker was sending a large force to the Shenandoah Valley, which Lee believed resulting in his sending his remaining cavalry in that direction thus depriving himself of his own eyes and ears; he had instituted much stricter security measures to deprive Lee of any useful information about his numbers and intentions. Thanks to Hooker's activities and policies Lee was very much in the dark about what the Army of the Potomac planned and thus had no way to deal with the situation, something that thoroughly irritated Lee. His success was built on his ability to discern his opponent's motives and inclinations, and Hooker successfully denied Lee any insight into what he was up to into late April.

Hooker also developed a very sound plan based on his intelligence and on the advantages he possessed at the time. Knowing that the Confederates were facing serious supply problems, Hooker determined to move around Lee's left flank to sever his supply line entirely. Given Lee's problems he would have no choice but to come out of his entrenchments along the Rappahannock and give battle — with Hooker's men on the advantageous defensive and Lee's making the bloody frontal assaults. Hooker knew too that he could not cross at U.S. or Banks' Fords because Lee had those Rappahannock crossings covered. So Hooker decided he would bypass those fords and quickly march the bulk of the army further up the river to Kelly's Ford, cross there and get into the rear of Lee's army. To keep Lee's attention along the Rappahannock while most of the army got around his left flank, Hooker would have General Sedgewick's VI Corps cross the Rappahannock to make it look like he was trying to cross and attack below Fredericksburg. By the time Lee figured out demonstrations below and around Fredericksburg were diversions, it would be too late. Hooker's main force would already be behind him and on his supply line. Lee would have to come after him or retreat and give up the entire Rappahannock line. Either way Hooker won. The plan was sound and with Lee having no firm idea what Hooker was up to it had an excellent chance of success, so perhaps "Mr. F.J. Hooker" can be forgiven, at least a little, for expressing such confidence that early spring day.[8]

Hooker began putting his plan into action on April 27. Much like Stonewall Jackson, Hooker wanted to keep his enemy in the dark as long as possible. To minimize the possibility that Lee would figure out the Army of the Potomac was on the move, Hooker had the regiments closest to the river remain where they were, acting normally. If Confederate pickets began reporting lots of movement on the other bank and then the pickets were suddenly not around, Lee would figure out that something was up and move to upset Hooker's plan. Lead elements of the Army of the Potomac pulled out and marched upriver past U.S. and Banks' fords and crossed the Rappahannock at Kelly's Ford on April 28 and had continued on, crossing the Rapidan River the following day. This force was marching southeastward toward a glorified clearing in the woods known as Chancellorsville and was heading for Lee's rear. So far Hooker's plans were going perfectly.

While most of the Army of the Potomac was executing their march around the Confederate left, the officers and NCOs of the 18th North Carolina went through the camp shouting for the men to "fall in!" It was April 29 and a sizeable Union force had appeared on the north bank of the river with the obvious intention of forcing their way across at Franklin's and Fitzhugh's crossings. Finally, it appeared that Hooker was making his move and that he was going to accommodate the Rebels by attacking them in their breastworks. Lee and Jackson did not realize it at the time but this was merely a diversion to hold their attention for a little while longer while Hooker's main force continued to get around the Army of Northern Virginia. The 18th North Carolina marched to meet the Federal threat but did not directly participate in the fighting on the twenty-ninth. Early's Virginians took the advance positions and opposed the crossing while Lane's North Carolina regiments remained behind in reserve if needed.

By the end of the following day, April 30, Lee's vision began to clear. The push across the Rappahannock the previous day did not appear particularly forceful, which was suspicious. More importantly, he had gotten a telegraph message from Jeb Stuart about a major Federal crossing of the Rappahannock at Kelly's Ford. Fortune had continued to smile on Hooker to that point; Stuart had sent the message the previous day, but one of the telegraph offices had shut down for the day so the message was delayed for twenty-four precious hours. Thus Lee was starting to see the precarious position he was in and that he had perhaps underestimated "Mr. F.J. Hooker." At least one historian has argued compellingly that Lee was in a tight spot by May 1 as much because of his own overconfidence as because of Hooker's plans. While Hooker deserves credit for planning and executing a flank march around Lee's army and for successfully deceiving Lee, the Confederate chief faced a tough spot because he had given Hooker no credit. Lee did not appear to have considered that his opposite number could or would develop a plan to get around his army and come directly after it. If he had, he would certainly have called back Longstreet and the bulk of his First Corps from southeastern Virginia, but he did not, figuring he could deal with Hooker with what he had available. He simply figured that Hooker would threaten his supply and communication lines; but he dismissed the possibility that his Yankee opponent would act as he would have under the circumstances and seize the initiative and maneuver his army into a position to boldly force his enemy into a major confrontation on favorable terms. So far Lee's overconfidence had played into Hooker's hands.[9]

On May 1 Colonel Purdie awoke, got dressed, and, as he put on his sash and sword, told Forney George to have the 18th fall in. Lee now understood that the Union demonstration on his right was just a diversion and that he faced a serious threat on his left. All of Jackson's corps except for Early's division were ordered towards Chancellorsville to deal with Hooker's moves. Of course, nobody in the regiment had any idea where they were going or what awaited them at the end of the march. One Tar Heel soldier summed up the infantryman's role, saying: "A soldier never knows where he is going, nor what he is going to do, until the moment for action comes. They have only to trust in the commanders and blindly 'follow their leaders.' On we went through mud and over stumps, stumbling about in the dark, to the great danger of our heads and shins."[10]

The 18th North Carolina got to the outskirts of Chancellorsville around 8:30 on the morning of May 1. The Light Division reached the field second in the marching column behind Robert Rodes' division. The Federals were having some success and outnumbered the Confederates even with the arrival of Jackson, whose orders were to blunt the Federal attack. Stonewall figured the best way to halt the Yankees was to go after them so he ordered an attack. The 18th North Carolina was on the scene to exploit any advantage or to help plug any gap that may develop along the Confederate front. Colonel Purdie offered encouragement to his regiment, fully expecting to be called into the fight at any moment. But the 18th did not see fighting on May 1. In a move that confused his officers (and angered a few), Hooker ordered his forces to disengage and pull back to the clearing around Chancellorsville when it met serious resistance from Jackson. Some, like General George Meade, wanted to continue pressing the Rebels despite the increased resistance. The tide of battle was still on their side; falling back gave Lee breathing room, which had always proven to be dangerous. Hooker, however, was content to have gotten around his enemy's flank. He also remained determined that Lee would attack him in their major confrontation and he did not intend to deviate from his plan. As Hooker saw things, pulling back a bit was not a terrible thing at all. His army would be in fortified positions and Lee would still have to attack him on ground and under conditions dictated by Hooker. Victory, and hopefully the destruction of the Army of Northern Virginia, would still be his.[11]

General Hooker was about to learn the lesson that others like McClellan, Pope, and Burnside had; giving Robert E. Lee any room to operate, no matter how little, was potentially fatal. When Hooker pulled back to Chancellorsville he effectively surrendered the initiative to Lee. The question then was what to do with it now that he had it. Popular mythology has the ever-aggressive Stonewall Jackson coming to Lee at the end of the day on May 1 with a daring plan to take his corps on a march to turn Hooker's right flank the following day. The more accurate version of events is that Lee had already determined that he was going to maneuver around Hooker and attack him, forcing the Union general to react to him, to take back the initiative and give himself the best chance to win the battle. The question was how best to achieve that. Lee was certainly not going to oblige Hooker and attack him in the center. The Federal left was well defended, anchored by the Rapidan; dense trees and undergrowth in its front would trap the attackers so that approach was out. Conversely, the Union right flank offered possibilities. According to Stuart's reports, the right

8. The Regiment Loses Its Colonel and Its Colors

flank was "in the air," meaning that no natural barriers stood in an attacker's way and the enemy had put up no defensive works worthy of the name. Indeed, General Oliver O. Howard's XI Corps, which formed the army's right flank, focused its attention on its front while having done almost nothing to guard against a potential attack from the right. Having learned of this weak spot Lee and Jackson spent the evening of May 1 determining how best to exploit it.

Jackson proposed and Lee approved a plan for Jackson to take his corps around Hooker's right flank, hopefully without the Federal commander finding out about it until it was too late to react to the move. Jackson's soldiers would move out at first light and march west (left) along the Furnace Road until it came to Catherine Furnace. There, the column would turn left (south), away and out of sight of the Federals on the Wellford Furnace Road for about two miles. They would then take a road that took them northwest where after about another five miles they would come to the Orange Turnpike just east of Wilderness Tavern and, most importantly, on the road leading straight through the XI Corps's unprotected flank and the heart of Hooker's force at Chancellorsville. If all went as it should, Jackson's men would roll up the Federal right flank, link up with the rest of the Confederates around Chancellorsville, and destroy Hooker, whose back would be against the Rapidan. That night the 18th North Carolina was told to get what sleep they could and to be prepared to fall in before first light to march against the enemy. They did not know it, but they were about to participate in another of those movements that the foot cavalry was so famous for and that the survivors would tell their children and grandchildren about.

First light came and went on the morning of May 2 with the 18th North Carolina not having moved. In fact none of Jackson's corps had moved at his usual early departure time; a series of delays kept the head of the column from beginning the march before 7:00. A.P. Hill's division brought up the rear of the marching column and did not begin its move until 11:00. While Lane's brigade was waiting for the other divisions to move down the road towards Catherine Furnace so they could fall in, the 18th North Carolina was formed near Willie Pegram's artillery, which had been attached to Hill's division. That morning the two sides traded artillery fire; two of Pegram's caissons were hit and exploded causing several casualties in the regiment. The men of the 18th were relieved when it was their turn to face left in column of fours and follow the rest of Jackson's force so they could get away from the artillery fire they had no defense against.

Marching conditions were perfect. The previous summer the regiment had made forced marches under extremely hot, humid conditions, where the dusty roads only increased the misery at Cedar Mountain, Second Manassas, and Sharpsburg. May 2 was a welcome contrast. The day dawned a little on the chilly side and warmed to a very pleasant sunny, breezy spring day. The 18th got its normal ten-minute break for each hour on the road but because speed was also needed, the normal hour for the mid-day meal was shortened to a fifteen minute respite. Jackson rode along his column, one North Carolinian remembered, encouraging his men, silently raising his cap to them and reminding them to remain as quiet as possible and to constantly "close up." "On we rushed," one of Lane's men recalled, "jumping bushes, up and down hill. We did not know and did not care where we were going ... but there is one thing we did know and knew for a certainty and that was, that Old Jack was going round the bulls horn but unless the bull kept his tail twitching very fast the old hero would have a grip before the sun went down." Normally being at the rear of the marching column meant that soldiers were bombarded and caked with the dust kicked up by hundreds of men and horses, but recent rains had dampened the roads and minimized the dust. This was not only a welcome thing for those marching near the back, it also greatly helped conceal the column. Jackson wanted the flank march to be secret, and very often columns this size could be seen miles away just by the amount of dust they created. At Sharpsburg the Light Division's massive dust cloud was the first sign Lee had of A.P. Hill's arrival on the scene.[12]

While the 18th North Carolina was "jumping bushes, branches, up and down hill," General Hooker visited his lines to make sure everything was ready for what he hoped would be a series of bloody, Fredericksburg-style attacks by the Confederates. When he got to Howard's position on his right he was not happy with what he saw that morning. Upon arrival he discovered what Jeb Stuart already knew, General Howard had made no preparation for the possibility of an attack on his flank aside from placing a couple of regiments and two artillery pieces facing that direction. When he got back to his headquarters at the Chancellor house, he sent a dispatch to Howard expressing his concerns. He told Howard:

> The disposition you have made of your Corps has been with a view to a *front* attack by the enemy. If he should throw himself upon your flank, ... examine the ground and determine upon the position you will take in that event, in order that you may be prepared for him in whatever direction he advances.

He further emphasized that the "right of your line does not appear to be strong enough. No artificial defenses worth naming have been thrown up, and there appears to be a scarcity of troops at that point, and not, in the general's opinion, as favorably posted as might be." General Howard assured Hooker that he had taken care of all of his commander's concerns but the reality of the situation was that he did nothing of the sort. When Jackson arrived on his flank that afternoon it was still in the air.[13]

By mid-afternoon on May 2 the front of Jackson's column arrived at the Plank Road three miles west of Chancellorsville and on Howard's flank. His original intention was to deploy and attack along the Plank Road, but cavalry reports from Fitzhugh Lee's troopers indicated that such a route took his column more towards Howard's front than his flank. After he took a look for himself, Jackson determined to take the cavalryman's advice and move a mile north and deploy along the Orange Turnpike. Because of the dense woods and underbrush, there was a limited amount of space, which made aligning the force to hit the Federal flank take several hours. But this was done without the Federals having any idea what was occurring. While Confederates were spotted near Catherine Furnace, Hooker misinterpreted the sightings as indications that Lee was retreating. With Lee thought to be backing away, concerns over the precariously perched right flank were forgotten as Hooker began to focus on chasing his retreating prey. Stephen Sears, who has produced one of the best studies of the battle, has pointed out that such a conclusion was extremely odd for Hooker to have jumped to. He had faced Lee before and at this point in the war Hooker should have known better than to think that the Confederate commander would give up so easily just because Hooker had stolen a march on him a couple of days earlier. Lee had proven himself to be nothing if not aggressive for the past year; he had been in a very tight spot the previous September in Maryland, too, but refused to back down without a fight. Why Hooker thought Lee would have acted any differently at Chancellorsville is a mystery and was a costly mistake on the Union general's part.[14]

By 5:00 Jackson's corps was deployed and he sent it forward into the woods along the Orange Turnpike straight for Howard's exposed flank. The 18th North Carolina, along with the rest of Lane's brigade, was at the extreme rear of the attacking force, having just arrived at the Turnpike. Much of A.P. Hill's force was actually still shaking itself out from its marching columns as Jackson sent in the bulk of his corps. As the regiment moved forward along the Turnpike, they heard the snapping of sticks and the tramp of thousands of men marching through the woods to their front on both sides of the road. Suddenly at around 5:30 firing erupted in front and they heard the famous Rebel yell as Southerners burst from the woods and descended on the XI Corps. The sudden and unexpected attack sent the Federals reeling and heading towards Chancellorsville as fast as they could get there. One of Jackson's artillerists exulted:

> The surprise was complete. A bolt from the sky would not have startled [the Federals] half as much as the musket shots in the thickets ... and then a solid wall of gray, forcing their way through the timber and bearing down upon them like an irresistible avalanche. There was no stemming such a

tide....The shock was too great; the sense of utter helplessness was too apparent. The resistance offered was speedily beaten down. There was nothing left but to lay down their arms and surrender, or flee.

A Pennsylvanian disgustedly and more succinctly wrote that the XI Corps was "rolled rearward, a helpless, crazed mob, intent on nothing but personal safety." A North Carolinian was more sympathetic. "They did run and make no mistake about it," he said, "but I will never blame them. I would have done the same thing and so would you and I reckon the Devil himself would have run with Jackson in his rear."[15]

Jackson's flank march is often portrayed as a complete success and route of Hooker's right. However, James I. Robertson, Jr., the most prolific student of Stonewall Jackson's career, has noted that in reality the flank attack was a little more complicated than the standard picture. For one thing, while the Unionists did fall back when first attacked, Federal resistance did stiffen and significantly slow Jackson down in his attempt to reach Hooker's main line and cut it off from the road leading to U.S. Ford, Hooker's main route of retreat. Robertson has noted too that often forgotten in the glory of the initial success of the flank attack "is the fact that it was rather badly organized and somewhat mismanaged." Confederate units were running over top of each other and became terribly confused and snarled, which seriously weakened the force of the attack. One Confederate admitted: "We were all mixed up so bad that we could hardly tell which Reg. or Brig. we were in. That however made no difference, as we never stopped to learn who did this or that. But our watchword was onward. Onward we went." Indeed, Jackson seemed so intent on just moving forward to cut the Federals access to the fords that would allow them to escape before dark that little time was taken to ensure that his force was attacking as a cohesive unit. The one thing officers seemed to remember Jackson saying the most that afternoon and evening was "forward" and "push on."[16]

As the sun was setting Federal resistance stiffened and the Confederates needed reorganization if they were to continue pushing on, and Jackson had every intention of continuing the pressure on the enemy. He was not in favor of consolidating his gains and being content with what his corps had accomplished so far, which was considerable. Jackson had the initiative and he meant to keep it. The Light Division had not participated in the first phase of the flank attack and was therefore still reasonably well organized. Jackson told Hill to move his division to the front and prepare to receive orders to continue advancing against the enemy. It was between 8:30 and 9:00 and the woods along the Orange Turnpike were becoming darker by the minute. Hill did as ordered, sending Lane's brigade to the front of Jackson's line where it deployed on either side of the turnpike. As the Tar Heels were moving east along the road, Confederate artillery began firing in the direction of Fairview Heights

8. The Regiment Loses Its Colonel and Its Colors

and the Yankee guns. Logically enough, their fire was returned, but at a much greater and more accurate rate. With Union shells screaming down the Plank Road at his men, Colonel Purdie yelled to his men to get off the road and lay down, something every other regiment in the brigade did as well. The Union guns put down "the most unmerciful artillery fire I was ever under during the entire war," according to one of Lane's men. Another said we "buried our faces as close to the ground as possible and I expect some of us rubbed the skins off our noses trying to get under it."

With the hot artillery fire coming down the road, Lane's advance came to a halt. That situation was contrary to Hill's orders. Hill had been in Jackson's dog house too many times already to get in there again so he went forward to find out why the North Carolinians were not moving forward. By all accounts General Lane got irate at Hill's question when, to him, it seemed rather obvious that there was nothing his Tar Heels could do with Yankees firing so vigorously down the road at them. Lane suggested to Hill that if he could get the Southern gunners to quit firing that the Federals probably would, too, at which point he could get his brigade out off the ground and moving forward again. Orders went back to the Confederate gunners to quit firing. Shortly after complying, the Federal shelling stopped as well. At this point Lane told Colonel Purdie to deploy the 18th North Carolina on the left (north) of the pike with the 28th North Carolina to his right and with the left anchored on the road. Across the road from the 18th was the 37th and 7th North Carolina while the 33rd North Carolina deployed as skirmishers 200 yards to the front.[17]

Despite the full moon the woods all around the 18th North Carolina were so dense and knotted that it was quite dark and ominous. Adding to the tense atmosphere along the Plank Road was the knowledge that they were out in front of Jackson's whole command and in close proximity to the enemy. General Lane visited the 18th's position and told Purdie "to keep a bright lookout" because they "were in front of everything & would soon be ordered forward to make a night attack." The 18th's colonel relayed the message to his officers; the men in the ranks gripped their muskets a little bit tighter. Assaulting the enemy, who could be clearly heard just a few hundred yards out front chopping trees and putting up defensive works, was dangerous enough but the idea of doing it at night was a frightening proposition. And of course there was the possibility that the Federals might suddenly appear out of the gloom in front of them in a night attack of their own.[18]

At around 9:30 Jackson and several aides rode forward along the Plank Road and through the 18th North Carolina's position toward the Federal lines. Jackson and his group took a road known as Mountain Road, which ran parallel to the Plank Road about eighty yards north of the Plank Road. Jackson still intended to launch a night attack and wanted to get a firm idea of his front for himself. He did not, as one historian has noted, have to do this personally but as one of his subordinates remembered, Jackson was "always a great hand to wander about.... He had to see for himself." Jackson and his entourage rode to about the midpoint between Lane's main line and the 33rd North Carolina's skirmish line where he remained for a few minutes before turning his horse and heading back to his own lines.[19]

As Jackson headed back events had been unfolding that made Lane's men increasingly nervous. On the far right of the brigade, part of the 128th Pennsylvania had stumbled into the 7th North Carolina. The Keystone State officers were not sure at first if they had come upon friend or foe so in an effort to bring some clarity to the situation the regiment's colonel came forward with a white flag asking if the men in front of him were for the Union. The 7th responded they were not, at which point the Pennsylvania officer attempted to go back to his lines, something the North Carolinians were not going to allow. The Union officer got very irritated, saying he was under the protection of a flag of truce. General Lane, who had recently arrived on the scene, responded it was a misuse of a white flag and therefore provided no protection from capture. It was ludicrous, he argued, for an officer to assume he could affix a piece of white cloth to something and safely stroll about the front lines gathering intelligence and then return once he had a better idea what he was facing. When the Federal officer was not returned, the situation got increasingly tense as the Unionists began threatening to open fire on the Southerners if their colonel were not returned.

As Pennsylvanians and North Carolinians argued and threatened each other on the right, more Yankees appeared on Lane's front. A Union horseman rode up on the 33rd North Carolina's skirmish line looking for General Alpheus Williams. He too was not entirely sure where the lines were and he asked if the men to his front were Unionists or not. The Tar Heels' response was musket fire, which hurried the officer back to the Federal lines. It also sparked return fire. In a matter of minutes the extremely tense atmosphere seemed to explode as what began as sporadic fire on the right of Lane's line became contagious and spread to the left from the 7th on the far right across the Plank Road to the 18th.

It was in this dark, smoky, frightening atmosphere that Jackson and his group, followed by A.P. Hill and his aides, rode straight towards the 18th North Carolina's position. What happened next is not altogether clear except for the ultimate results. According to the regiment's adjutant, William H. McLaurin, Colonel Purdie heard movement out front and called McLaurin to go with him to investigate, at which point they came upon a captain of the 33rd North Carolina. As they were discussing troop dispositions "a few shots were fired" on the right and front of where they were standing. "At this juncture," McLaurin remembered,

8. The Regiment Loses Its Colonel and Its Colors

Tangled wilderness where Stonewall Jackson was accidentally wounded by members of the 18th North Carolina. Library of Congress.

> Colonel Purdie and myself started for our line, making our steps fast and long. Firing began along the brigade. Before we reached the Eighteenth it fired a terrific volley. How we escaped was wonderful. Horses with riders, and horses without came into the line with us.

This was the famous (or infamous) volley that so grievously wounded Stonewall Jackson and killed several members of his and A.P. Hill's staff. According to McLaurin, Colonel Purdie was not on hand when the order to fire was given. In 1901 James Lane reinforced McLaurin's version that Purdie was not with the regiment when it mistakenly opened fire, saying that at the time Major John Barry was in charge of the regiment and gave the order to fire into the oncoming horsemen.

Both McLaurin's and Lane's recollections are at odds with Captain Alfred

Toler's recollection. Toler, who commanded Purdie's old Company K, said that as he remembered that night,

> the brave Colonel Purdie gave the order "Fix bayonets; load; prepare for action!" as fast as the command could be given. When [Jackson] was within 100 yards, perhaps, of our line, the Colonel gave the command, "Commence firing," and from that moment until notified ... that we were firing on our own men, the firing was kept up by the entire regiment with great rapidity."[20]

There are a couple of problems with Toler's recollection of the evening that suggest his memory was faulty. For one thing, two other eyewitnesses corroborate the version where Colonel Purdie was not with the regiment when the famous volley was unleashed. Furthermore, John Barry himself felt extreme guilt over giving the command to fire even though it was the sort of tragic accident that often happens in combat. "Colonel Barry," Lane recalled at the turn of the century, "who was one of my bravest and most accomplished officers, always thought Generals Jackson and Hill were both wounded by his command." Barry family history tells of his being so guilt ridden that he never fully recovered from the events of that night and explained his untimely death in 1867 at only twenty-seven years old. What probably gave Barry the most discomfort was not so much that he made a mistake but that after one of the couriers shouted out that the regiment was firing on friends he was heard to respond: "It's a lie! Pour it into them, boys!" Toler also said that there were no skirmishers in the 18th North Carolina's front, which was certainly not the case, either. In fact, not only was the 33rd North Carolina out front, the officers knew it was there.[21]

After the war James Lane was understandably touchy about any criticism of his brigade generally or the 18th North Carolina specifically for wounding Stonewall Jackson, something many then and ever since have speculated cost the Confederacy the war by seriously wounding the man who was arguably Lee's best general. In the early twentieth century Lane lashed out at the critics, saying that his "brigade was charged by some of the heroes of the rear with being unduly excited on that occasion, because the 18th, under a misapprehension caused by the darkness, had fired upon its friends ... [and] yet it stood its ground under ... terrific and prolonged artillery fires which doubtless made those self-constituted critics of the rear quake...." Venom aside, Lane was essentially correct in his defense of the brigade and the 18th North Carolina. His men had a proven record of bravery, and criticisms that the 18th was "unduly excited" or acted like jittery green troops were and are unfounded. The simplest explanation of events is, as is often the case, probably the most accurate. There can be no doubt that the men and officers of the regiment were on heightened alert; General Lane and Colonel Purdie had even informed the regiment to be especially ready since they were now Jackson's front line.

Combine that knowledge and instructions with the eerie, inky darkness, several brushes with Federal units on the right and front, and being close enough to the enemy that their commands could be heard through the woods, and it is easy to see that Purdie's men's nerves were taut. In this same atmosphere firing erupts and is definitely coming from the enemy's direction followed by "the tramp of thirty horsemen advancing through a heavy forest at a rapid gait, [which] seemed to the average infantryman like a brigade of cavalry." Under the circumstances it was not surprising that John Barry reached the conclusion that with the enemy firing at them and a sizable number of horses galloping from the enemy's direction that Union cavalry was trying to get to or through their line.[22]

Whether or not the officers and men of the 18th North Carolina realized at that moment that they had seriously wounded Stonewall Jackson is not clear either. Some accounts have them being aware while others have them being informed of it later. Whether they did or not, their night was not over anyway. Between midnight and two o'clock General Daniel Sickles ordered two separate attacks on Lane's position, which were both repulsed. Much of the fighting was done on the 28th's and 18th's front where the two regiments "behaved with commendable courage and zeal," according to General Henry Heth. The 18th was not so fortunate as the 28th North Carolina, which captured an enemy flag in fighting where the only aiming was at the muzzle flashes in the darkness, but they did manage to bag a few prisoners, one of whom was an aide to General Alpheus Williams. The Yankees accomplished nothing in their forays and for the three or four hours before sunrise on May 3 an unsettling calm settled over the woods. Nobody in the 18th North Carolina slept in the intervening hours; they had heard the Northerners' axes working earlier and knew that when day broke they would attack an entrenched enemy.[23]

During the pre-dawn hours General Heth, who had taken over command of the sector after Hill was wounded by a piece of artillery, redeployed Lane's brigade. The 37th and 7th and part of the 33rd North Carolina moved to the north side of the road. The 18th North Carolina was next in line with the 28th North Carolina on the 18th's left. At 5:30 Archer's, Lane's, and McGowan's brigades launched their attack on the Federal works opening the final phase of the Battle of Chancellorsville. Lane's brigade was in the center with McGowan's South Carolinians on his right; his North Carolina regiments advanced in line of battle with their flags waving defiantly screaming the Rebel yell. One account of the battle has the Tar Heels charging the Federals yelling "Remember Jackson!" as well. Whether the regiment's members knew they had wounded Jackson is not clear but word of his wounding was apparently known by the following morning.

The 18th North Carolina marched straight into extremely heavy musket and artillery fire as they attacked the Yankees behind their breastworks, taking casualties with every step. One of the first was Corporal Andrew J. Proffitt, one of the western Carolinians from Wilkes County who had joined the regiment the previous August. He was shot carrying the regimental colors and in the post-battle report was listed has having been killed, though other records have him being captured indicating that he was merely wounded. The 18th's colors were then taken up by the recently promoted Corporal Owen J. Eakins who took it over and into the Federal breastworks as the 18th North Carolina charged them.

Having successfully gotten into the Yankee works, the 18th North Carolina found it impossible to remain there very long. As Eakins waved the regiment's colors, the Federals raked them with artillery, opening "a murderous fire of shell, grape, and canister upon [them]." Making matters worse (and hotter) for the regiment was the fact that the Federals had managed to repulse the Confederates on Lane's right totally exposing that flank to particularly nasty enfilading fire from Union guns. And as the cannons were doing their bloody work, Union reinforcements arrived and applied additional pressure on the 18th North Carolina's front and flank—a familiar feeling for the regiment. The first Confederate attack was faltering and Lane gave orders for his bloodied regiments to pull back to re-form in the woods to the rear. "We were ... ordered to fall back," Forney George reported, "and just then our gallant colonel (T.J.) Purdie, encouraging his men both by work and example, was killed instantly by a Minie ball passing directly through his forehead." Unfortunately for Corporal Eakins, he did not hear the order to pull back and remained a few minutes still waving the battle flag until Lieutenant Alfred Rowland of Company D — barely more than a boy, having enlisted in Robeson County when he was only seventeen back in the spring of 1861— risked his own life to go alert Eakins to get back to the woods. Major Barry said Eakins "was probably the last man in the regiment to leave the field. He had gone but a few feet when he, too, was killed...." Unfortunately by the time Rowland realized what had happened it was too late to go back for the regiment's colors; the position was full of Yankees. The 18th North Carolina could do little as the 7th New Jersey grabbed their flag as a trophy. Driving the Yankees would have to be left to the rest of the army; the 18th North Carolina, along with the rest of Lane's brigade, was done at Chancellorsville as far as active fighting was concerned.[24]

The horrors of war were not over, though. When the regiment fell back to regroup in the woods near where they had camped the previous night, they found them on fire. Stories of the Wilderness being ablaze and consuming the dead and dying have become synonymous with that 1864 battle but it was not the first time this tangled area of Central Virginia was set afire by the shot and shell of the opposing armies. Lane reported:

8. The Regiment Loses Its Colonel and Its Colors

The woods we entered were on fire; the heat was excessive; the smoke arising from burning blankets, oil-cloths, &c., very offensive. The dead and dying of the enemy could be seen on all sides enveloped in flames, and on the ground on which we formed was so hot as at first to be disagreeable to our feet.[25]

And despite the great odds, and thanks to some questionable decisions on Hooker's part and downright egregious ones on Howard's, Lee was victorious at Chancellorsville. In fact most have viewed it as his greatest victory. On May 7 a much-relieved commanding general addressed his troops:

With heartfelt gratification the general commanding expresses to the army his sense of the heroic conduct displayed by officers and men during the arduous operations in which they have just been engaged. Under trying vicissitudes of heat and storm, you have attacked the enemy, strongly entrenched in the depths

An unusual flag with battle honors on two sides. This one was captured at Chancellorsville, May 3, 1863. North Carolina Museum of History.

of a tangled wilderness ... and, by the valor that has triumphed on so many fields, forced him once more to seek safety beyond the Rappahannock.

While the mood in much of the rest of the Army of Northern Virginia was ebullient over their recent triumph over "Mr. F.J. Hooker," the mood in the 18th North Carolina was decidedly somber. Not since their first battle at Hanover Court House had the regiment been so roughly handled. The regiment lost thirty-four killed and ninety-nine wounded, and every field officer was either killed or wounded with the single exception of, as Lane referred to him, "the gallant young [Major John] Barry." While other regiments bragged of running the enemy and gathering trophies, the 18th had been forced to withdraw and lost their colors, a truly demoralizing thing for Civil War regiments. As if all those things were not bad enough, they bore the bur-

Second side of the 18th's flag captured at Chancellorsville. North Carolina Museum of History.

den of knowing that their regiment had seriously wounded one of the Confederacy's best generals. Though Lane told his men, "I shall always feel proud of the noble bearing of my brigade in the battle of Chancellorsville — the bloodiest in which it has ever taken a part," and despite accolades from General Heth, who said, "I cannot conceive of any body of men ever being subjected to a more galling fire than [Lane's North Carolinians]," the battle would never hold anything but bitter memories for the regiment.[26]

While all the members who gave their lives were missed, certain losses were more difficult than others on a regiment. This was certainly the case with Colonel Purdie's death. All evidence points to the conclusion that his loss was a severe blow to the unit. Purdie had been through every battle with the regiment and had led the men through most of them. He led from the front and never asked his men to do anything or go anywhere he would not do or go himself and as a result had been wounded at Fredericksburg and killed at Chancellorsville. Post-battle reports referred to him numerous times as courageous and cool under fire; Lane had referred to him in his post–Chancellorsville report as the "fearless Purdie." Despite his relative youth, Purdie also took a paternal interest in his men's welfare, even spending his own money to get shoes and clothing for them. This concern for their well being was rewarded, though he did not always seem to see it that way, by quick election to higher rank from lieutenant to lieutenant-colonel in less than a year while others were voted out. A May 9 letter captures the feeling many had over the loss of their colonel:

> Poor Tom Purdie I never was shocked so much as when I heard of his death. He was killed just to my right charging the same breastworks [where] I was wounded. General Lane was nearby him when ... the ball entered his head. I was glad to know his remains were ... taken home. His death has cast a gloom over the 18th. [B]oth officers & men unite in saying it is the greatest loss the regt ever sustained.

An obituary printed in the *North Carolina Presbyterian* read, in part:

> All the members of the 18th Reg., N.C. Troops, will testify to his kindness, and at late hours of the night he would visit their tents to quell any disorder; his powers of persuasion were so great that he seldom had to use harsh means to bring a soldier to his duty.

The anonymously written piece went on to say: "I believe I speak a universal sentiment, he was one of the bravest men in the Army of the Southern Confederacy." Even allowing for the rather flowery and maudlin style of the period, the obituary likely did capture the Tom Purdie that the members of the 18th North Carolina remembered. Purdie's body was brought home to Bladen County, and his well-attended funeral was held at Purdie Church, which still stands. He was interred in the family cemetery at Purdie Hall in Bladen County.[27]

The *Presbyterian* obituary also printed an accusation that has come to be a part of local lore regarding Thomas Purdie and his death at Chancellorsville. In the final paragraph the writer claimed that the "vandals occupied our ground and stripped him of his coat." Ever since, the story of how Purdie's corpse was wantonly robbed of his coat has been repeated and is included in literature at the Averasboro Battlefield Museum where one of Purdie's early war uniforms is on permanent display along with other of his wartime personal effects. Whether the story is true or not is impossible to say with certainty. The writer who made the claim in the newspaper is known only as "W," so it cannot be determined if he was actually a member of the 18th and, even if he was, if he was present and actually witnessed Yankees robbing the body. Furthermore, one letter to a family member from a friend actually at Chancellorsville says: "Tom Purdie's body has just arrived from the field. I will have a coffin fixed to send his body on." No mention is made of his uniform coat or anything else missing. It also seems at least a little questionable that some Yankee, no matter how greedy for a nice-looking officer's coat to send home as a souvenir, would have gone out corpse robbing where a battle was currently raging and from which his side was about to be thrown. That was the sort of thing that tended to go on in quieter sectors, not to mention on fields one actually controlled. Finally, one has to wonder why the "vandal" in question would have taken the time to undo Purdie's sword belt, which would have been fastened over the colonel's uniform coat, and left the valuable sword and scabbard (currently displayed with the other Purdie memorabilia at the Averasboro Battlefield Museum in Harnett County, North Carolina) on the field to take a coat.[28]

Whether Colonel Purdie's body was shipped back to Bladen County and made the trip from Wilmington up the Cape Fear to Purdie Hall with or without his officer's frock coat will never be definitively proven. And at the time nobody in the regiment was concerned about it one way or the other. The Battle of Chancellorsville was just the beginning of the campaigning season and the Federals were not whipped yet. It was time for new men to move up and take the place of those who had fallen and get prepared for their next move. Given Lee's proclivities a move would probably not be long in coming.

Chapter 9

Difficult Days: The Gettysburg Campaign and the Winter of 1863–1864

When General Joseph Hooker informed President Lincoln that the Army of the Potomac had disengaged from the enemy and retreated across the Rappahannock, the president was shocked and dismayed to say the least of it. "My God! My God! What will the country say! What will the country say!" Lincoln responded when he heard the news of yet another defeat in Virginia. One thing was clear to the commander in chief and that was that he was going to have to meet with Hooker quickly to determine precisely what had gone wrong and, more importantly, how his general determined to turn things around.[1]

Being the political animal it was, a number of key high-ranking officers in the Army of the Potomac determined that the first thing to do was get rid of Hooker. Hooker (more specifically Hooker's political views) had never been popular among the conservative McClellanites, and those who still remained with the Army of the Potomac practically salivated at the opportunity Chancellorsville provided to pull strings and get him removed from command. In a communication to Hooker in mid-May, Lincoln informed the general and even he was aware of the political maneuvering, saying to Hooker: "I must tell you that I have some painful intimations that some of your corps and Division Commanders are not giving you their entire confidence." Such political backbiting was as unprofessional as it was unseemly. It was those officers' duty to obey their commander regardless of how they felt about him personally, professionally, and politically. But this sort of thing had marred the Army of the Potomac from the beginning, and there was no reason for it to suddenly cease. And to be fair, General Hooker had very little room to complain; he had been just as guilty of playing politics and undermining the army's commander in late 1862 and early 1863. Now, having to bear the responsibility and burden of a major defeat he found himself vulnerable to attack by those who never wanted him in command of the army in the first place.

Lincoln appears to have been willing to give Hooker the benefit of the doubt and try him at least one more time in the days immediately following Chancellorsville. After all, he had tried McClellan several times even though he never got anything positive out of the Young Napoleon. Though there is no direct evidence that Lincoln thought in these terms, he was certainly intelligent enough to understand that constantly changing generals inhibited cohesion among the army's command structure and hindered its effectiveness. Rapid and constant turnover at the higher levels kept the commanding general from getting to know his officers' abilities and liabilities, things critical for the commander to learn about his subordinates. Hooker could not learn such things in a few weeks or after one battle. Furthermore, Lincoln must have been aware, on some level, that he could not expect the leader of the Army of the Potomac (whoever it was) to be as aggressive as he wanted if he had to worry that one slip up, one defeat, could cost him his job and his reputation. Aggressiveness meant taking chances, but knowing that gambling and losing on a given field got a general hauled in to Washington to be grilled by the Joint Committee on the Conduct of the War and most likely fired certainly discouraged the sort of boldness Lee exhibited on a regular basis. Thus, in the days immediately following Chancellorsville Lincoln seemed reluctant to appoint a third commander of the Army of the Potomac in six months.

Hooker's days at the Army of the Potomac's head were numbered, though. Part of this had to do with the heavy lobbying by certain key officers for his removal. More of a problem for Hooker, though, was that the supreme Union military commander, Henry Halleck, despised Hooker and was never shy about exercising whatever influence he could to get Hooker reassigned. During May and most of June Hooker and Halleck sniped at each other with Hooker ultimately telling Lincoln to make a choice between him and Halleck. By the time Hooker threw down his "him or me" challenge, Hooker had cooked his own goose. When Lee's army began to move in early June and was known to be strung out between the Shenandoah Valley and Fredericksburg, Hooker failed to attack anywhere. Lincoln figured that Lee had to be vulnerable somewhere, but his general seemed content to merely follow a roughly parallel route without going after Lee even once, action that was depressingly reminiscent of McClellan. Hooker reinforced that unfortunate parallel by begging for reinforcements and complaining that he was outnumbered and used the supposed numerical disparity as an excuse for inaction. Hooker's lethargy following Chancellorsville was simply too much. Lincoln did not feel he could support Hooker as commander of the Army of the Potomac any longer. He was insubordinate to his own supervisors, he had lost the faith of his subordinates, and, most importantly, he permitted Robert E. Lee to do whatever he liked unmolested. On June 28, after trying to give the job to at least three other officers who refused to take the high-profile, pressure-cooker job, General George Gordon Meade assumed command of the Army of the Potomac.[2]

The Army of Northern Virginia also underwent significant personnel changes after Chancellorsville, but not because of political intrigue and maneuvering. With Stonewall Jackson's death a replacement to lead the Second Corps had to be appointed. Jackson was replaced by one of his most competent subordinates and one who had been with Jackson's army for most of its existence, General Richard Stoddard Ewell. In deciding to promote Ewell to take over the Second Corps, Lee also decided to make another significant change to the Army of Northern Virginia. He concluded that the two corps structure was too large and unwieldy for a single commander so he decided to create a third corps out of part of the old First and Second Corps. For command of the new Third Corps Lee chose one of his most pugnacious generals and one who had led the largest division in the Army of Northern Virginia, A.P. Hill. Hill's Light Division was the heart of the new Third Corps, which consisted of Dorsey Pender's and James Lane's North Carolina brigades, McGowan's South Carolina one (now commanded by Abner Perrin), and Thomas's Georgians and Tennesseans.

With Hill now a corps commander a decision had to be made as to who would lead the old Light Division. Two choices presented themselves as the most obvious, Henry Heth and Dorsey Pender. These two men were the senior division commanders, but while Heth was, by all accounts, a good soldier, he was also very new to the Army of Northern Virginia, having only been with the army for about three months. Conversely, the North Carolinian Dorsey Pender was a known quantity who had developed a solid record of leadership and personal bravery within the division. In recommending Pender for promotion to division command, Hill pointed out that Pender "has fought with the Division in every battle, has been four times wounded and *never* left the *field*, has risen by death and wounds from fifth Brigadier to be its senior, has the best drilled and disciplined Brigade in the Division, and more than all, possesses the unbounded confidence of the Division." Pender had certainly earned the promotion and deserved his opportunity to command a division. As often happens with promotions, though, not everyone was satisfied. Shortly after his promotion, Pender told his wife that James Archer felt he had been passed over unfairly, relating to her: "I fear my promotion has caused [General James] Archer to be cool towards me. His manner the last time we met was not as cordial as heretofore, and he seemed very much embittered and rather down on Gen. Hill and I suppose because I will not join him in the latter, he will grow cool towards me."[3]

Of course changes among the officers were not confined to the corps and division levels. At the Battle of Chancellorsville the 18th North Carolina had lost all of its field officers except one, Major John Decatur Barry. Barry was a young twenty-four-year-old banker from Wilmington who had volunteered for the Wilmington Rifle Guards in August 1861 as a private. When the regiment re-formed in April 1862 Barry was one of the enlisted men elected to the officer corps, becoming Company I's captain. Though he was the only field officer to escape injury at Chancellorsville, he had been wounded the previous year at Frayser's Farm. When the 18th's leadership changed because of Colonel Cowan's resignation in November 1862, Captain Barry was promoted to Major Barry. With the death of Colonel Purdie and the resignation of Lieutenant-Colonel Forney George, Major Barry became the 18th North Carolina's fourth and final colonel. His second-in-command was another young officer, John W. McGill. McGill was an eighteen-year-old student born in Sampson County living in Bladen County when the war broke out. He volunteered right away, was elected second lieutenant of the Bladen Light Infantry and ultimately earned promotion to captain of Company B. Like Barry he too had been wounded at Frayser's Farm, suffering a painful wound to his foot. Despite his youth McGill had exhibited sound enough leadership under fire to be promoted to lieutenant-colonel of the regiment after Chancellorsville.[4]

Chancellorsville was arguably Robert E. Lee's greatest victory but when viewed objectively and dispassionately, it was not decisive. Hooker and the Army of the Potomac got away and would not only live to fight another day but had the luxury of expecting reinforcements to fully replace the Chancellorsville losses. The Yankee army in Virginia was still a threat and the victory had done nothing to bring the Lincoln administration to the negotiating table or encourage foreign intervention in any meaningful way thanks in part to off-setting Confederate reverses in the West. And the battle had been costly to the Army of Northern Virginia. Stonewall Jackson may have been the most famous loss, but the sheer volume of fighting men and field officers lost hurt Lee's army significantly. While the North could replace its losses relatively quickly, the South's ability to do the same was steadily eroding. When Lee drove the Army of the Potomac from the gates of Richmond the previous summer he had a force of 92,000 and the disparity between him and McClellan was not dramatic at between 13,000 and 14,000. After the Army of Northern Virginia took some time to lick its Chancellorsville wounds, Lee would have only 80,000 and the disparity between him and his opponent was growing to something closer to 30,000. Though it was true that Union replacements would be green while most of Lee's soldiers were veterans, the increasing manpower gap was a serious problem and it was one that was only going to get worse the longer the war dragged on.[5]

Lee's critics have looked at these numbers and concluded that his decision in the summer of 1863 not to dig in and play defense was a critical mistake and his fatal flaw. Instead of looking for new ways to go on the offensive, the iconoclasts argue, Lee should have been thinking in terms of how best to conserve his army's strength. While the argument is not without merit, Lee had some pretty sound reasons for not throwing up breastworks and sitting tight in 1863. As he explained to President Davis the previous summer, a totally defensive tactical scheme would merely prolong inevitable defeat. The North had the manpower and the materials to surround Southern cities and armies and bomb and starve them into submission if Confederate forces just sat there and allowed them to do so. Grant was about to prove that very point at Vicksburg, which had been considered so formidable that it was referred to as a "Gibraltar." General Pemberton may have lost relatively few men in losing Vicksburg, but he did lose it and it was a devastating loss for the Confederacy. The same Fabian strategy would play out wherever it was implemented, so Lee refused to consider it while he had a strong enough force to actively defeat the enemy. He was convinced that fighting not to lose was the surest route to defeat while fighting to win offered the surest chance for success. As he explained to Davis when he lobbied for approval to resume offensive operations after Chancellorsville, "There is always hazard in military movements, but we must decide between the positive loss of inactivity and the risk of action."[6]

There were other reasons that the Army of Northern Virginia ought to move and look to engage the enemy, on favorable terms, of course. The most immediate reason was that the army's current position along the Rappahannock was simply not a good spot to stay indefinitely. He could not just stay put and permit the Federals to launch offensive operations against his army, as was surely the plan. Lee had to disrupt those offensive operations, and the best way to do that was to move and force Hooker to react to his changes. Hooker had already demonstrated that it was possible to get around the army and there was always the possibility that the Federals could again move down by water to the Peninsula and be in Lee's rear and threatening Richmond. Then there was the problem with supplies. Ever since the Confederates got to the Rappahannock, they had been short on food, a situation that certainly was not going to improve with two massive armies in the area. In fact, Lee wanted to move the army into Northern territory partly as a way to feed his men and horses at the enemy's expense. Provisionally speaking the Army of Northern Virginia would be in better shape in Pennsylvania than Virginia, which was being stripped bare.

Lee also proposed to Davis that taking his army into the North was one of the soundest ways to affect Northern politics in the South's favor. So long as Lincoln and his party and the war Democrats were in control of Washington, the chances that the United States would negotiate an end to the war with Confederate independence were slim to none. The Confederacy's best chances lay in getting more Copperheads elected. Success on Northern ground would go a long way to discouraging Northern morale, especially since so much attention was focused on the East and where most Americans viewed as the barometer for how the war was progressing or not progressing. Whipping Yankees in their own country would, Lee believed, be an excellent "means of dividing and weakening our enemies" by giving "the rising peace party of the North" better ground to sustain their argument that the war was being horribly managed by the current leadership. Though the Copperheads, so called because of their poisonous viewpoint, did not advocate Southern independence, they were the ones most likely to listen to proposals for halting the fighting and opening negotiations. "When peace is proposed to us it will be time enough to discuss its terms," Lee told Davis, but the first step in securing independence was halting hostilities and opening talks. And if those talks were opened while a victorious Southern army was sitting triumphantly on United States soil, the South could and would negotiate from a position of strength.[7]

Success on Union ground also held the possibility of offsetting the dire situation in Mississippi. General Ulysses S. Grant was besieging Vicksburg and it seemed a matter of time before this critical river city fell to Union forces. Morale would plummet in the Confederacy and soar in the North. By taking Vicksburg the Union would have total control of the Mississippi River and effectively remove the entire Trans-Mississippi region from the rest of the Confederacy. This would surely look to foreign governments and the Northern voting public like the North was getting the upper hand, which would undermine whatever support existed for intervention on the South's behalf. The Vicksburg situation was bad enough, in fact, that the suggestion was made that Lee send part of his army there to help save the city. Lee rejected the proposals, however, arguing a number of compelling points that his critics have dismissed in favor of casting him as stubbornly dedicated to protecting his precious Virginia. But Lee pointed out that he was already outnumbered by the Army of the Potomac and it did not make a great deal of sense to further weaken his army before a huge enemy in the midst of the summer campaign season when that enemy was most likely to act. Furthermore, logistically there was no guarantee that any reinforcements could reach Vicksburg in time to save it. And there was Lee's lack of faith in Pemberton's abilities to use whatever reinforcements sent to him effectively. It was better, he argued, to go north and beat the enemy on his own ground. That would offset any morale problems suffered by Vicksburg's fall and allow the Confederacy to still portray itself as a viable nation and military power capable of leaving its borders and defeating an enemy in his own country.[8]

Having discussed all the possible benefits of resuming offensive operations and heading for the North, Davis approved Lee's plans and the beginning date for what became the Gettysburg Campaign was set for June 3. During the first two weeks of June, Colonel Barry and the rest of the 18th North Carolina felt increasingly lonely along the Rappahannock line. Lee did not want Hooker to know that he was evacuating the position until he was well to the northwest. Doing that made it more likely that Hooker would be pressured by Lincoln and Halleck to be more concerned about the Confederate threat to Washington than with taking the open opportunity to rush for Richmond. A.P. Hill's Third Corps drew the job of remaining in the lines to keep the Yankees' attention while the First and Second Corps slipped away towards Culpeper Court House and the Shenandoah Valley. Fortunately, since they were facing the entire Army of the Potomac by themselves, the 18th North Carolina and the rest of the Third Corps did not see much activity from the Union side other than a probe across the river in early June. "We have nothing in the world new," one of the soldiers wrote from Fredericksburg, "but all feel that something is brewing and that Gen. Lee is not going to wait all the time for them to come to him."

When it came time for Hill's force to slip away, Pender's division was the last to leave the area on June 15. The 18th crossed the Rapidan River at Eli's Ford the next day. The division followed Ewell's route northwesterly towards and down the Valley, which Ewell had cleared of Federals at Second Winchester. The door into Maryland and beyond was open to Lee's army. On June 23 the regiment found itself in a very familiar place, Shepherdstown, Virginia, where it had helped send part of the Federal pursuit running back for the Maryland shore the previous September. The 18th North Carolina was getting ready to cross the Potomac with the rest of the division when their corps commander's proclamation was read to them. "We will move at 2 o'clock to cross the Potomac and conquer a glorious peace on their own soil!" Hill's brief words of inspiration and encouragement were greeted with cheers and Rebel yells as the Third Corps began splashing into the Potomac headed for the Maryland shore and beyond. General Perrin wrote of the day: "I do not suppose that any army ever marched into an enemy's country with greater confidence in its ability to [conquer] and with more reasonable grounds for that confidence." Lieutenant-Colonel Arthur J.L. Fremantle, a British officer attached to Hill's corps provides one of the best descriptions of what the 18th North Carolina looked like as it crossed into Maryland in the summer of 1863: "The soldiers ... are a remarkably fine body of men, and looked quite seasoned and ready for any work. Their clothing is serviceable ... but there is the usual utter absence of uniformity as to colour and shape of their garments and hats; grey of all shades, and brown clothing, with felt hats predominant."[9]

When Lee took his army into Maryland and Pennsylvania, he instructed his corps commanders to forbid the men from indiscriminately plundering from civilians. In the years following the war, Lost Cause mythology boasted that Lee's orders reflected his and his Southern army's superior moral qualities. Forgotten by those who repeat the myth today is that part of Lee's reason for going into the North in the first place was to live off the enemy. Lee expected to live off Northern civilians' supplies; he simply wanted any and all confiscated items to be collected by duly appointed quartermasters in an orderly way. If the 80,000 men he brought with him took off in every direction foraging for themselves, not only would discipline break down, but it would make the collecting of provisions for the army far less efficient. To be sure Lee did not want the Army of Northern Virginia to be perceived as a bunch of vandals, but he was far more concerned with maintaining order and discipline on a dangerous raid into the enemy's territory and maximizing provisions via orderly confiscation than with ensuring that his men did not upset the locals too much by taking things that did not belong to them.

That certainly seems to be the way Lee's subordinates viewed the situation. Their understanding of the orders was that so long as the confiscating and plundering did not get out of hand and undisciplined nothing was going to be said — and nothing ever was. One officer said that "although positive orders were issued prohibiting soldiers from disturbing private property, [the army] paid no attention to any order of the kind, and took everything they could lay their hands on in the eating line." Another Confederate boasted: "We press every thing that we can think that will be beneficial to our cause and country." Another wrote that "we killed, captured, and destroyed everything that came in our way." A member of Lane's brigade recorded:

> Yesterday and the day before our soldiers plundered far and wide — taking butter, milk, apple-butter, fruit, chickens, pigs and horses and everything they could get their hands on. The people are frightened out of their senses "take anything you want but don't hurt us" is their cry. They are afraid to protest against anything.

In addition to helping themselves to food and other provisions, two of the best historians of the war generally and the Gettysburg Campaign specifically, James McPherson and Stephen Sears, have documented that Lee's army also rounded up thousands of Pennsylvania blacks and sent them south to be sold as slaves.[10]

Whether the 18th North Carolina was specifically involved in kidnapping blacks for sale into slavery in the Confederacy is not documented, but the regiment certainly helped itself to what it could find in the Pennsylvania countryside just like the rest of the army did. Many Southern readers, especially those who still defend "the Cause," will mistakenly take this as an indictment of their ancestors. This is not the case. They were in Pennsylvania to live off the locals and they did so. In the final analysis, the 18th North Carolina — like the rest of the Army of Northern Virginia — did less damage and brought less mayhem and misery to the local (white) population than other invaders from the pages of history such as the Vikings or the Mongols. But the romantic legend that these Confederates treated Pennsylvanians with kid gloves taking only what they absolutely needed to survive is copiously undermined by contemporary Southern and Northern sources.

During the last rainy, muggy days of June, the 18th North Carolina continued marching up the Cumberland Valley with the rest of the Third Corps, following the course of the Cumberland Valley Railroad, which wound northeasterly through the towns of Greencastle, Chambersburg, and Carlisle before it fed into the Northern Central on the west bank of the Susquehanna River and opposite the Pennsylvania capital of Harrisburg. Ewell already had most of the Second Corps around Carlisle, just twenty miles west of Harrisburg while Jubal Early's brigade was at the historic city of York about twelve miles south on the Northern Central Railroad. When Lee united Hill and Longstreet with Ewell, he could threaten Harrisburg or possibly Philadelphia directly. With the rail network in that part of the state he could also threaten supplies and communication between Washington and much of the Northeast. Such movements would force the Army of the Potomac to follow him and attack him, and when it did Lee would make sure it was on ground he had carefully chosen to inflict the decisive defeat that had been so elusive.

Lee's ability to be so effective against his enemies to this point had rested on a number of factors not the least of which was excellent intelligence from Jeb Stuart's cavalry. Unfortunately for the Army of Northern Virginia its eyes and ears were bogged down in Virginia, forcing Lee to march virtually blind through the enemy's countryside. On June 28, the same day that General Hooker was removed from command, Lee got word from one of Longstreet's favorite spies, Henry Harrison, that the Yankees were much closer than Lee supposed. The Army of the Potomac had been keeping pace with the Rebels, had already crossed the Potomac, and was camped around Frederick, Maryland. This was disturbing intelligence. Lee had thought up to that point that the Unionists were still slowly shuffling far behind in Virginia. The first thing that needed to be done with the Federals following more closely was to unite the army. To that end orders went to Ewell to get his Second Corps together and bring it by the most direct route possible to the area around Gettysburg, which was centrally located between Ewell and the rest of the army and was served by numerous roads. Once the Army of Northern Virginia got there, Lee could get with his commanders and plan the next phase of the campaign.

A.P. Hill's three divisions — Heth's, Anderson's, and Pender's — were in front of Longstreet's corps and turned right at Chambersburg onto the Chambersburg Pike connecting that town to Gettysburg twenty miles to the east. On June 29 the 18th North Carolina marched near the rear of Hill's column through the Cashtown Gap and bivouacked for the night near Cashtown itself at the little town of Fayetteville. Despite the misty, humid conditions the regiment's division commander was excited, writing to his wife, "Everything seems to be going finely. We might get to Phila. without a fight, I believe, if we should choose to go.... Confidence and good spirits seem to possess everyone."[11]

The following day, June 30, the 18th spent the morning drying out their blankets and ground cloths and checking and re-checking their muskets while Longstreet marched his corps to the area. Nobody in the regiment knew at the time that while they were enjoying a respite from marching, a detail from Heth's division, led by a fellow North Carolinian, James Johnston Pettigrew, was about to discover that the Yankees were much closer to the Army of Northern Virginia than anyone in the high command thought. General Pettigrew marched his men down the Chambersburg Pike to reconnoiter Gettysburg, assured that the most trouble he would run into was local militia. However, after marching several miles from Cashtown, Pettigrew ran into soldiers who deployed along his front and looked and acted like veteran soldiers, not local militia. He was correct; they were Union cavalry under one of the best officers Meade had, General John Buford. For his part, Pettigrew had no idea exactly who had deployed along his front, but he had enough experience to distinguish trained soldiers from militia. Knowing that current orders from Lee were to not pick a fight with any Federals while the army was divided, Pettigrew turned around and headed back to Cashtown where he told his division commander, Henry Heth, what he had seen. Heth refused to believe that Pettigrew had seen what he claimed. When A.P. Hill entered the conversation he took his old West Point friend's side and said the Pettigrew must have been mistaken; all the latest intelligence had the nearest Yankees at least fifteen miles from Gettysburg. Nothing Pettigrew said could convince Hill otherwise so when Heth asked permission to resume the mission the following day with his entire division his old friend granted it immediately.[12]

Shortly after dawn on July 1 the 18th North Carolina began getting its bivouac packed up and into their bedrolls. Most of these veterans had long since discovered the importance of traveling as light as possible and that bedrolls were much lighter and easier on the shoulders than knapsacks. At about seven officers and NCOs walked through the misty rain telling the men to get their gear on and fall in. At eight the 18th, with the rest of Pender's division, was on the Chambersburg Pike heading for Gettysburg. The mist and fog began to clear as the sun rose, but the day promised to be extremely humid and quite warm.

While Colonel Barry and his regiment were clearing their camp and collecting their gear, General Heth was about to discover that he should have listened to General Pettigrew the previous day. Heth's division marched for Gettysburg several hours earlier than Pender and Anderson and at seven-thirty one of Buford's troopers fired one of the several "first shots" from his skirmish line along Herr Ridge, about one mile west of the town. It being Buford's objective to slow the Confederate advance on Gettysburg to give lead elements of the Army of the Potomac time to get to the area, the troopers opened with their carbines from the ridge. At this point Heth probably ought to have realized, as Pettigrew had the previous day, that he was facing real Yankees as opposed to Sunday soldiers and should have countermarched back to the Cashtown area since Lee's orders to not bring on an engagement until the army was unified had not been superseded. But he did not. Rather, he decided to shake out his two lead brigades into a battle line that stretched over a mile on either side of the Chambersburg Pike, a maneuver that ate up nearly two hours.

With Joseph Davis and James Archer deployed, Heth ordered them forward to drive the Yankee horsemen from Herr Ridge. The outnumbered cavalrymen drifted back from the ridge and across Willoughby Run to Buford's main line along McPherson's Ridge, about a half mile east of Herr Ridge and just a mile west of the center of Gettysburg. Even with rapid-firing carbines the outnumbered troopers were not a match for fully deployed infantry but they had already bought sufficient time for Union I Corps brigades to arrive to take their place. Along McPherson's Ridge Solomon Meredith's famed Iron Brigade arrived and pitched into James Archer's, stopped it in front of McPherson's Woods, and drove it back across Willoughby Run towards Herr Ridge, capturing its extremely irritated commander in the process. On the left (north) side of the Chambersburg Pike, Davis's brigade also stalled and fell back after some initial success. Having halted Heth and the Confederates, a late-morning lull settled over the field and woods west of Gettysburg punctuated by each side's artillery fire.

The 18th North Carolina did not know exactly what was going on ahead of them on the road but after marching several steamy miles the regiment could hear the unmistakable rumble of cannon fire. They continued to march, the sound of artillery getting louder with each step. When Pender's column got to within about a mile of Herr Ridge, Lane ordered his brigade to deploy its battle lines on the left side of the road. The 7th North Carolina was the far right regiment with its right resting on the pike. Next to it, on its left was the 37th North Carolina, then the 28th, the 18th, and the 33rd North Carolina anchoring the brigade's left. While deployed for battle the regiment marched forward for another mile reaching the area just below Herr Ridge.

During the mid-day lull in the infantry fight, Heth had determined that he would send in his other two brigades, Brockenbrough's Virginians and Pettigrew's huge North Carolina brigade. At the Battle of Gettysburg Pettigrew's brigade was the largest on either side because most of the regiments in it had seen relatively little action and had not yet been decimated by casualties; three days in Pennsylvania changed that considerably. Brockenbrough and Pettigrew were both ordered to attack McPherson's Woods from the south side of the Chambersburg Pike. Pender was to support the attack, so in order to be in proper position, the 18th North Carolina and the rest of the brigade marched by the right flank to the south side of the road where they formed the far right of Pender's line below Herr Ridge. The alignment was the same from left to right, 33rd, 18th, 28th, 37th, 7th, as it had been on the north side of the pike. Perrin's South Carolinians were on Lane's immediate left and Scales' North Carolinians were next to Perrin. The 7th North Carolina, though, was formed at a right angle to the rest of the brigade facing south because, as they had been doing all morning, cavalry (8th Illinois) had been harassing the attacking Confederates' right flank.

At 2:30 the battle in front of the 18th North Carolina resumed. Pettigrew's Tar Heels advanced and began the extremely difficult job of trying to convince the Yankees in McPherson's Woods, which included the tough Iron Brigade, to retreat. The regiment was close enough to the battle that, as they watched, stray Minnie balls whistled by their heads although no one was injured by any of them. Determining whether their fellow Tar Heels were getting the upper hand was difficult to do with the smoke of one of the hottest firefights of the entire war obscuring the scene. For nearly two hours the men of the 18th North Carolina listened to the furious battle going on just 200 yards in front of them and waited for their turn to go in. The Confederate flags faltered and fell numerous times but Colonel Barry's men cheered when they saw them quickly picked up and pushed toward the Northerners in the woods. It was a truly savage fight with some Confederates and Federals firing at each other from less than fifty yards, neither side willing to yield. The I Corps Yankees, though, were facing their second wave of attacks so with ammunition running low and lacking immediate reinforcements the stubborn men of the I Corps began to fall back to Seminary Ridge.

It was three-thirty and the Union forces in the area were all falling back; it was time to finish the job. Colonel Barry shouted for his regiment, at this point no larger than some 400 men, typical of other veteran regiments, to fall in. Shortly afterward the soldiers of the 18th North Carolina heard the orders "Shoulder, arms! Forward, march!" The plan was for Scales, Perrin, and Lane (Thomas was held in reserve) to take their brigades and sweep the Yankees before them, but events did not go according to plan. Scales and Perrin advanced through Pettigrew's and Brockenbrough's exhausted men and into massed artillery along Seminary Ridge, which unleashed a terrible fire of grape shot and canister that shredded Scales's North Carolinians. A Wisconsin captain was posted near the 5th Maine Light Artillery saw the destruction of Scales's line firsthand.

> These guns were brimmed with shell or double shotted with canister; they were carefully posted by the best field artillerymen in the army; every man was at his station; and they were awaiting this very opportunity. The charging Confederates were brave men — in fact, no braver ever faced death in any case, and none ever faced a more certain death! Almost at the same moment, as if every lanyard was pulled by the same hand, this line of artillery opened, and Seminary Ridge blazed with a solid sheet of flame, and the missiles of death that swept its western slopes no human beings could endure. After a few moments of the belching of the artillery, the blinding smoke shut out the sun and obstructed the view.

The Wisconsin officer's grim view was no exaggeration. As Scales later reported, "Our line had been broken up, and now only a squad here and there marked the place where regiments had rested." One of his regiments, the 34th North Carolina, left the Cashtown area that morning with 180 men and was left with only thirty by the day's end.[13]

Perrin's South Carolinians were also severely bloodied during their part of the assault on Seminary Ridge, one that after heavy loss saw them get around the Union left and force it back and into the town. But the glory was bought at a very high cost. Perrin went into the day's battle with 1,500 men and he lost 1,000 of them in their attack below the Lutheran Seminary the afternoon of July 1. One Palmetto State veteran reported that the "Union troops fired low, and their balls swept close to the ground on the dishlike field to their front.... Men never fell faster in this brigade." The 14th South Carolina's lieutenant-colonel, Joseph Brown, recalled that the ground he and his men fought on "was swept at every point by the deadly minnie balls." General Perrin was proud of his brigade's fighting that afternoon, and he had good reason to be. But he was also outraged because he believed his losses were higher than they should have been because of an inexcusable lack of support on his right. While he fully understood that Scales on his left was hit hard, Perrin was livid with General James Lane, who was supposed to be on his right but was nowhere to be found in the heat of the battle. "If we had any support at all we could have taken every piece of artillery they had and thousands of prisoners," he angrily wrote to Governor Bonham of South Carolina.[14]

So what happened to the 18th and the rest of Lane's brigade, which was supposed to be on their comrades' right? Precisely what happened after they marched out for Seminary Ridge is not entirely clear, but what is clear is that these Tar Heels played no meaningful role in the fight below the seminary. Instead of marching with their left on Perrin's right, the brigade drifted to the right and southward, most likely reacting to the presence of the 8th Illinois Cavalry. Apparently Lane feared the 400 Yankee troopers more than he really should have. A regiment of infantry was sufficient to deal with a few hundred dismounted horsemen, but Lane slowed the regiment down several times to focus his entire brigade's attention on them. Some accounts even have Lane to form a hollow square to fend off the threat of a massed cavalry attack. Whether the 18th formed a hollow square with the other regiments of Lane's brigade is not clear, and it certainly would have been odd for Lane to have ordered such an obsolete maneuver since the brigade had faced an actual cavalry charge the previous August at Cedar Mountain and mauled it. What is not in dispute is that while their fellow division members were shot to pieces on Seminary Ridge's western slope, Lane's men dithered about in the right rear of the other two brigades. Unlike the situation in Scales' and Perrin's brigades, when the 18th North Carolina bivouacked for the night along Seminary Ridge, they did so with every man they had marched out of Cashtown with that morning.[15]

July 1 was a clear tactical victory for the Confederates. The Federals from the I and XI Corps who had arrived throughout the day were all thrown back and through the town to seek the shelter of Cemetery Ridge south of Gettysburg. As the 18th North Carolina bedded down for the night with their enemy just a few hundred yards east of them, there was no guarantee that the fight would be renewed the following day. Meade's Yankees were beaten but they also had established a strong defensive position that stretched from Culp's Hill south along Cemetery Ridge to Little Round Top in the shape of what many historians have described as a fishhook. Culp's Hill was the barb, Cemetery Ridge the shank, and Little Round Top as the eye. Furthermore, the entire Army of the Potomac was now on the scene, which gave the Federals the numerical advantage over the Army of Northern Virginia. For these reasons General Longstreet argued against renewing the battle the next day by attacking the Yankees. From his perspective it was a much better idea to maneuver around Meade's left to put the Rebels between the Yankees and Washington, dig in, and force the bluecoats to attack them à la Fredericksburg. No, Lee said, "If the enemy is there tomorrow, we must attack him." An angry Longstreet flirted with insubordination in his reply, telling his commander that if Meade was there tomorrow, "it will be because he is anxious that we should attack him — a good reason, in my judgment, for not doing so."[16]

The second day's fighting at Gettysburg was another bloody one for the Confederates who attacked Meade's right at Culp's Hill and left at Little Round Top. Unfortunately for the Southerners, their bloody assaults did not meet with the same success they enjoyed the first day. The attacks were supposed to be coordinated with A.P. Hill supplying support in the center from his division's position along Seminary Ridge. Only Anderson's division among Hill's Third Corps saw any action on a day marred by poor communication among the Confederate high command and excellent reactions by the Federal officers from one side of their position to the other. The 18th North Carolina again saw no significant action as Pender's entire division remained deployed but unused along Seminary Ridge. Their position was not completely safe; there was a considerable amount of artillery fire in their sector of the field. In fact as General Pender was riding along his lines, probably expecting to be sent in before the day was out, he was struck in his left thigh by a shell piece causing what turned out to be a mortal wound. Still, considering the tremendous casualties this battle had inflicted on much of the rest of the army over the course of two days, the 18th North Carolina had so far been spared from the carnage.[17]

The night of July 2 General Meade met with his generals at the Leister House he was using as his headquarters to discuss the day's fighting and what to do next. He and his generals agreed that it was best to remain where they were rather than move to attack Lee's army. The day's fighting had been hard and costly, but they had won the day and their position was a strong one. The advantages belonged to the Federals, they reasoned, and there was no reason to leave their position and engage in costly attacks unless the Army of Northern Virginia moved to cut their communication with Washington. Let Lee and his Rebels come on if they were so inclined. They would be waiting to punish them if they did.

Attacking the Yankees was precisely what Lee had on his mind that night. Again his chief subordinate and best general, James Longstreet, thought the decision was unsound for the same reasons he thought attacking the Yankees on July 2 was a bad idea. He still wanted to maneuver around Meade's left and force the Army of the Potomac out of its position and make it attack the Confederates on more favorable ground. Lee was not interested in alternatives; he had made his decision and he was getting extremely tired of Longstreet arguing with him every time he made a decision to attack the enemy. This battle within the Battle of Gettysburg was extremely detrimental to the Army of Northern Virginia in Pennsylvania, and both men share the blame. If Longstreet was sulky and uncommunicative, and he was, General Lee was unreasonable and impulsive in rejecting out of hand his chief lieutenant's viable alternatives to a bloody assault. Given his army's battered state and his limited intelligence regarding Meade's army, his intransigence is hard to justify. Based merely on the assumption that since the July 2 attacks had taken place on Meade's flanks the Yankees must be weak in the center, Lee issued orders for an attack up the middle the next day believing that his army, which had accomplished amazing feats in the past, would pull off another miracle on July 3.[18]

Late on the night of July 2 or perhaps early the next morning, Colonel Barry told his company officers to make sure their men were ready with full cartridge boxes and to get some rest because there was to be an assault on Cemetery Hill and they would be in it. The plan for what has been inaccurately remembered as "Pickett's Charge" had two wings, the right wing under the direct command of General George Pickett and the left under direct control of General Pettigrew, who took over command of Heth's division when Heth was wounded during the fighting on the first day. Pettigrew's larger wing deployed in the woods behind Seminary Ridge with the four brigades under Burkitt Fry (Archer's), James Marshall (Pettigrew's), Joseph Davis, and John Brockenbrough from right to left. About 150 yards to the rear and right of the front brigades were two supporting brigades, James Lane's on the left and Colonel William Lowrance (Scales' command) next to it on the right under the command of Isaac Trimble who took over for the mortally wounded Dorsey Pender. Choosing Lane's brigade to be part of the assault made perfect sense; it had been only very lightly engaged during the previous two days, but some of the other choices were ill conceived. Putting in Thomas's brigade, which had seen no action at Gettysburg, made a lot more sense than choosing Scales's remnants under Colonel Lowrance and which had been thoroughly mauled by Union artillery on July 1. Fry, Marshall, and Davis were also leading decimated brigades. Marshall was commanding what was left of Pettigrew's Tar Heels who had been in one of the hottest and bloodiest firefights of the war on McPherson's Ridge two days earlier.[19]

Before the infantry began their dangerous quarter-mile trek across open ground towards their massed enemy on the high ground of Cemetery Hill, the 18th North Carolina and the rest of Pettigrew's assault force lay down as Southern gunners opened the most intense artillery barrage the war had witnessed to soften up the Federals on the hill. The Confederate guns were an impressive display of force as they deployed. One Union officer was both impressed and a little unnerved by what he saw that morning: "Our whole front for two miles was covered by batteries already in line or going into position. They stretched — apparently in one unbroken mass — from opposite the town to the Peach orchard, which bounded the view to the left, the ridges of which were planted thick with cannon. Never before had such a sight been witnessed on this continent, and rarely, if ever, abroad." At just after 1:00 p.m. that "unbroken mass" opened fire. "Turn your eyes which way you will the whole Heavens were filled with Shot and Shell, Fire and Smoke," a Connecticut sergeant wrote. Union General John Gibbon said, "The whole air above and around was filled with bursting and screaming projectiles, and the continuous thunder of the guns...." One Northern colonel remembered: "The roar was continuous and loud as that from the falls of Niagara." A Pennsylvania officer was so awed by the display that he had difficulty finding words to describe it, saying that "there is no other expression but terrible to designate the character of their fire."[20]

The artillery fire was indeed frightening sounding, but unfortunately for the Southerners it was not as effective as Lee hoped it would be. The fault was not so much with the gunners as with the quality of Confederate ordnance. Many Southern shells had faulty fuses that caused them to explode too early or too late. Sometimes they did not explode at all. Thus, while Confederate batteries furiously shelled the Yankees atop Cemetery Hill for a full and terrible two hours, so many shells exploded at the wrong time or sailed over them to explode in the rear that they did not accomplish the goal of softening the Union center so that a strike by the 13,000 men under Pickett and Pettigrew could pierce the Federal center and be exploited by other brigades from Longstreet, Hill, and Ewell. When Pettigrew's force emerged from the wood line along Seminary Ridge, the Federal artillery and infantry would be waiting for them.[21]

It was 3:00, warm and humid as the six brigades under Pettigrew and Trimble emerged deployed for battle with flags waving. It was an impressive sight, but the Rebels in this part of the field had to advance across open terrain, cross the tall fences along the Emmitsburg Road, and ascend Cemetery Hill to attack their enemy who was massed behind a low stone wall. The parallels to Marye's Heights the previous December were obvious. One Bay State captain echoed many Yankees' thoughts when he wrote: "The moment I saw them I knew we should give them Fredericksburg. So did everybody." In his report of the battle Louis G. Young of Pettigrew's staff would also compare the July 3 charge to the failed Federal assault back in December, calling it a Fredericksburg in reverse.

The march from Seminary Ridge to the Emmitsburg Road took Pettigrew's men twenty minutes to cross. At that range they were out of musket range but they were perfect targets for the nearly 200 Yankee cannons that did not suffer from the same ordnance problems the Confederates did. As soon as the Southerners began their assault, the Northern cannons belched forth a continuous stream of fire that ripped huge holes in the attackers' front lines. Marching 150 yards behind the main line, the 18th North Carolina's men had a perfect view of the terrible effects of the Yankee guns. An Ohio soldier remembered, "Arms, heads, blankets, guns and knapsacks were thrown and tossed in the air.... A moan went up from the field, distinctly to be heard amid the storm of battle...."

Despite the losses Pettigrew's line continued on. When they reached the Emmitsburg Road they came within musket range and the Yankees added a continuous and murderous small arms fire to the canister rounds. Federal soldiers in front of Pettigrew massed to lay down maximum musket fire on the Southern attackers. Some of the men in the front ranks along the stone wall fired and moved to the back to reload and make room for loaded muskets to come forward while others remained, taking freshly loaded muskets from the rear ranks. It was truly terrific. A Connecticut soldier boasted to his wife that "...such a volley of rifles we gave them you cannot imagine. Soon the first line was shattered to pieces, and with shouts of derision we awaited for the next, [and] served them the same way." Not surprisingly General Trimble said the brigades in front of him "seemed to sink into the earth under the tempest of fire poured into them."

The 18th North Carolina had a terrible view of the smoky, blood-soaked field in front of them. They marched over and around the dead, trying to avoid wounded and mangled comrades. But as Lane's brigade got to the scene there was nothing to be done. The Federals' artillery and small arms fire had effectively stopped the assault at the Emmitsburg Road. Pockets of Rebels bravely crossed the road and forced their way to within a few yards of the stone wall but that was as far as any of them got. In his report of the battle, James Lane, as usual, expressed great pride in his brigade's performance in the Pickett-Pettigrew Charge. "My command never moved forward more handsomely. The men reserved their fire, in accordance with orders, until within good range of the enemy, and then opened with telling effect...." But as the brigade got to and across the Emmitsburg Road the lead brigades had already been shot to pieces. Lane had nobody to his left or right and within a few minutes he was forced to order his brigade to turn and get back to the relative safety of Seminary Ridge as quickly as possible.[22]

It is not entirely clear what role the 18th North Carolina played in the Pickett-Pettigrew Charge at Gettysburg. The regiment certainly stepped out of the trees with the rest of the brigade, but there is reason to believe that somewhere along the way the regiment stopped. According to one of the best students of the battle, Stephen Sears, confusing orders caused only three of Lane's brigades to proceed forward with the rest of the assaulting force, though it is not clear which regiments were held back. It is very possible and perhaps likely that the 18th North Carolina was one of the regiments held up and did not get quite as far as the Emmitsburg Road. In his post-battle report General Lane listed his losses at 660, almost half of the 1,355 men under his command.

Given his brigade's light combat until July 3, these losses were almost exclusively incurred during that day's charge. But the 18th North Carolina lost only four killed at Gettysburg, suggesting that the regiment was one of the ones that Sears says did not advance with the rest of the brigade, which was fortunate for them as it turned out.[23]

With the failed charge of July 3, Lee's Pennsylvania Campaign came to a bloody and decidedly unsuccessful end. Finally the Army of the Potomac could celebrate a true victory over Robert E. Lee, something that it had yet to accomplish. On a rainy July 4 the armies sat staring at each other but neither was in any condition to do much else. Lee, blaming himself for the loss, had to get his army back to the safety of Virginia and sadly sent orders to have his corps begin moving southward. The 18th North Carolina formed part of the army's rear guard during the retreat and was among the last of Lee's army to cross the Potomac on July 17 at Falling Waters. "There it stood alone," General Lane wrote years later and with some romantic exaggeration, "until every other command had crossed safely; then it retired to the Virginia shore in perfect order, and General Heth, in honor of such unusual fortitude and success, doffed his hat to these veterans as they proudly marched by him in columns of fours."[24]

In the wake of the bloodbath that was Gettysburg, it was inevitable that changes in the command structure would again occur. The 18th did not see any change in the regiment itself because it was barely engaged during the three days of fighting, but the division had lost its commander, Dorsey Pender, to a mortal leg wound. Most of the regiment no doubt expected that their brigade commander, James Lane, would be promoted to division command. Lane, the most senior brigadier in the division, was passed over in favor of Cadmus Wilcox. Wilcox was a native North Carolinian, had ably led an Alabama brigade to that point,

Cadmus Wilcox took command of the 18th's division in mid-1863. Library of Congress.

and was a West Point graduate but he was from outside the division. Why Lee felt more comfortable with Wilcox than Lane at the head of Hill's old Light Division is not known for certain. Perhaps Lane's questionable movements on July 1 were still so fresh in the commander's mind or maybe Lee's preference for West Pointers in the uppermost ranks explains choosing Wilcox over Lane, whose record was generally sound. Then again, something as simple as the fact that Wilcox and A.P. Hill were personal friends going back to their college days played a role.[25]

In addition to filling vacant officer posts in the late summer and early fall of 1863, Lee had to make sure his army was as strong numerically as it could be, something that was getting increasingly difficult. Battle casualties and sickness could not be helped but desertions could be; the army commander determined that a sterner line had to be taken to discourage desertion. While Lost Cause mythology portrayed the Confederacy as a monolithic entity where all of its sons fought nobly for the sacred cause of independence, the objective fact is that thousands of Southerners did *not* support "the Cause" and deserted rather than risk their lives for one they did not consider particularly grand or holy. Some just found military life too demanding. Conscripted soldiers from other parts of the state may have never felt at home in the regiments they were assigned to and left. Simon and William Deal of Company A could have fit one or a combination of these variables. They were drafted into service the previous August from the western part of the state, and when the Army of Northern Virginia came through the Valley following the Gettysburg debacle they both reported to a Winchester hospital and simply disappeared.[26]

In addition to all of the normal reasons for desertion, North Carolina soldiers may have been particularly tempted by the existence of the most articulate peace movement that existed during the war. While all states in the Confederacy (and the United States for that matter) had peace advocates, the movement led by Raleigh editor William Holden was by far the largest and most articulate. Many Tar Heel soldiers believed that their friends and family no longer supported the war and would shelter them from Confederate authorities if they could make it home. The 18th North Carolina's members were well aware of the peace movement and they vehemently disapproved of it. The regiment had its share of deserters like every other regiment, but the regiment was drawn from the part of the state that had exhibited early and vocal support for secession prior to the Fort Sumter crisis and the desire for independence had not waned among the core of the regiment. In August 1863, while camped at Orange Court House, Colonel Barry voted on behalf of the regiment in favor of a resolution sponsored by several other North Carolina regiments, to repudiate the state's peace movement, which the group condemned as "disgraceful to the fair name of our state."[27]

Whatever the reason the hemorrhaging of men through desertion, it had to stop. Earlier, more lenient policies were dispensed with following Gettysburg; Lee no longer had the luxury of extending clemency to those who left the ranks. Previously it had not been uncommon for deserters to be given prison sentences or even pardoned if they voluntarily returned to duty. The 18th North Carolina, having served a significant amount of time under Stonewall Jackson, probably had no idea that deserters ever got anything but shot, something that would be more common as summer turned to fall in 1863. Despite the regiment's support for the war itself, the men and officers did not relish having to witness the executions of deserters. One soldier from the Old North State expressed his feelings in a letter to his wife: "[Death by firing squad] is much more shocking to men than in battle, for in battle the blood is up and men excited and as no one expects to be hit positively, he feels a hope, ... But in these military executions the blood is cool and the doom of the victim certain and it freezes the blood to witness it." A Virginia sergeant wrote to his sister after witnessing an execution, telling her it was one "of the awfullest sights I ever saw."[28]

In September the 18th North Carolina had to witness the execution of several men from their own regiment and brigade. On September 19 the regiment marched out with the rest of Lane's brigade to view the shooting of two deserters from the 33rd North Carolina. After the men were shot the regiments were forced to march past the bodies still tied and slumped at the posts they had been tied to as a means of reinforcing the new zero tolerance policy for desertion in the Army of Northern Virginia. A week later three men from the 18th, William P. Lee and Elkana Lanier of Company C and Elkana's younger brother, nineteen-year-old Jacob, of Company A, were captured. Lee was a conscript who had deserted the previous summer within days of reporting for duty. Upon capture he was sentenced to be shot along with the Laniers. The Lanier brothers, unlike William Lee, had stood in the ranks for nearly a year before deciding they had had enough and deserted. How Lee took his fate is unknown but the Lanier brothers were quite calm and resigned to their fate, believing that God would take care of them. Elkana told his wife not to worry: "I can take it tolerably patiently, knowing that the Lord died for me." The younger Jacob was remarkably calm about his fate. In one of his last letters he said, "There is not a man in the regiment that will say we got justice, but the officers have determined to have a better disciplined army than heretofore, and so it must need be that they make an example of some to check the remainder, and it has fell to our unhappy lot to be an example." After bidding a "Farewell to friends and the world," Jacob was tied to a post and shot alongside his brother and William Lee and four others from Lane's brigade on September 26, 1863.[29]

With winter coming and the campaigning season coming to a close, the 18th North Carolina established winter quarters just south of the Rapidan River at Liberty Mills in Orange County during the second week of November. The sprit in the regiment was generally good at this point. Meade had been too timid to attack after Gettysburg and the pursuing Yankee army had been held north of the Rapidan. The regiment had also been fortunate to miss the bloody mess Hill made of the attempt to inflict a significant injury on the Army of the Potomac at Bristoe Station. As the weather turned colder the regiment built and turned into their huts and cabins on the river's south bank. The quality of the huts varied greatly, and a North Carolina newspaper correspondent described those of many regiments as crudely built, "but Col. Barry's of the 18th, are very nicely built.... Indeed Col. Barry's camp is a model, and universally admired."[30]

Winter was a relatively safe time in the soldier's life but it was also a time of boredom. Officers did their best to keep their men busy with drill and dress parades; the men did have to perform picket duty, but these activities became mind-numbingly routine after a short time as well. So it was not surprising that when the snow began to fall the men broke up winter-quarters monotony with snowball wars — "fights" is too small a word for what these affairs often became — where entire regiments assaulted one another. Though they generally started in good fun, they could become dangerous once the battle blood got up, which happened in November. During this particular battle the 18th teamed up with the 33rd and 7th North Carolina and assaulted their brethren in the Twenty-eighth and Thirty-seventh. At some point the fun got out of hand:

> Some disgruntled spirit, at last, threw a rock in his snow-ball and brought blood. This dastardly act was promptly resented, and went to such an extent that the men rushed for their arms, and it took the best efforts of the officers and level-headed men for a while to prevent the rebel yell, and snow-ball from being followed by real powder and ball.

The danger of someone getting shot over a rocky snowball was real enough that General Lane himself rode into the middle of the melee to calm the situation down and sent the soldiers back to their quarters before anything untoward happened.[31]

The fun and excitement of snowball fights aside, the winter of 1863/1864 was extremely difficult for the 18th North Carolina, as indeed it was for everyone in Lee's army. Clothing supplies were in increasingly short supply, and food shortages were often acute. The area around Liberty Mills had been stripped bare over the past two years, and the single track rail line could barely bring enough food for the army. One Virginian in the army wrote home that rations were "scarce as hen's teeth" and North Carolina General Stephen Ramseur told his brother that the men got by on a little over a pound of flour and a quarter pound of meat per day. A Tar Heel sergeant related to his family that rations were "regular enough but getting enough is the thing." Another Rebel told his relatives that his rations were "barely enuff for one meal per day." General Lee was aware of the problems and greatly concerned by it, complaining to Richmond officials: "Short rations are having a bad effect upon the men...." Times were definitely lean in the Army of Northern Virginia.[32]

Clothing was also not as plentiful as it needed to be for many men in the regiment. In January 1864 an article appearing in the *Fayetteville Observer* urged civilians to help out the fighting men, describing the cold conditions and lack of suitable clothing for the men in Lane's brigade:

> The bleak winds and driving rains and sleets which this cold winter has brought with it ... find their way through stouter garments than clothe our piquets, and would benumb the hands and feet of those who wear gloves and shoes.

The article went on to relate that "blankets and shoes are particularly needed; but other articles of clothing would by no means be inappropriate contributions."[33]

As they had done throughout the war, the women of southeastern North Carolina did what they could to help clothe the fighting men at the front. In early January Company F sent a note of thanks to the Laurel Hill Soldiers' Aid Society "for their very timely and liberal donation of clothing...." While all the southeastern counties donated clothes to the 18th North Carolina, Robeson County was particularly well organized and regular in its clothing donations to Liberty Mills that winter. In late January a member of Company D thanked Miss Bettie J. Rowland for six pairs of pants, thirteen pairs of shoes, eight blankets, 107 pairs of socks and "a large supply of under clothing." Miss Bettie had a special place in the regiment's heart because the January donation was "not the first time that the soldiers of Robeson County have been the recipients of her kindness: ever thinking of the welfare of the shivering legions of the South, she has been earnestly laboring to make them more comfortable....." Colonel Barry added his thanks to Miss Bettie and the ladies of Robeson County "for the spirit of patriotism evinced, as well as for their consideration for the comfort and well being of these gallant men now under my command." Colonel Barry finished with high praise for those women and their county, saying:

> [I]f each county in North Carolina would follow the excellent example exhibited by the good people of Robeson, not many of our soldiers this winter

> would be required to perform their tours of picket duty, as now, without shoes, blankets, ... or the assurances of the sympathy and remembrance of those at home whose liberty and property they are battling to establish and defend.[34]

Despite the difficult conditions, morale and confidence among the soldiers in Lee's army remained high as the spring campaigning season drew near. This is probably best reflected in the 18th North Carolina by the resolutions the regiment unanimously adopted when it reenlisted for the duration of the war in February 1864.

> Resolved, by the officers and soldiers of the 18th Reg't N.C.T. that we do cheerfully tender to the Government, our services for the period of the war, pledging our lives and our sacred honor, all that we possess, that we will never lay down our arms until the last enemy upon our soil shall be destroyed or driven from it.
> Resolved, that the spirit of submission which we regret to say seems to have seized the hearts of many bad men in N.C., will if persisted in prove ruinous to our cause, dangerous to our liberty, and disgraceful to the fair name of our State. We therefore express our entire disapprobation of the course of those traitors, and earnestly appeal to them to desist from their ruinous policy, and sustain our government and leaders.
> Resolved, that in President Davis and Gov'r Vance we recognize the able statesmen, virtuous rulers, and true patriots, and pledge ourselves to sustain them throughout these trying times.

Upon adoption of the resolutions the regiment presented them to General Lane who could not have been more proud of the regiment. In a formal statement of appreciation to the 18th North Carolina, General Lane told the regiment:

> It were not possible to read the eloquently patriotic resolutions which were unanimously adopted to day by you, without emotions of pride and gratitude — of just pride, that I have the honor to command such men; of well merited gratitude in the Nation's behalf and mine, for this exhibition of high resolve and patriotic action at the time of the nation's greatest need.[35]

The 18th North Carolina had endured great adversity as it looked to the spring season. The Yankees had decisively beaten Lee for the first time, and food and clothing deficiencies made the winter of 1863/64 very difficult. Yet the army had survived the setback in Pennsylvania, which was how most in the regiment viewed Gettysburg. And surviving on skimpy rations and clothing had become a source of pride in the Army of Northern Virginia. Despite losses, the Army of Northern Virginia was still as strong numerically as it had been at Fredericksburg and Chancellorsville, fields where the Northerners were thoroughly whipped. There was no reason to think this army of veterans would not whip them again as the weather warmed and the roads dried. What the 18th North Carolina and the rest of Lee's army did not realize was that the war was about to assume a more desperate character; General Ulysses S. Grant was on his way to Virginia.

Chapter 10

Desperate and Relentless Fighting: Wilderness to Cold Harbor

While Grant made his way east, General George Meade was going through the excruciating experience of having his every decision and move minutely examined and questioned by officials in Washington, something that went hand in hand with command of the Army of the Potomac. He knew, because President Lincoln had been very blunt about it that his victory over Lee in July, while welcome and cause for celebration, was viewed as ultimately incomplete and, in some quarters, as worthless because the Army of Northern Virginia had escaped to fight another day. Allowing Lee to hold him in check across the Rapidan certainly did not help reassure Lincoln that Meade had the sort of pugnacity — the killer instinct — he wanted in whatever general led the Army of the Potomac. Meade knew as well as anyone that commanders who were perceived not to be up to the task of destroying Lee's Army of Northern Virginia did not command for long. He had better do something offensive against Lee before 1863 was out and that left little time.

Meade decided in early November to go on the offensive and get Lee out of his entrenched position along the south bank of the Rapidan. He wisely did not consider the possibility of trying to bull his way across the river and through the Confederate works on the south side of the river. He decided, rather, to maneuver Lee's men into the open by getting around the Confederates' position on the right. His basic plan was to have the Federals cross the Rapidan east of Lee's position at two fords, Germana and Ely's, march west along the Orange Turnpike, and get on the other side of a little tributary called Mine Run, which put the Yankees on Lee's unprotected right flank. The Confederates would have to fight on Meade's terms or they would have to flee southward; either result was positive and helped put the Unionists in Virginia in control of the theater as the year closed.

The plan was certainly sound enough, but the elements conspired against General Meade and denied the element of surprise he counted on. He intended to move his soldiers on November 24, but heavy rains the night before postponed the march for two days, which gave Lee time to react to Meade's move. The night of November 26 the 18th North Carolina drew two days' rations and moved out in brutally cold weather at two-thirty A.M. on November 27. The brigade's historian noted that the temperatures in late November were well below freezing with some accounts putting the temperatures near zero. Water froze in the men's canteens, and their breath congealed in their beards and froze them solid. Colonel Barry's men tramped twenty-two hard, cold miles along the Orange Turnpike to the banks of Mine Run, and began entrenching immediately in preparation for the expected enemy attack from the other side. A Federal soldier across Mine Run from the 18th remembered: "Jackson's old corps had worked like beavers all night and kept themselves in a sweat 'to give the Yanks a warm reception' in the morning."

The expected attack did not come. During the last remaining days in November the pickets traded shots and did their best not to freeze to death. In fact the only real threat the 18th North Carolina faced at Mine Run was the bitter, bone-chilling cold. Those on the picket line had the worst experiences because fires were forbidden so close to the enemy lest it be spotted and draw fire. The temperatures were well below freezing, but to make things just that much more unpleasant, snow and rain took turns pelting the unprotected soldiers. Fortunately the pickets were relieved every thirty minutes rather than the normal two hours to keep the men from freezing at their posts. Ultimately Meade decided that the Confederate works were too formidable and that he could accomplish nothing but getting men killed to show officials in Washington that he had "done something" against the Rebels, so he turned around and headed back across the Rapidan, ending his Mine Run Campaign. Washington viewed it as a failure, of course, but his men appreciated Meade's respect for their lives and lauded the decision not to waste them. As for Colonel Barry's men, they were glad, too. William Barlow wrote to his wife happily: "The Yankees concluded they could not whip us and went back across the river, and we came back to camp." There, though, rations were short but their quarters were quite snug. Another veteran remembered how after the Federals pulled back on December 1, he and the rest of the 18th North Carolina "gladly returned to our winter quarters at Liberty Mills and spent the winter there."[1]

Meade's rarely mentioned Mine Run Campaign had no tactical or strategic significance in any traditional sense. But the aborted attempt to turn Lee's right and strike a blow at the Army of Northern Virginia certainly undermined whatever faith Lincoln may have retained in Meade's abilities as a major army commander. Meade had not done a particularly poor job; he was still the only leader of the Army of the Potomac to have decisively beaten Lee in battle. But he had let that Rebel army escape and had either been moving away from it or balking at engaging it ever since. To Lincoln it appeared that here was yet another example of excessive caution in the Army of the Potomac's high command. It is no coincidence that by late 1863 Lincoln chose to bring his most successful general and a man who shared his opinion that Lee's army was the principal target to the East.

That figure was, of course, General Ulysses S. Grant. Despite his lack of prewar success in much of anything and early attempts by selfish, politically minded individuals to undermine him, he had forged an impressive record of success as a military leader. His most recent example of snatching victory from the jaws of defeat in eastern Tennessee, combined with Meade's perceived dawdling in Virginia, led Lincoln to call Grant to Washington for promotion to the rank of lieutenant-general, a rank not held since George Washington last held it, and supreme command of Union military operations. Upon receiving the promotion and new authority, Grant decided to travel with Meade and his army instead of remaining in Washington. Partly Grant did not relish the thought of waging war from behind a desk, but based on Meade's record over the previous five or six months the Army of the Potomac could use an infusion of aggression. George Meade technically remained the commander of the army but as would become increasingly obvious in the spring of 1864, Ulysses S. Grant would be its de facto leader.[2]

During the winter of 1863/1864 Grant was thinking about how to decisively defeat Lee. Too often Grant has been depicted as a simple brawler with little capacity for high-level strategic or tactical vision. Nothing could be further from historical reality. While he fully grasped the manpower and material advantages the Union possessed and intended to use them to their full benefit and capacity, he did not, as his critics would have it, simply start tossing waves of blue-coated Northerners at the Confederates until they surrendered because he knew he could afford the losses longer than Lee could. If simple butchery was all Grant had in the way of strategic vision he would have told Meade to have his army ready to bull its way across the Rapidan and attack the entrenched Rebels on the other side as soon as the weather cleared in the spring. But Grant had no intention of shoving masses of men across the Rapidan to assault the Confederate lines, which stretched from Liberty Mills, where the 18th North Carolina called home that winter, five miles west of Orange Court House, along the south bank fifteen miles east to where Mine Run feeds into the Rapidan. Rather, he decided to maneuver Lee out of his formidable works along the river by turning his right flank and threatening his rear, the same basic plan Meade had in November but did not execute. When the weather permitted, Grant wanted the Army of the Potomac to move quickly around Lee's right and dip below Mine Run to threaten the Southern flank and rear. This would get Lee out of his works and force him to fight Grant out in the open on Grant's terms and where the Northern general could use all of his material and manpower advantages to demolish the Army of Northern Virginia. It was the sort of sound strategy that Lee employed and has received full (and deserved) credit for, while Grant is often seen as devoid of that sort of military finesse.

Lee too was thinking about the spring campaign season and, as was typical of the Army of Northern Virginia's leader, he was thinking about how to go out and whip his opponent. He knew the odds were steadily getting longer. But he still believed that digging in and playing defense merely prolonged the inevitable while going after the enemy and defeating him offered the best chance of undermining Northern morale and support for the war. If he could pull off another big win, it might seriously undermine or threaten Lincoln's reelection campaign, something every bit as critical to ultimate success as tactical military victories. Surveying the situation as spring 1864 approached, Lee attempted to do what he was so good at, which was to discern his opponent's plan, move to block it, and turn it to his advantage. The Federal commanders could do one of several things but Lee thought the idea that offered the best chance of success was to turn his right flank; it is what he would do in the same situation. Heading around the Confederate left lengthened Federal supply and communication lines and made them more vulnerable, and a headlong series of attacks across the river where Lee's men were securely dug in would only bring another Fredericksburg. A turning movement around his right made the most sense of all the options. Knowing that was one thing, doing something about it was another. Lee looked at the area below Germana and Ely's fords, the most likely crossing points, and knew the Army of the Potomac had to navigate through the area known as the Wilderness to attack him. If Lee intercepted the Yankees in the dense tangle of thickets, swamps, and scrub oaks, many of their advantages would be effectively neutralized. Cavalry and artillery would be all but useless and having a two-to-one advantage in infantry did not matter much in a place where maneuver was extremely difficult.[3]

When the 18th North Carolina's members looked at themselves, they saw a lot of rather thin specimens who were something less than hearty and well clad, but they also saw mostly hardened veterans who had been tested on many battlefields and had tasted victory more often than they had defeat. Numerically the Army of Northern Virginia was as strong as it was the previous spring, and if the Army of the Potomac was replacing its losses, and even increasing its numbers — many of those increases were in the form of green recruits — Lee's men believed that outnumbered veterans could more than hold their own against more numerous rookies. Towards the end of March 1864 one of the regiment opined: "Old Sol and the southern breezes are rapidly hastening the Spring Campaign. The Roads are almost as dry as in August. Our boys are jubilant at the present condition of *Dixie*." Then there was Lee, the trump card as far as his men were concerned. One Rebel along the Rapidan wrote home in early 1864: "Our army here is in the highest spirits and ready to meet the enemy at any day that we may be called on by our leaders." "Nothing is surer," he went on, "than our ultimate success." There would be hard fighting in the spring and summer of 1864 but they thought it would be the final summer of the war and that the survivors would return home heroes of a new republic.

In hindsight this elation and confidence in ultimate success may seem strange, especially to those who view Gettysburg and Vicksburg as crushing emotional and military defeats signaling the beginning of the end. As spring 1864 approached, most Confederates did not see their situation as irretrievable. Few, even among those who fought there, thought Gettysburg amounted to anything more than a setback. They did not see it as the "high water mark" of Confederate fortunes. Besides, since Gettysburg Meade was so scared of Lee that he had stayed across the Rapidan in the following weeks and he had retreated from Mine Run in November rather than fight. The Federals were defeated at Chickamauga in September; Union offensives in Florida and Louisiana failed; Confederate General Robert Hoke captured Plymouth, North Carolina, in April 1864; Confederate General Nathan Bedford Forest was racking up victories at the same time in Mississippi and western Tennessee. War clerk John B. Jones wrote in his famous diary of the high Southern spirits as spring 1864 drew near, writing that "in Louisiana, Florida, West Tennessee, and North Carolina the enemy have sustained severe defeats.... [T]he work of concentration goes on for a *decisive* clash in Virginia.... Our men are confident, and eager for the fray." "We are still flushed with the pleasing anticipation that this summer will cast the die for our deliverance from Yankee tyranny," one Rebel soldier wrote to his mother, while another said Lee's men "are in the highest kind of spirits and confident of victory. All believe that this campaign will *end the war*."[4]

The fight was on its way during the first days of May. The plan for the Army of the Potomac was to cross the Rapidan at Germana and Ely's fords quickly and then turn west around and below Lee's entrenchments at Mine Run. The toughest obstacle was one that many Federal officers were familiar with, the Wilderness below the fords and between the old Chancellorsville battlefield and Lee's army. If the Yankees got bogged down there they would lose their many advantages, so the plan was to move through the Wilderness quickly before Lee was fully aware of the move and trapped them. During

10. Desperate and Relentless Fighting

the pre-dawn hours of May 4, the Federal army began to move across the Rapidan and made good progress during the day. The right wing that had crossed at Germana Ford bedded down for the evening at Wilderness Tavern, situated on the Orange Turnpike about four miles west of Chancellorsville, where the left wing under General Winfield Scott Hancock bivouacked.

In later years critics, including officers like Hancock, pointed to a couple of crucial early missteps in the campaign. One of the more surprising things was that neither Grant nor Meade suggested some sort of diversion in Lee's front to hold his attention while the army moved to flank him. Instead, they seemed to think that Lee would sit tight in his works and let the Federals do whatever they liked. Also, plans for May 5 called for the Army of the Potomac to consolidate its position in the Wilderness to create a line running from the Rapidan south to Shady Grove Church three or four miles below Wilderness Tavern. Given the dense terrain, a better plan would have been to get through the morass, consolidate the various corps, then move forward against the Confederates. Slowing down in the Wilderness on the assumption that Lee would sit behind his works turned out to be a mistake that provided the Southern leader with additional time to react.[5]

Lee made good use of the opportunity; he had actually done little to disrupt Federal movements early on, and the Army of Northern Virginia was quite spread out in late April and early May. General Richard Ewell's Second Corps was closest to the enemy and moved east on the Orange Turnpike to Robertson's Tavern five miles west of Wilderness Tavern on the turnpike on May 4 with Hill's Third Corps behind. General Henry Heth's division took the lead, for the Third Corps followed by Wilcox's division on May 4. Lane's North Carolinians were the lead troops in Wilcox's column for the march towards the Wilderness. The 18th North Carolina made another of those long marches they had become accustomed to, covering twenty miles from midday until they reached their destination of Verdiersville where they stacked arms and unrolled their blankets and collapsed for the night, not quite ten miles from the Yankees at Wilderness Tavern.

While Grant thought of flanking Lee, Lee thought of the very same thing and ordered Ewell's Second Corps to march east on the Orange Turnpike and engage the enemy in the woods around Wilderness Tavern. He wanted Hill's Second Corps to drop down from Verdiersville to the Orange Plank Road, which ran roughly parallel to the turnpike, to where it intersected with the Brock Road a couple of miles south of the Yankees at Wilderness Tavern. This put Hill in a position to threaten the Union left flank at the tavern. Then, making use of the Catharpin Road below the Plank Road, Longstreet's First Corps, just back from Tennessee, would slam into the Federal left and rear and either roll it up entirely or send the Army of the Potomac back across the

Rapidan. Since Longstreet's corps was marching from Gordonsville and could not be available until May 6, Lee's plans for May 5 were for Ewell and Hill to simply keep the Federals occupied and in the Wilderness until the First Corps arrived to deliver what Lee hoped would be the killing blow.[6]

The fighting of May 5 in what became the Battle of the Wilderness was not, because of the terrain, one massive fight on a single field but was more of a battle with separate but connected sectors. One part of the fighting was done on the Orange Turnpike around Wilderness Tavern by Ewell's Second Corps while in the other sector Hill's Second Corps fought along the Orange Plank Road. The Federals attacked along both fronts throughout the afternoon of May 5 and the fighting was furious at each. For most of the afternoon, the 18th North Carolina did not directly participate in any of the bloody work for most of the afternoon. Lee was justifiably concerned about the three-mile gap between his two corps and wanted to seal it. At the moment Wilcox's division was supporting Heth, so Lee had that division go back to Parker's Store and to head north up Parker's Store Road to bridge the gap between Hill and Ewell. Lane's brigade was again in the lead and at 4:30 in the afternoon was just above the Chewning Farm and within sight of General John B. Gordon's brigade, Ewell's left flank. Here the regiment waited, wondering if they would be sent into the furious fighting going on all around them.[7]

As the sun dipped below the treetops, the fighting intensified along Heth's front. All afternoon Heth's outnumbered division held on against repeated Union attacks but he and his men had about reached their limit. Meanwhile, Hancock's Second Corps arrived and fed more brigades into the fight along the Plank Road, pushing Heth to the breaking point. Heth needed help to hold on, and the only division available was Wilcox's. Lee was uncomfortable recreating a gap between the two corps, but there was no choice. He had to send Wilcox into the battle and hope his men could hold until nightfall brought an end to the fighting. If they could keep the Yankees from breaking through, Longstreet would arrive during the night and significantly strengthen Confederate odds.

Given their position near the rear of the column, the 18th heard the increasing roar of battle as they marched south past the Chewning place and took a left onto the Plank Road past the Widow Tapp farm. The regiment double-quicked to the scene and deployed on the right (south) side of the Plank Road behind Alfred Scales' brigade, which went in first to help stem Hancock's advance. More could be heard than seen not only because of the dense growth and the descending sun but because of the smoke of thousands of muskets firing until they were too hot to handle. A Federal soldier described the volume of small arms fire as "simply terrific. The musketry was continuous and deadly along the whole line." Another Northerner who fought along the Plank Road echoed the description:

The musketry was terrific and continuous.... Usually when infantry meets infantry the clash of arms is brief.... One side or the other speedily gives way. Here neither side would give way, and the steady firing rolled and crackled from end to end of the contending lines, as if it would never cease. But little could be seen of the enemy. Whenever any troops rose to their feet and attempted to press forward, they became a target for the half-hidden foe, and lost severely.

Lane's North Carolinians entered the noisy, smoky, and bullet-filled fighting with the 37th North Carolina posted on the right flank facing the Plank Road at about six-thirty. As the Confederate firing escalated in Hill's front, Lee's aide, Charles Venable, was heard to say: "Thank God, I will go back and tell General Lee that Lane has just gone in and will hold his ground until other troops arrive tonight." Next to the Thirty-seventh the alignment ran from left to right as follows: 7th, 33rd, 28th, and 18th North Carolina. In the dense growth the brigade quickly found that its right flank was exposed. To meet the threat, Colonel Barry ordered two companies to turn right to guard the flank, but as more Federals appeared the entire regiment was faced by the right flank and got involved in a furious firefight to keep from getting flanked and destroyed or captured. Within the next few minutes Lane found that the left flank was unsupported as well and ordered his brigade to fall back to the hastily constructed works on the road.[8]

Darkness brought an end to the fighting along Hill's front and the 18th North Carolina collapsed where it was. In later years a controversy developed over who was responsible for the failure to fortify the line along the Plank Road the evening of May 5. Whoever was responsible, the Confederate Second Corps was allowed to rest where they were after a tough day's fight where every one of Heth's and Wilcox's regiments were thrown in. Works were not strengthened, and little effort was made to align regiments against an attack that would almost surely to come the following day. The expectation was that Longstreet was due at any moment during the night and his corps would take over the Plank Road front and be ready to meet the Yankees by first light.

The problem was that Longstreet's corps did not arrive that night, and at dawn Hancock attacked. The Rebels were in no position to put up much of a fight about it, either. Many of the men in the 18th North Carolina were out or nearly out of ammunition and with "arms so badly fouled from the firing in the engagement of the 5th that but few of them would fire." As General Lane tried to align his brigade perpendicular to the Plank Road, his left resting on it, Hancock attacked and plowed through Scales' men. Lane's still-forming regiments did not last any longer; they fired a few shots and retreated down the Plank Road. The 18th did try to rally and blunt the Federal attack by falling into line with General Henry "Mud" Walker's Virginia brigade but they and the Virginians quickly found themselves pushed back in the direction of the Widow Tapp's farm and beyond.

As Hill's front broke, Longstreet's corps arrived on the scene and slammed into Hancock's front. The First Corps not only halted the advance along the Plank Road but managed to hurl it back, unfortunately at the expense of General Longstreet who was severely wounded eerily close to the place Jackson had been wounded the year before. Hill got control of his corps and realigned them between the Tapp and Chewning farms and played no further role in the fighting at the Wilderness. Had Grant's plan been implemented fully, there would have been fighting along that front, plenty of it. General Burnside's recently arrived Ninth Corps was supposed to attack through the gap between Ewell and Hill while their corps were engaged and roll up and destroy one or both of their flanks, potentially crippling the Army of Northern Virginia for good. Burnside mismanaged his role and the 18th North Carolina saw no further fighting on May 6; for them the Wilderness was now part of the regiment's history, another battle honor for their flag.[9]

The regiment's casualties for the Wilderness were forty-three killed and wounded and another fourteen missing, which for this battle was getting off easily. Still, the losses were significant. Precise numbers for the 18th North Carolina going into the battle are not available but the regiment likely did not have more than 400 or 450 men (and probably not quite that many), making their losses somewhere between 12 and 15 percent. General Lane, as usual, praised his regiments in his report. In discussing the officers he made special mention of Colonel Barry, who commanded the regiment in battle for only the second time since succeeding Thomas Purdie almost a year to the day after his death. Given the terrain and the sustained combat the regiment engaged in, this was a truer test for Colonel Barry's abilities than Gettysburg had been. In Lane's view Barry passed the test with flying colors, writing in his report that the 18th's colonel, "is deserving great praise for the manner in which he handled his Regiment in protecting our right flank on the 5th. He has shown himself fully competent to fill a more responsible place than that which he now holds."[10]

The men of the 18th North Carolina, like the rest of Lee's army, felt that they had won another victory over the contemptible Army of the Potomac. Lincoln could bring Grant in from the West if he was so inclined but that would not change anything as long as Yankee generals had to keep dealing with General Lee; or so they thought in early May. As one of Lee's Tar Heels opined, Grant was discovering that "this army is composed of different material from our western army." From the Southern perspective they had thwarted Union plans (yet again) and inflicted heavier damage on the Union force (again). Lee had lost 11,000 but Grant lost almost twice that number, which

10. Desperate and Relentless Fighting

was a greater casualty toll than the Confederate commander had inflicted on General Hooker in the same area the year before. They "fought us right tight," a Georgian recorded, "but we drove them off leaving a great many dead bodies & wounded subjects." General Wilcox, the 18th's division commander, boasted that "no battle of the war was fought with more valour on our part," and North Carolina General Bryan Grimes wrote that the enemy "have been active but have accomplished nothing at all.... They are regarded as badly whipped and greatly demoralized." A Mississippi private probably captured the confidence of Lee's army after the Wilderness when he asked rhetorically: "Can men such as these under such a General ever be subjugated?"[11]

Grant certainly thought so. If Southerners gloated that Grant was finding Lee a considerably more difficult assignment than he had faced before, the Army of the Potomac and its opponents were about to find out that Grant was made of sterner stuff, too. Unlike many of the officers under him, Grant was not intimidated by Lee or his reputation and he thought the soldiers in the Army of the Potomac were certainly good and brave men, which they were. But they had not been led aggressively enough to get the job of defeating the Army of Northern Virginia done. If the Army of the Potomac's full power could be used and unleashed on Lee's men, victory would be a matter of time. Even if they endured a setback or two, like in the Wilderness, they would win if they kept the pressure on the Rebels. Understanding that setbacks are merely part of war, Grant intended to keep using his powerful machine to move forward to grind his enemy down. He intended to give these eastern veterans another shot at Lee's army, and soon, which, though it promised more fighting, showed Grant's confidence in the soldiers and that the army finally had a man in charge of it who would let them at the enemy and not run scared every time the army got a bloody nose. One Union soldier's diary entry shortly after the Wilderness expressed a universal feeling among the fighting men under Grant: "I do not know that during the entire war I had such a real feeling of delight and satisfaction as in the night when we came to the road leading to Spotsylvania Court House and turned right." Years later a Maine veteran remembered: "I was truly happy we were advancing, which indicated that we had not been beaten. The rank and file wanted no more retreating, and from the moment when we passed the roads that led to the Rappahannock fords and continued straight to Spotsylvania, I never had any doubt that General Grant would lead us on to final victory."[12]

As Grant had told Lincoln even before the Battle of the Wilderness, when he went into the field with the Army of the Potomac he intended to keep moving forward and keeping the pressure on Lee's ever-shrinking army and that "whatever happens, there will be no turning back." Earlier generals like McClellan, Pope, and Hooker had bragged that they would keep after

Lee with a brutal relentlessness that would assure victory. Grant was not boasting, however; he was merely explaining to Lincoln what his intentions were. And he meant what he said. The Wilderness had not gone as well as he had hoped, but Grant did learn from it at least that he would have to increase his role from merely advising Meade to taking de facto control of the Army of the Potomac for the rest of the war. Despite the bloody losses, which Grant sincerely abhorred, the army would move forward and around Lee's right flank to Spotsylvania Court House. If he got there he would be between Lee and Richmond and would threaten Lee's supply lines by being between Lee and Hanover Junction. This would, Grant hoped, pull Lee out of position and force him to give battle in the open on the Union commander's terms, where he could inflict a serious blow and bring the war a giant step closer to a successful conclusion. On the morning of May 7 Grant ordered General Meade: "Make all preparations during the day for a night march to take position at Spotsylvania Court House"[13]

Grant's plan called for Gouverneur Warren to march south along the Brock Road for Spotsylvania Court House the night of May 7 and get there before Lee knew what he was up to by the following morning. Officers from A.P. Hill's staff, though, noticed that Union artillery was moving southward, and cavalry reports began to come in that Grant was indeed headed for Spotsylvania Court House. Fortunately for Lee he had a couple of means to block Grant from reaching his planned destination. One was his cavalry, which could ride down and hinder Warren's troops as John Buford's Union troopers had at Gettysburg. Another was a road Lee had cut through the Wilderness that connected the Orange Plank Road with a section of the Catharpin Road leading to Spotsylvania Court House, a shortcut to the area if he used it quickly enough.

On May 8 and 9 Lee and his cavalry did both. On May 8 troopers under the general's nephew, Fitzhugh Lee, swooped around Warren's vanguard and deployed before it about two miles north of Spotsylvania Court House. In what may have been his best day as a commander, Fitz Lee and his horsemen successfully halted the Federal movement and held the Unionists at bay until a division led by General Richard "Fighting Dick" Anderson, who had also taken command of the First Corps after Longstreet's wounding, arrived to reinforce the troopers. The next day, May 9, Anderson's men entrenched and threw up formidable and complex breastworks of logs covered with earth and abatis of sharpened logs facing the attackers; field fortifications were getting more sophisticated in the East. While they dug and prepared for the inevitable Federal attack, the Army of the Potomac deployed, and the rest of Lee's army rushed down the improvised shortcut to extend Anderson's works and have their full force above the Court House to inflict more massive losses on Grant's force. By the end of the day the Rebel front was directly in Grant's way and,

10. Desperate and Relentless Fighting

as one historian has described the scene, it "resembled a ragged V, the flanks bent back to meet attacks from either left or right and a strong salient in the center, protruding northward." Wilcox's division formed the army's left flank, extending the defensive line southward from the salient soon to be famous as the "Mule Shoe" to near Massaponax Church below and east of Spotsylvania Court House. Lane's North Carolina brigade was posted on the division's far left next to General George Steuart's brigade and aligned in the following order from left to right: 28th, 18th, 7th, 33rd, and 37th. This position faced eastward and placed them about 1,000 yards south of the Mule Shoe's right-hand side.[14]

Grant would not be blocked and if Lee was in front of him he would look for a way to pierce the Confederate line and strike a debilitating blow to the Army of Northern Virginia. The Mule Shoe salient was chosen as the key point of attack for May 10 and would be led by a young Massachusetts brigadier named Emory Upton. Upton had come up with a plan to successfully take an entrenched position that presaged tactics that would be used on the Western Front in World War I by his grandson's generation. Upton's innovative plan called for speed and concentrated power at the point of attack. The Federal soldiers would march forward at the double-quick with uncapped muskets to keep the wave from stopping to fire and ensured that it reached the enemy works quickly and with fewer casualties. Upon reaching the Rebel works the first wave would fire and use their bayonets to cut a hole in the enemy line through which the brigades that had followed the first group would explode and widen allowing for a decisive victory and hopefully the destruction of a significant part of Lee's army.

May 10 dawned as most of the mornings had the previous few days — chilly, damp, and foggy. Upton's force moved out according to plan and rushed the Confederate works along the northern section of the Mule Shoe. The fighting was fierce, much of it at close quarters. Upton's attackers breached the line, but Lee deftly moved reinforcements to the Mule Shoe from other areas and threw the Yankees back. Grant's hoped-for breakthrough failed that day, but Upton's plan showed much promise and had created a hole in the Southern line. Grant decided that the attack could have worked had more men been dedicated to the effort. He therefore determined that despite the mounting casualties he would hit the Mule Shoe again but with greater force. Lee had parried him again, but Grant viewed May 10 as but one act in a grander play that would end in Union victory if he just kept trying. And so long as he kept trying Lee had to dance to Grant's tune, taking away Lee's greatest weapon, his ability to maneuver and force others to react to him.[15]

May 11 was eerily calm, though unseasonably wet and cold. The men of the 18th North Carolina thought that today would be their day to fend off one of Grant's massive attacks. He had tried one point and failed, and they were learning that Grant did not give up just because he got a bloody nose. Besides, they knew very well that Burnside's Ninth Corps was just a few hundred yards in front of them. But aside from the smattering of picket and sniper fire, the regiment's most difficult battle that day was to keep dry and warm, a battle most of them lost in their muddy trenches—one more precursor of World War I. Grant was going to attack, but he took May 11 to get his force in position for a massive punch he would deliver on the 12th.

As the shivering and mud-encrusted men of the 18th North Carolina were watching the last stars disappear from the sky as dawn approached, they heard the "Huzzah" of charging Yankees from their front and to their left; Grant's massive attack on the Mule Shoe had begun. The Union assault was overwhelming. At the Mule Shoe's apex, soon to be famous as the "Bloody Angle," Federal soldiers rolled over General Witcher's brigade as well as General Steuart's on Witcher's right. This quickly put the 18th North Carolina in a precarious position. Lane's brigade was next to Steuart's and with his brigade overwhelmed and collapsing on the left, Lane's left-most regiments, the 28th and 18th, suddenly found themselves horribly exposed. One veteran of the May 12 fighting remembered: "The rattle of musketry became so incessant that it was like peal after peal of thunder, long and continuous, vibrating up and down the great lines and echoing from front to rear." These regiments were in a hopeless situation and dozens of soldiers from both were quickly captured in the Yankees' morning breakthrough and hustled to the Federal lines where they would begin their difficult journey to prison camps at Point Lookout, Maryland, and Elmira, New York.[16]

The fighting at the Angle was vicious and would continue into the early evening. According to Grant's plan, Burnside's Ninth Corps was to play a role in applying significant pressure to Lee's right, but for most of the morning those regiments had done very little. During the morning fighting General Lane had sent skirmishers forward to feel Burnside's position, and they reported that the Union general's left appeared to be very lightly defended. With this information Lee determined to disrupt Grant and attack his enemy's left in the early afternoon with Wilcox and Heth. At 2:00 Lane's brigade, supported by Colonel David Weisiger's Virginians from William Mahone's division, came upon Federal artillery and Lane determined to take it. In the attack several Federal guns were in danger of being captured, but the Tar Heels were forced to fall back under tremendous canister fire. Lane regrouped and moved his brigade to his left and ran into Colonel John Hartranft's brigade of General Orlando Willcox's division. Lane's North Carolinians descended on the surprised Yankees, taking a number of prisoners from the 17th Michigan and sending the 51st Pennsylvania flying. The two other regiments, the 50th

Pennsylvania and 21st Michigan, made a stand before they too retreated. The fight did not last long, but it was close quarters and bloody. A Pennsylvanian remembered: "The bayonet and butt end of the muskets were freely used." Lane had gotten into the Yankee line and disrupted it a bit but that was all he could do with the force he had and he had to return to the trenches content with having taken prisoners and a flag.[17]

Lane was again proud of his men in his reports and, as he and other officers often did, he engaged in a bit of hyperbole.

> It is impossible for me to speak in too high terms of my command in repulsing [the] terrible attack of the enemy — men could not fight better, nor officers behave more gallantly — the latter regardless of danger, would frequently pass along the line and cheer the former in their glorious work. We justly claim for this brigade *alone* the honor of not only successfully stemming, but rolling back this tide of Federal victory which came surging furiously to our right.

Lane's North Carolina veterans fought with their typical courage but, the Federal tide was hampered more by Burnside's balky handling of the Union left than by Lane's brigade alone. The 28th and 18th North Carolina lost the most on May 12 with the 18th losing 157 men, roughly half the regiment. The overwhelming majority of those losses were captures when the Federals came surging over the Confederate works in the morning attack on the Mule Shoe. Of the 157 men lost in the regiment, 140 were captured. The regiment was left with less than 200 men, but unlike earlier in the war, these losses were not replaced, at least not fully. The 18th North Carolina, like so many of Lee's regiments, would continue to dwindle away to a glorified company, constituting a regiment in name only.[18]

While the battle against Burnside's Yankees was concluded, a new one erupted between Lane and Mahone. At the heart of the matter was who was to get credit for capturing the 17th Michigan's flag. Mahone argued that the honor belonged to one of his soldiers, Private Thomas Savage of the 41st Virginia while Lane contended that Lieutenant James Grimsley of the 37th North Carolina had taken the trophy. The matter would probably not have been as acrimonious as it was had not the fiery Mahone not ridden to the scene of battle as it was ending, casting loud and public aspersions upon the honor of Lane's men specifically and the state of North Carolina generally. As Lane's brigade was returning to its lines, Mahone galloped in and jumped to the conclusion that they were fleeing the scene to leave Weisiger's Virginia brigade to fight alone. Spotting Lieutenant-Colonel John McGill of the 18th North Carolina, "Little Billy" demanded to know, "Where in the hell are you taking these men to?" Before McGill could inform the general that they were pulling back as ordered, Mahone began screaming that Lane's "damned North Carolinians were deserting his brave Virginians" and angrily ordered him to turn around. McGill, incensed at the insults to his men and state, recalled informing Mahone that he "might 'go to hell' or anywhere else, but as for me I would form with my command."

Adding to the ill will Mahone had instigated was the accusation that Grimsley was stealing an honor due his "brave Virginians" by claiming the 17th Michigan's flag. Lane angrily dismissed Mahone's ability to have any idea who captured what, railing that Mahone's activities on the afternoon of May 12 amounted to "riding around on horseback in the edge of the woods, near the Fredericksburg Road, abusing my brigade, generally, and claiming for his own most, if not all, of the prisoners that were brought to the rear...." Lane's undiplomatic tone notwithstanding, he was correct in pointing out that Mahone had not been in a position to know who had captured any flags that afternoon. Colonel Barry of the 18th North Carolina, who commanded the division after Lane was wounded at Turkey Hill the first week of June, echoed the point firmly but diplomatically, saying in a June 10 report on the matter: "With all due respect to Gen Mahone, I beg leave to say that he has jumped at his conclusions too hastily." Furthermore, Lieutenant Grimsley had physical possession of the flag. When the question was raised regarding ownership of the Michigan flag, Grimsley declared (in the presence of several general officers): "I captured this flag with my own hands and I can whip the man who says I did not!" During the second week of June, Colonel Barry concluded his evidence in favor of Grimsley having captured the flag, writing:

> While I would not wittingly deprive any brave and gallant Virginian, or any Brigade from any state of any of their dearly won and highly prized honors and fair name, (Mahone's Brigade is doubtless entitled to and possesses its full share) I cannot quietly consent to seeing any man of this Brigade deprived of any of his laurels by such evidence as is contained in these papers.

Ultimately Lieutenant Grimsley got to keep his honor, but Lane never forgave Mahone for his insults to his brigade and to the Old North State. He remained a bitter personal and political enemy of "Little Billy" for years to come.[19]

As the fighting around Spotsylvania Court House came mercifully to a close on May 12, those remaining in the ranks of the 18th North Carolina collapsed exhausted into their muddy trenches and contemplated how different the war had become since Grant entered the picture. The war had never been easy to endure, but since Grant came east it had taken on a new and terrible relentlessness they had not experienced before. Previously, horrifying battles had often been followed by extended periods of rest as the Yankees pulled back. Those days appeared to be over and the soldiers were introduced to stress levels caused by miserable living conditions and constant, often fierce, contact with the enemy that no previous American soldiers had faced. Writing of the horrible and dangerous conditions behind the works a Southerner recorded: "We lay all day and night long in the Breastworks in mud five inches deep with every kind of shot & shell whistling over us, among us *in us* and about us, so that it was as much as your life was worth to raise your head above the works." One Southern staff officer summed the situation up nicely when he wrote: "This is the eighth day of rain and the fifteenth in which our troops have been in the line of battle. The great days of fighting were on the 5th, 6th, 8th, and 12th." A Georgia soldier told his wife: "This is the 9th day of the fight and no likelihood of its stopping yet.... The fighting was terrible on the 6th, 10th & 12th not so severe on the other days."[20]

These conditions began to have detrimental physical and mental effects on the soldiers on both sides. A Confederate captain wrote that the army was generally confident, feeling that it had successfully sabotaged Grant's designs, "but the extraordinary fatigues & exposures of 21 days & nights of marching, fighting, watching, & lying in the trenches begins to tell on them, in the loss of flesh, & sunken eyes, & falling asleep anywhere just as soon as they become still." Civil War–era Americans had no terms for what the soldiers around Spotsylvania Court House were experiencing; they would have to wait for the next century when "shell shock," "combat fatigue," and "post-traumatic stress disorder" would come into the military lexicon. For the survivors of the first weeks of May 1864, there was nothing left to do but prepare for the next wave of fighting. One Rebel spoke for many when he wrote home after Spotsylvania: "Grant is certainly a far more fearful adversary than any of his predecessors." The only question would be where and when the next big fight would be fought.[21]

Once again Grant determined to try to move around Lee's right to put the Army of the Potomac between Lee and Richmond. Lee deployed his army in something like a convex line facing north and northeast with Hill's Third Corps forming the left side. The 18th North Carolina was at or across the Virginia Central Railroad just a quarter mile north of Atlee's Station above Mechanicsville and facing the Totopotomoy Creek. During the last few days of May, there was skirmishing along the Totopotomoy Creek but nothing more significant than that. Grant had no intention of seriously trying to go around Lee on the Confederate left. His target was Cold Harbor, a strategic point where five roads came together and where the two armies had bloodied each other back in the summer of 1862.[22]

As he had at the Wilderness and Spotsylvania, Lee again beat Grant to his destination with the First Corps under General Anderson. The Confederates dug in facing east and waited for Grant's attack and the rest of the army to arrive and extend the defensive line to the right. While the 18th North Carolina was pulling out of its lines along the Totopotomoy the Federals

18th North Carolina's battle flag captured in summer of 1864, most likely at Spotsylvania Court House. North Carolina Museum of History.

attacked at Cold Harbor on June 1, breaking through briefly before being driven back. Grant had proven, though, that blunting his assaults and sending his soldiers back where they came from would not discourage him. He would try again so it was imperative that Hill's corps arrive.[23]

They did the following day, June 2. Heth's division was ordered detached from the rest of the division to strengthen Jubal Early's left side of the Confederate works. The remaining divisions — Wilcox's and Mahone's — were ordered to form the far right and anchor it on Turkey Hill. Turkey Hill was seen by both commanders as an important spot to occupy not only because it provided a view of the fields between the armies but also because it was an

10. Desperate and Relentless Fighting

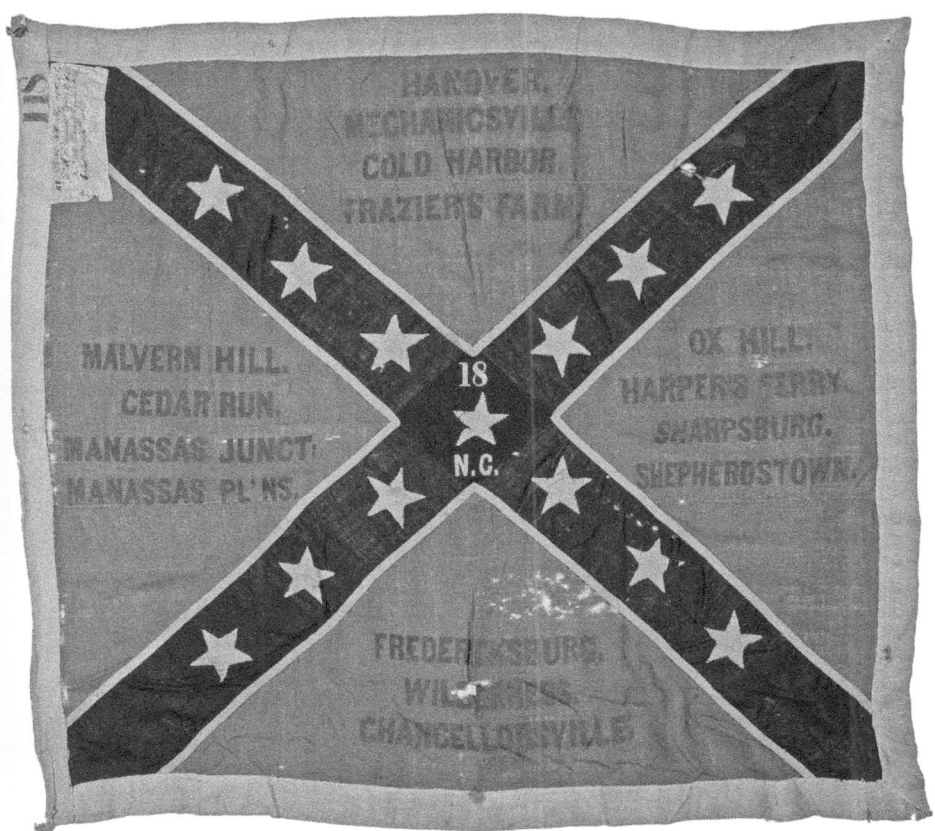

The 18th flag captured at Spotsylvania (Courtesy NC Museum of History).

excellent place to deploy artillery to fire down on the enemy. The hill itself was located just to the east of the Watt House that Union General Porter had used as his headquarters during the Battle of Gaines's Mill. Lane's brigade, along with three others, was ordered to charge Turkey Hill, drive the Yankees who were trying to establish themselves on it, and secure it as the anchor for the Confederate right. The Confederate assault on Turkey Hill was a small but important part of the Battle of Cold Harbor that successfully gained the rise for Lee's army and a large section of artillery that made turning the army's right virtually impossible. Casualties in the charge were light in terms of numbers but General Lane, leading from the front, was seriously wounded. Colonel Barry was also wounded on July 2. The details are not clear, but the records say that he was "on a reconnoitering tour" when a Federal sharpshooter drew down on the 18th North Carolina's colonel and hit his right hand. Barry's wound was severe enough that he had to turn command of the regiment over to Lieutenant-Colonel John W. McGill until he was able to return to duty in January or February.[24]

Having driven the Federals from Turkey Hill, Lane's North Carolinians did what both sides did without being told since the Wilderness; they threw up breastworks, dug trenches, and waited for Grant to attack. Just before dawn the following day, June 3, Grant's attack came to the left of Lane's position. The Union assault at Cold Harbor was one of the most notorious mistakes of the entire war, one that Grant himself acknowledged was a mistake that he wished he had never ordered. Thousands of Northern soldiers, many with their names pinned to the backs of their coats because they knew their chances of survival against well-entrenched Rebels were slim, rushed the center of Lee's line only to be mowed down in droves. The 18th North Carolina, on the far right of the position on Turkey Hill, did not actively participate in defeating Grant's doomed charge but they heard the battle rage and probably hoped the Yankees would try such a suicidal assault of their works. Such an attack did not happen. For the next two weeks the two sides remained behind their works, in some places within fifty yards of each other, waiting for something to happen.

On the one hand, the relative inactivity following Cold Harbor was a welcome relief from the near-constant marching, digging, and fighting. At various points along the lines soldiers declared informal and unsanctioned truces where they agreed not to shoot at each other as long as they were on picket duty. As had happened since the war's beginning, soldiers met between the lines and traded with each other and there are even accounts of soldiers fishing along the opposite banks of the Chickahominy. A New York veteran explained:

> The Rebs and our men got tired of shooting and *stopped* without any arrangement between them.... One of our men exposed his hat on a ramrod above the works, the Rebs did not shoot, by and by he exposed his head a little; then a Reb showed his, no shooting — then one exposed a little more, then the other a little more & so on till both stood up in full view of the other and then others tried it without any trouble, then they began to talk backwards & forwards and then on both sides began to get up on the works & then to walk out toward the other works and so on until they were having a nice friendly chat. Men all left their guns in the pits and met as friends (some say shaking hands and drinking together but that I don't know about) and were laying down on the top of the works.

Such instances were not universal and were usually broken up very quickly when officers arrived to break up the fun, something many infantrymen believed officers lived to do.[25]

Informal truces and the chance to rest represent the positive side of the inactivity immediately following Cold Harbor. Sharpshooters on both sides made moving about extremely dangerous; many soldiers on both sides were killed during mundane tasks like going for rations or even answering the call of nature. Adding to the danger was that posed by Yankee artillery. Normal cannon fire was dangerous enough, but the Federals also had an early version of what would be called a trench mortar in World War I, something called a Coehorn mortar. These were much smaller versions of the normal siege mortars that could be carried to the trench line by a squad of four men. Depending on how the fuse was cut, the mortar rounds could be lobbed into the enemy lines to explode overhead, scattering deadly iron fragments, or burrow into the ground to blow a large hole that killed and maimed soldiers unfortunate enough to be crouching in the vicinity. After the war a Southerner who was at Cold Harbor recalled that the Yankees "could elevate those short pieces just a little toward us from straight up, and drop those death-dealing shells almost in our ditches...." Another Rebel recalled:

> The boys called them "Demoralizers." And they were demoralizers too! For a man to sit behind a bank of earth and hear one of those old mortars belch, look up and see the shell going up toward the skies until out of sight, knowing that it was going to come down and perhaps burst in the air just above the ground and the instruments of death send hither and thither over a line of helpless men — such surely was demoralizing.[26]

Another element adding to the misery of the lines around Cold Harbor was the horrible odor of death. For days following the battle the bodies (and the wounded) lay between the lines decomposing in the hot sun because no agreement could be reached between Grant and Lee for doing something with the dead and wounded. Most of the bodies were Union but Grant refused for several days to formally ask Lee's permission to send out teams to bury the dead and retrieve the wounded because to have done so would have been conceding defeat, which he did not want to do. Union fortunes were not going well in the Valley: Sherman had yet to strike a decisive blow on the Army of Tennessee or to take Atlanta; there was no good news of Union activity further to the southwest; and Grant did not want to officially concede defeat in arguably the most important theater, certainly politically speaking, with the 1864 elections looming. Conversely, Lee wanted formal acknowledgement that Grant was defeated to bolster Southern morale while undermining it in the North. And since the bodies and wounded were mostly Grant's, he insisted on a formal request of the field's victor. Meanwhile the bodies decomposed and made life in the trenches hell for the soldiers. One Confederate remembered that the stench "was so nauseating that it was almost unendurable; but we had the advantage, in that the wind carried it away from us to them."

Eventually Grant was forced to relent after trying several times without success to get Lee to permit burial and retrieval parties without making it look like the vanquished was asking the victor's permission. A delegation was sent from the Federal lines in front of General Wilcox's sector on the Confederate right to work out the details with the Southern high command. With one of General Winfield Hancock's pillow cases on a stick, Colonel Theodore Lyman and Major William Mitchell yelled over that they were on a mission of mercy to try to discuss details for the removal of the dead and wounded. This part of Wilcox's line happened to be manned by Lane's men. Major Thomas Wooten of the 18th North Carolina ordered a cease fire along his front and pulled himself over the works along with a party of about twenty men to meet Lyman and Mitchell to make sure their claims were legitimate. Later Lyman remembered that the Tar Heels he met with between the lines were thinly clad with few of them looking as if they had anything approaching a "uniform" appearance as one would have found in the Army of the Potomac. On the contrary, he described Wooten and his entourage as some of "the most gipsy-looking fellows imaginable." "Gipsy-looking" or not, Wooten determined the mission was legitimate and sorely needed and permitted the Northern officers to pass. Mercifully burial parties began their work over the next few days easing the stench of death and decay that had hung so heavy over the Cold Harbor field.[27]

Chapter 11

Petersburg: The Final Campaign

When General Grant broke contact with the Army of Northern Virginia the second week of June, his goal was still to force Lee out of a strong position and to continue to apply constant pressure to the army. He gave momentary consideration to moving the Army of the Potomac around Lee's left and decided it was fraught with too many problems, not the least of which was extending the distance between the army and its supply lines. Besides, if Grant took the army south around Lee's right he could accomplish much more without risking supply bases and lines. If the Union force got across the James River, it could make for the important rail city of Petersburg. With five major rail lines coming together in the city, Grant could force Lee to come to him by threatening the Army of Northern Virginia's (and Richmond's to a significant degree) supply routes. One of the most critical was the Weldon Railroad connecting the Confederates with North Carolina and the state's still-open and vital port of Wilmington. Threatening Petersburg was, Grant determined, just the thing to help bring the war to a successful conclusion.

Very often the military actions around Petersburg between mid-to-late June 1864 and the first of April 1865 have been misunderstood and mislabeled as a siege. That term conjures images of relatively passive soldiers glaring at each other waiting for one side to give up. The word certainly does not convey a sense of active campaigning in the traditional sense. And, as perhaps the best historian of the Petersburg Campaign, Earl J. Hess, has argued, "Petersburg was less of a siege than it was a traditional field campaign with some limited aspects of siege warfare. While a number of contemporaries used the terminology of sieges when referring to operations at Petersburg, engineer Nathaniel Michler asserted that "no regular siege was intended." General Grant especially did not envision sitting around starving out the enemy; he, in his usual aggressive way, constantly looked for ways to maneuver the Con-

Death in the trenches of Petersburg, summer of 1864–spring 1865. Library of Congress.

federates into decisive battle. Indeed, as Hess and Noah J. Trudeau have both demonstrated very persuasively, Petersburg was an active Federal campaign, the longest of the war, with distinctive offensives and battles designed to get through or around the enemy's defenses. In a very real sense the Petersburg Campaign, when understood as an extended series of attempts to break through or get around an entrenched enemy to achieve decisive results, had more in common with the Western Front of World War I than any of the campaigns of the American Civil War.[1]

11. Petersburg: The Final Campaign

The 18th North Carolina certainly experienced Petersburg as an active campaign. While the regiment spent its share of time in the city's trenches, it was not assigned to any one section of the works to defend as some units were. Rather, the 18th North Carolina, along with the rest of Lane's brigade, was more of a "flying column." Whenever Grant made a move, Lee, as he had done against many earlier Federal opponents, shuffled troops to counter the threat; few commanders were as good as Lee (and no one was better) at shifting troops to meet emergencies. Throughout the Petersburg Campaign the regiment moved back and forth across the James River to deal with Union movements, engaging the Yankees in a number of generally forgotten skirmishes and battles. These firefights, which were sometimes quite intense, are perhaps seen as having done little more than prolong what was by then inevitable defeat. But one should understand that, at least through the end of 1864, the soldiers of the 18th North Carolina were not so pessimistic. They had inflicted massive casualties on the Yankees while avoiding a major defeat. Many, including some Northerners like Grant and Lincoln, believed that if the Army of Northern Virginia could continue the trend through the fall the Northern people might elect a government in November more amenable to ending the war — on Southern terms. True, it was a long shot, but as long as they could stay in the field defying the Yankees, killing and maiming them in large numbers, anything seemed possible.

Though the regiment may have had higher hopes of ultimate success than circumstances, especially with the benefit of hindsight, there were certain grim realities the unit and the Confederacy could only ignore for so long. Most obviously was the fact that the 18th North Carolina was, like many others, a shell of its former glory. Grant's Overland Campaign, especially Spotsylvania Court House, had taken a serious toll on the regiment, and the Union commander's early efforts to take Petersburg had whittled the unit down as well. At the beginning of May the 18th North Carolina had twenty-five officers and nearly 400 men fit for duty. At the end of June the rolls showed only ten officers and 132 men present for duty. This was not out of line with the other regiments in Lane's brigade: the Seventh was down to 256 men, the Thirty-third had 222, and the Thirty-seventh was apparently the largest with 344. (The 28th North Carolina's rolls are unavailable, but given their heavy losses while posted next to the 18th at Spotsylvania the regiment was also severely under strength.) Now the 18th would have to do what it could as little more than a glorified company.[2]

Following the horrendous battle at Cold Harbor, Grant and Lee occupied opposing lines for nearly two weeks before Grant, again looking for a way to outmaneuver his opponent and put the Army of the Potomac on the move again around Lee's right and closer to Richmond. Extricating his army while in such close proximity to his enemy was extremely risky, but Grant managed to get the Yankees moving during the evening of June 12, 1864, without Lee's knowing about it. The next day Lee was reported as extremely irritated at Grant's ability to stay a step ahead of him and keep the Virginian from divining what he was up to, thus limiting his ability to act decisively. A Southern artilleryman wrote: "When we waked on the morning of the 13th and found no enemy in our front we realized that a new element had entered into this move — the element of uncertainty.... [Even] Marse Robert, who knew everything, did not appear to know just what his old enemy proposed to do."[3]

One thing Lee did know was that if the Army of the Potomac was on the move he could damage it if he could hit it while in motion. Orders went through the 18th North Carolina's camp to fall in the morning of June 13 to catch at least part of Grant's army while it was stretched out along roads southeast of Richmond. "The day was intensely hot," one of Lane's men remembered, "so that it required unusual vigilance in officers, and unusual exertion in the men, to execute the frequently repeated order to close up and keep in four ranks. As it was, a good many straggled." Reports came to Lee of a significant Federal force near the old Frayser's Farm battlefield, and A.P. Hill's men went to meet it and block the approaches to Richmond from that direction. The Yankees there were from Gouverneur Warren's Fifth Corps, which was actually serving to screen the rest of the army's move south across the James River, and contact was made near an establishment called Riddle's Shop. A brief but sharp firefight occurred there in the late afternoon and early evening with what Colonel John McGill described in his report as "severe artillery fire," but the 18th North Carolina was lightly engaged in the fighting at Riddle's Shop. Depending on which report is used, one or three men in the regiment were wounded at Riddle's Shop, most likely by artillery fire. During the next few days the regiment helped to throw up defensive works stretching from White Oak Swamp to Malvern Hill that would help cover the approaches to the capital south of the Chickahominy.[4]

Meanwhile Lee tried to work out Grant's objective; was he intent on moving against Richmond directly on the north bank of the James or more indirectly by threatening and taking Petersburg? During the third week of June Lee got his answer as Grant launched what Hess has called the First Offensive against the Petersburg defenses between June 15 and 18. The Union assaults were ineffective, proving that the Yankees could not take Petersburg by frontal assault even when the city was thinly defended; the works, which had been erected two years earlier, were too formidable for that. No doubt the oversized company that now constituted the 18th North Carolina took heart that Grant could still be thwarted by smaller numbers.

With Grant concentrating before Petersburg Lee ordered Hill's Third Corps south of the James on June 18. The twenty-two-mile march was as difficult as any the regiment had performed during the war. As one member of Lane's Carolinians recalled, the march

> began without breakfast and became one of the most severe that the brigade endured throughout the war. Under the severe heat, the men choked on the thick clouds of dust raised with each step. Each man's clothes and face was soon blanketed with a powdery gray mantle. A scarcity of water led to fights at every well passed by the marching column.... The brigade stretched out for miles as soldiers fell by the way side with every mile, unable to maintain the pace demanded by the officers.

The 18th North Carolina entered Petersburg around 6:00 P.M. on June 18, 1864, and immediately went, with the rest of Wilcox's division, to the far right of the Confederate defenses. The division deployed on William Mahone's right and its right flank rested nearly on the important Weldon Railroad and faced to the south. Given the importance of that rail line as a major supply artery for Lee's army and the Confederate capital, it was a matter of time before the regiment was called on to help protect it from Federal threats to cut it.[5]

Grant was indeed planning something in that sector for his Second Offensive. This move was not about sending scores of men against entrenched positions to breach the Confederate defenses. This Second Offensive was designed to do a couple of important things from the Federal perspective. One goal was to squeeze off supply lines; the Weldon Railroad was the most obvious route to be cut but there were other roads like the Boydton Plank Road and the smaller Halifax Road that served as supply arteries coming into Petersburg from the south — particularly North Carolina and the vital port of Wilmington. Grant intended to use two corps, Hancock's Second (his favorite for any sort of offensive operations) and the Sixth Corps to not only sever supply lines from points south but also to continue working to extend the Union position further around Lee's right. In effect, the Yankees would push south and west of Petersburg and dig in, extending the Union's fortifications before the Rebels to stretch Lee's already-thin lines.

By June 21 the Federals had reached the Jerusalem Plank Road, which ran south out of Petersburg and parallel to the Weldon Railroad two miles west of the plank road and dug in. The Sixth Corps formed on the left, the Second next to it on the right (north) of the Sixth Corps. The following day the Yankees made their move. It was an extremely hot and muggy day with some temperature readings registering in the upper 90s while others reported temperatures over 100 degrees. Mahone and Wilcox were ordered to check the Federals west of the Jerusalem Plank Road. As he watched the Union soldiers advance, Mahone recalled from his days as a railroad engineer a ravine that ran directly from the Confederate works across the Second Corps front.

He pushed three of his brigades south along the ravine out of sight of the Yankees and attacked the Second Corps and, with support from Wilcox's division, intended to roll it up and destroy it.

Mahone's plan had much to recommend it, and fate seemed to be lending him a hand. The terrain between the Jerusalem Plank Road and the Weldon Railroad was dense and swampy making it impossible for large bodies of troops to remain in contact with each other — as in the Wilderness. The Second and Sixth Corps quickly lost contact with each other in the thick woods, and Mahone got in front of the Second Corps and extended beyond its left flank by three on the afternoon of June 22. While Mahone's division was making ready to pounce on the Second Corps, Wilcox's division moved in line of battle towards the Sixth Corps. As the men and officers of the 18th North Carolina were sifting through the gloom and the thick undergrowth, the wild sound of the Rebel yell rang out in their front and left; Mahone was attacking. Mahone's men thoroughly surprised the Yankees and sent them running back towards their trenches along the Jerusalem Plank Road as fast as they could run. But Mahone's initial success could not be followed up because Wilcox did not support the attack. Rather, he remained in front of the VI Corps, which posed little threat, and cited (rather lamely) that the thick brush had slowed him down. Mahone was incensed that his opportunity to destroy Hancock's corps had been lost because Wilcox dithered about in the woods doing almost nothing of any importance. The utter surprise with which Mahone burst upon the Federals and the light casualties in Wilcox's sector (the 18th North Carolina lost two killed and 1 wounded) seem to suggest that, unlike his Spotsylvania ranting, he may have had a point. At least Grant's attempt to extend his lines to the Weldon Railroad had been stopped.[6]

With his Second Offensive ending ineffectively, Grant decided to take some time to figure out what to try next. Some of his subordinates were content to settle into a siege, something the Confederates actually feared would happen because they knew that would make defeat a mere question of time. Grant had no such intentions; he wanted to restore mobility to operations in Virginia because it suited his style and philosophy about how to win and also because he understood the potential political fallout if the campaign became a siege. Northern voters would not understand, or perhaps not care, that despite static appearances Grant had moved his army to within a few miles of Richmond, had completely taken away Lee's ability to freely maneuver, and was steadily eroding Southern resources and morale. All they would see was large casualty lists and continued Confederate defiance, which could very well result in a change of administration in Washington in the November election. Until he determined just what to do next he was content to allow the Army of the Potomac to strengthen its fortifications.

The 18th may have gotten a respite from active campaigning and fighting, but life in the trenches of Petersburg were no better than they had been at Cold Harbor. One North Carolinian from the brigade found conditions both dangerous and uncomfortable during the end of the June, complaining:

> The works we are now in are so close to the enemy's lines we can't stick up our heads without getting shot at. We are in the open field. No shade's over us in the boiling sun & the hottest weather I ever did see & no rain. We have had no rain in over a month ... it is horrible to be in this place. We are first shot down, day or night, any time. Our sharpshooters & the enemy are all the time looking for each other. As soon as a man shows his head he is plugged at & often killed or wounded. It is a perfect state of horror here.

One Confederate echoed the comments about the hot, dusty conditions in the trenches, commenting that the "boys look as though there was a heavy frost on their hair & whiskers." One of the regiment's men related to the home folks: "We have intensely hot weather and until yesterday afternoon, have had a drought for more than six weeks, which made the roads suffocating with dust...." Yankee accounts complain of the same problem. A Pennsylvanian wrote: "You see nothing but dust, you smell dust, you eat dust, you drink dust. Your clothes, blanket, food, drink, are all permeated with dust." While the boiling sun and dust was difficult to deal with, when the rains came the relief was quickly tempered by the problems summer thunderstorms brought to the ditches the men called home. Cold rains chilled the men to the bone and filled the trench floors with mud that was sometimes knee deep. Given the circumstances of life in the trenches, the men of the 18th North Carolina were probably glad that they were not assigned permanently to a particular sector of them. Marching and moving constantly was no fun either, but it must have been at least marginally better on some level than being confined to the same fetid position for months at a time.[7]

Towards the end of July the brigade again moved to a different sector, this time to Chaffin's Bluff along Richmond's outer defenses. The area was quiet for most of July until increasing numbers of Federals began arriving in the middle of July. Grant had a new plan and this one had two key components. North of the James from a bend in the river known as Deep Bottom, Hancock and Phil Sheridan would focus Lee's attention there and pierce the Rebel works if possible while in front of Petersburg a tunnel was dug to plant a mine to blow a hole in the Confederate line. The mine was the centerpiece of the Third Offensive (July 26–30) while Hancock and Sheridan had essentially diversionary roles. If things went as planned, Petersburg would be depleted as Lee shifted units to Deep Bottom. Then, when the mine was exploded, Union forces would rush through the gaping hole in the defenses, and overwhelm the thinned force in front of Petersburg causing the city to fall. Richmond would be at Grant's mercy while, and more importantly, placing the Army of Northern Virginia between the jaws of two wings of the Army of the Potomac.

Lane's brigade, still commanded by the 18th's Colonel John Barry, was posted on the left side of the Confederate defenses near the Darbytown Road. At the end of July the main Yankee force prowling along that road from the north was Phil Sheridan's cavalry, whose job was to wreck the Virginia Central Railroad and, if possible, raid into Richmond itself. On July 27 the Federals tried to break through the Confederate position at Deep Bottom without success. During the fight Colonel Barry was wounded; circumstances and seriousness of the wound are not recorded. Lane's brigade went to Brigadier-General John Conner.

The situation north of the James could not be permitted to continue. Lane's brigade along with McGowan's and Henegan's got orders to leave their trenches and attack the Federal right flank near Fussel's Mill to force Hancock back across the James. Sheridan and Hancock also thought of getting around their enemy's flank in precisely the same area. The next morning just before sunrise the three Rebel brigades moved out through low wet terrain in the direction of Fussel's Mill. Lane's brigade was aligned from left to right: 7th, 18th, 37th, 28th, and 33rd.

The Confederate attack was not well coordinated. The brigades quickly lost contact with each other and hit piecemeal allowing Federal soldiers and Sheridan's troopers fighting dismounted, the ability to hold their ground against the disjointed attacks. Adding to the Confederates' problems was the fact that major gaps existed between the three brigades, with one of the larger ones between Lane's and McGowan's on the right. Taking advantage of the situation the Yankees rushed between the gap to get on the Tar Heels' right flank. Conner tried to get the brigade to change front to the right to fight its way out of the situation, but this added to the confusion on the field and made a bad situation worse as Federals poured in fire from two sides with the right-most regiments taking the brunt of the punishment. The situation was a complete mess and the brigade had no option but to pull back as quickly as they could to their defenses, which they did, but not before the brigade lost eleven men killed, forty-nine wounded, and seventy-seven missing, most of whom were captured when the Federals counterattacked.

Though the fighting at what is sometimes referred to as Deep Bottom or sometimes First Deep Bottom (Grant tried again in this area in August) and Gravel Hill was not the best moment in the regiment's history, the Federal efforts on the north side of the James were thwarted. Hancock was not able to pierce the defenses stretching from Chaffin's Bluff to New Market Heights.

Grant had managed to force Lee to shift forces away from Petersburg to weaken the lines, but when he detonated the mine that created the famous Crater on July 30, that operation ended in failure as well after a truly terrifying and bloody fight at close quarters. This ended Grant's third attempt to restore mobility to operations in the Richmond-Petersburg theater.[8]

While history records that the Confederacy had just nine months to live in August 1864, the situation did not look particularly promising from the Federal perspective. Lee appeared to be parrying Grant at every turn; General John Hood was keeping Sherman at bay outside Atlanta; and Jubal Early was doing a fine job clearing the Shenandoah Valley of Federals with the Second Corps. In fact, Early was not only driving Yankees down and out of the Valley, he was roaming about Maryland and Pennsylvania, sacking Chambersburg on July 30 and scaring most Washington officials half to death. Then there were the casualty lists. Between May and the end of July the Army of the Potomac had lost nearly 85,000 men causing Lincoln to issue a call for another 500,000 soldiers to feed into the war effort. Politically all of these things were the incumbent party's worst nightmare. If the situation did not change positively soon, there was every reason to believe that the Northern voters would express their frustrations at the ballot box in November. Neither Grant nor Lincoln was panicked by the military situation in the late summer of 1864 but both certainly understood the political stakes. Grant would, therefore, try again to make progress along the Richmond-Petersburg front for political as well as military reasons.[9]

Grant's Fourth Offensive (August 14–25) was not different strategically, or tactically for that matter, from the Third. The Army of the Potomac would again operate on both of Lee's flanks with Hancock and Sheridan again trying to break through in the Deep Bottom sector north of the James while General Warren took the Fifth Corps west beyond the Jerusalem Plank Road to the Weldon Railroad to permanently extend the Union's fortified lines and, again, stretch Lee's forces ever thinner. On August 14 and 15 the Federals north of the James maneuvered for position up to Fussell's Mill and attacked on the extremely hot and humid morning of August 16. The 18th North Carolina and the rest of the brigade had been positioned on the right of the Confederate line, closer to Deep Bottom when the Federal attack broke that morning. The Unionists at and above Fussell's Mill were initially successful and threatened to flank the Rebels on their left. Lane's brigade along with McGowan's was ordered to the far left to help stem the Union tide swarming over the Confederate defenses above and west of the mill. General Field, still standing in for the wounded James Longstreet, managed to rally the retreating Confederates along the Darbytown Road and with them and the reinforcements arriving from the right he was able to organize a counterattack that drove

Hancock's Federals out of the Confederate works and back to their starting point. The 18th North Carolina was to the right of most of the heavy fighting, its job being primarily to help extend and protect the Confederate left flank, and sustained very light casualties at Fussell's Mill.

Federal operations around Deep Bottom and Fussell's Mill did not go well for the Yankees, but Warren's operation along the Weldon Railroad was extremely successful. The Fifth Corps secured a position on the railroad at Globe Tavern and repeatedly deflected Confederate attempts to force it back towards the Jerusalem Plank Road. After two days of staring at their enemy from their fortifications, Hancock pulled his force back across the James River on August 20 to build on Warren's success along the Weldon Railroad. He set out to destroy more of the Weldon below Globe Tavern, which he would do from a base along the track at Reams' Station, about five miles south of Globe Tavern.[10]

The third week of August Hancock arrived at Reams' Station with 6,000 soldiers and sixteen cannons, assigned the job of destroying track eight to ten miles below the station. When he got there General Meade alerted him to Confederate forces in significant numbers moving towards his position; Hancock delayed the original order to tear up track south of Reams' Station until he knew what the Rebels were up to. Unfortunately for the Federals there, Hancock did very little to prepare for the possibility of an attack. Earl J. Hess has pointed out that on the Union side "everyone seemed to be easily lured into thinking that ... eroded parapets would do in a pinch." In reality the works around Reams' Station, erected the previous June, were a dilapidated mess. In some places the parapets were less than three feet high and lacked revetting (supports to keep the works from sliding). Hancock ordered some trees cut down and thrown on top of some of the parapets and to have some abatis thrown out front of the position facing west but that was all. That inattention to proper fortification cost the Federals at Reams' Station dearly on August 25 when Confederates under Cadmus Wilcox — who briefly commanded the Third Corps because Hill was too ill to command himself — arrived northwest of the station.

That morning the 18th North Carolina awoke and made quick preparations as dawn broke to march from their bivouac at Holly Point Church southwest of Petersburg. They had marched from the north side of the James the previous day amid rain and mud and this morning threatened more of the same. By midday the regiment made it to the area northwest of Reams' Station where the brigade deployed from left to right: 7th, 28th, 37th, 33rd, and 18th. There the brigade, which represented Wilcox's left flank, remained in a section of heavy woods next to Scale's, Anderson's, and McGowan's brigades. At two P.M., Wilcox sent Scales and Anderson forward against Hancock's works but they were thrown back after getting caught in the open and raked by infantry and artillery fire. After that repulse Wilcox determined to settle in and wait until additional troops (and artillery) under General Henry Heth arrived.

General Heth arrived less than an hour after the first Confederate assault on the Reams' Station position failed and assumed command of the Confederate operation. Between four and five P.M. Confederate sharpshooters from several brigades, including Lane's, made life difficult for the Federal soldiers and lethal for artillery horses who were particularly targeted by the Southern marksmen. The riflemen drove in Northern pickets, clearing the front of the Federal works near the railroad. At that point, around five-fifteen, Heth ordered a thirty-minute artillery barrage that was followed by a full-scale assault by nearly 2,000 Confederates, including the 18th North Carolina. The Confederate left found the going extremely difficult between the abatis and being in the open under artillery and musket fire; in fact, this side of the line was initially forced back to the wood line where they had started. At that point General William MacRae decided to either get his North Carolina brigade into the Union works or destroy it in the attempt. Screaming the Rebel Yell, MacRae's men dashed forward and pierced the Yankee line, turning the tide of the fighting as Mother Nature added her own version of artillery in the form of a booming thunderstorm. Encouraged by MacRae's success the Confederates that had initially turned back regrouped and returned to the fight. With MacRae's men inside the Union works and widening the breach on the western-facing parapets, the 18th and the rest of Wilcox's brigade swept around and over the works facing northwest. With Rebels swarming into their defenses Hancock's men faltered and fell back.

The fight at Reams' Station on August 25, 1864, was a spectacular tactical success for the Confederates. Hancock's losses were 600 killed and wounded and 2,000 captured; Confederate losses were just over 700. Confederate casualty figures for the last year of the war were spotty and losses for the 18th North Carolina were light at one killed and four wounded. One of the wounded was Calvin Davis, a young Bladen County native who had volunteered at age twenty-one in 1861. He had served with the regiment continuously except for the brief time he spent recovering from a wound after Cedar Mountain and was a popular member of Company K. Davis's wound was mortal and a friend wrote that when his commanding officer visited him after the fight it "was evident that his moments were few; he spoke calmly of his approaching end, and told his officer to write to his parents and tell them 'not to take it hard, for many had the same affliction to bear.'" So, the memoriam continued, "To the charge of a sister State we committed his body; may she guard well her treasures, for the Old North State has transferred many of her richest jewel to her keeping."[11]

At Reams' Station the Rebels also attacked an entrenched enemy successfully (though the works were not particularly formidable), infusing the Confederates with renewed confidence. Yankee works, which were continually moving around their right, were not impregnable after all. General Lee was particularly pleased with the results of Reams' Station and felt compelled to write to North Carolina Governor Zebulon Vance to praise the North Carolinians' conduct in the battle, which was largely fought by Tar Heel units and it was MacRae's North Carolina troops that turned the tide of battle. "I have frequently been called upon to mention the services of North Carolina soldiers in the army," Lee wrote, "but their gallantry and conduct were never more deserving of admiration than in the engagement at Reams' Station on the 25th instant." And, though many North Carolinians then and since thought Virginians were faint in their praise of Tar Heel soldiers, a Petersburg newspaper was effusive in its appreciation of North Carolina troops following Reams' Station:

> The soldiers of North Carolina have from the day of the first Manassas down to that of Reams,' fought with a valor that was never surpassed, and they have well entitled themselves to the admiration and gratitude of their country. In every battle in which they have engaged they have acquitted themselves nobly. There are no truer and more indomitable soldiers than they, as a score of bloody fields in this war gloriously attest. At Reams' they formed nearly the whole attacking force and again distinguished themselves as they always have done and will continue to do to the end of the war.[12]

Looking back, battles like Reams' Station were good for Southern morale in that they gave hope that Lee could thwart Grant's plans indefinitely and in so doing help ensure Lincoln's and the Republicans' defeat in November. Indeed, Grant and Lincoln were concerned about the very same thing. But looking at the situation from a purely military perspective, Reams' Station showed very clearly that Lee was reduced to buying time and hoping for the best in November. Hancock had been embarrassingly defeated and had lost a far larger number of men than the Rebels, but the Confederates lacked the manpower to make the defeat truly decisive. Worse, they did not have the power to counterattack while their opponent was reeling and destroy a major enemy force.

The Confederates around Petersburg lacked the numbers to do much more than react to Union advances and push them away, temporarily as it ultimately turned out. They could not strike back and force the Federals to abandon their positions and plans for stretching around the Confederate flanks. Within three weeks of Reams' Station, in fact, the Federals had control of the Weldon Railroad from Globe Tavern to below Reams' Station and were preparing to push west again towards the Boydton Plank Road and South Side Railroad.

Between September 29 and October 1, 1864, Grant continued to stretch Lee's defenses by working on both sides of the Richmond-Petersburg Line. South of Petersburg and west of the Weldon Railroad the Federals had dug in five miles from the Confederates' Boydton Plank Road Line; both sides' works ran in a southwesterly direction. Between the Federal and Confederate positions were two farms that became landmarks over the next few days. Halfway between the two forces lay the Pegram farm and to the north of that, about a mile from the Confederate works was the Jones farm. On September 30 Union units advanced and met the 18th and other Confederates around the Jones farm. Lane's North Carolinians helped to keep the Federals from gaining a foothold at the Jones farm but they were unable to throw the Yankees back to their original works in a counterattack the next day at the Pegram farm. The October 1 fight at the Pegram farm was marred by confusion and miscommunication; when the orders came for Lane's men to attack, the 18th North Carolina was the only regiment that actually did. Not surprisingly, the already-decimated regiment was easily driven back. The ultimate result of the Union offensive on the Confederate right was that the Federal line was successfully extended about three miles closer to the Boydton Plank Road and the South Side Railroad. Again, Union losses at Jones Farm were higher, about three times higher (3,000 to 1,310), but still the Northern lines advanced around Lee's right. One historian of the campaign has pointed out: "Altogether, Butler's and Meade's armies filled 48½ miles of earthworks fronting Richmond and Petersburg by mid–October."[13]

For the remainder of the fall 1864 and early winter of 1864/1865, the 18th North Carolina manned part of the Boydton Plank Road Line between Scale's and McGowan's brigades northwest of the Jones farm. That winter of 1864/1865 was a difficult time for the Confederacy generally and the 18th North Carolina specifically. The Confederate States of America had shrunk considerably by the end of 1864 and Lee could do little more than fend off Grant's assaults while Sherman marched to the sea and commenced his Carolinas Campaign. Lincoln's reelection meant that the North would not offer to negotiate an end to the war. Manpower shortages, always a problem for the Southern cause, were starkly reflected in the meager replacement numbers entering Lane's brigade. In 1862 the brigade replenished its ranks with over 1,400 new men but during the last months of 1864 a mere 442 men were added. The smallest regiment, the 18th North Carolina, got most of the new men: 147.

Many of the new men, and quite a few veterans, were not inclined to stay and see the war out, however. Despite a resolution adopted by the regiment in February to devote "our property, our lives, and our honor and our all, never to submit to Abolition tyranny nor Yankee rule," desertions climbed, peaking in February when Wilcox's division alone lost roughly 400 men to desertion. While descendents of Tar Heel soldiers prefer to repeat, and often do, the famous boast: "First at Bethel, Furthest at Gettysburg, Last at Appomattox," they generally prefer not to be reminded that the Old North State also posted very high desertion rates, especially at the end of the war. On more than one occasion Lee expressed concerns about the desertion rates among North Carolina soldiers. At one point during the Petersburg Campaign Lee wrote to the secretary of war: "The desertions are chiefly from North Carolina regiments, and especially those from the western part of that State." A New England soldier wrote home: "Almost all the deserters that we get now seem to be from the Old North State." But just as the boast is both true and misleading, the story of desertions among North Carolina soldiers is also true and more complicated than simple numbers.

When looking at numbers there is no doubt that North Carolina regiments were significantly more prone to desertion than regiments from other states. In some cases men deserted because they had never been dedicated to the cause in the first place. Of the 147 new recruits the 18th North Carolina received in late 1864, fifty-nine deserted. The regimental rosters clearly indicate that a lot of those who went over to the enemy to end their service were latecomers whose commitment to the cause was not as strong as their comrades.' Conversely, a look at the records shows that some of those who ultimately deserted were soldiers who had posted enviable and noble service records suggesting that not all deserters were shirkers or anti–Confederate. Bladen County native John W. Monroe, for example, volunteered in May 1861 at the age of twenty-eight. He was wounded and captured at Chancellorsville and paroled. Upon rejoining the regiment he was promoted twice before taking the oath of allegiance in February 1865. Alfred Bullard of Company D joined in May 1861, too, and served faithfully until shot in the shoulder, right breast, and right leg at the Wilderness. Despite such wounds he returned to duty in October and went over to the Yankees in January. Henry Barefoot of Company H also deserted and took the oath in February after having served since April 1861, during which time he was wounded at Hanover Court House and Gettysburg. Others who deserted had solid war records, which often included being wounded and earning promotions. Among the deserters were men like Anderson Guyton, George G. King, and Adam Shook of Company B; Lamar Bryan, Solon Lorenzo Gore, and Harman H. Hickman of Company C; William Townsend of Company D; Richard T. Brown of Company E; and William H. Sykes of Company K.[14]

Some deserted for the same reasons other Confederate soldiers deserted towards the end of the war; to many it seemed, especially after Lincoln's election, that the cause was lost. All that remained to be recorded in the history books was the date and time of death. One Tar Heel veteran noted: "I think that everybody can see that this war can't be carried on much longer, and it looks as if the soldiers are determined to end it some way for there is more or less running away every night and going to the Yankees steady." But North Carolina soldiers had the additional concern that their families were about to be visited by General Sherman. Sherman had cut a wide swath of destruction through Georgia, and it was even worse in South Carolina. If Sherman's army got increasingly destructive with each state he entered, North Carolina was in for a terrible amount of suffering. This concern was particularly acute for many of the men in the 18th North Carolina. Having been originally raised in the southeastern part of the state, the veterans from those counties knew that their homes and families would be threatened first. This was particularly true for the New Hanover men. Wilmington was a major and obvious target; with three regiments originating in the New Hanover/Wilmington area, it is not surprising that at least some of those soldiers felt their first obligation was to protect their families. One North Carolina soldier expressed that sentiment very well in a letter to his wife in the late winter of 1865:

> I have lived [as a] soldier long enough now not to dread its vicissitudes personally, but the thought of my family being cut off from me, and in the enemy's lines makes my heart heavy indeed. Your condition just now, my wife, rendering you so helpless to yourself whilst I have no command of my time is enough to destroy not only the wits, but the composure of a husband.

For some in the 18th North Carolina the thought of one of Sherman's bummers prowling around their house (and their wife) ultimately proved too great and, feeling they had done their service for the country, were off to take care of their most important priority.[15]

Conversely, many, especially among those who had been conscripted into the regiment late in the war, left because it was fairly easy to do and life in the trenches was difficult. For men whose commitment to the war effort was cool to begin with, the temptation to end their unpleasant experience was just too great. With short rations and abysmal living conditions, some decided that slipping over to the enemy during picket duty — the most common time soldiers deserted during the Petersburg Campaign — seemed like a good way to improve their lot. Another common time for Confederates to desert was during wood gathering details. The area around Petersburg was mostly under cultivation so the trees available to use for fuel were in short supply, and getting shorter the longer the armies remained in the area. Truces to gather wood offered an additional easy opportunity to put the experience of trench life in the past. The Yankees were well provisioned and General Grant dangled additional inducements to would-be deserters as a way to weaken Lee's army. Grant made it known that deserters who took the oath of allegiance would not have to serve in the Union forces where they may wind up fighting relatives or being captured and punished by the army they deserted. Confederate deserters would also be paid for all the arms and equipment they brought with them when they deserted.

The reasons for desertion were numerous and sometimes more complicated than at first glance. It is certainly true that many of those who deserted from the 18th North Carolina during the winter of 1864/1865 were shirkers or anti–Confederate to begin with. The late-arriving conscripts had no attachment to the unit and were probably treated with a certain amount of disdain by core members who viewed them as cowards who were content to let others do their fighting. Others, like those with solid service records, likely concluded that the cause was lost by February 1865 (they were not blind to certain objective realities) and determined not to die in vain. Then there was the direct threat Sherman posed. That danger, combined with the relative closeness of their homes, must have been a significant factor pulling men from the ranks in early 1865. Thus, it would be an over simplification to brand all who deserted the 18th North Carolina during the Petersburg Campaign as simple shirkers or cowards, though it did apply to at least some. The majority of those remaining with the company-sized unit that represented the 18th North Carolina at Appomattox were hard-bitten veterans who had served the regiment since 1861 or mid–1862.

During the winter and early spring of 1865 the 18th North Carolina manned a section of the Boydton Plank Road Line a few hundred yards north and west of the Jones farm. On the regiment's left was the 33rd North Carolina and the 37th North Carolina was on the regiment's right. As Grant stretched Lee's lines, the distance between men and units in the trenches had gotten increasingly wider. Generals Wilcox and Heth were responsible for defending an eight-mile stretch with barely 9,000 men or 1,150 men per mile. That meant that in many places instead of a solid wall of muskets defending a sector, there was a porous line with defenders as much as several yards away from each other. In late March the Eighteenth stretched itself even thinner as troops on the right moved farther west to deal with Grant's moves on Five Forks. The result was that the troop density along the Boydton Plank Road declined by nearly 25 percent from 1,150 men per mile to a skeletal 880 men per mile. One North Carolinian in the Boydton Plank Road works remembered that they "would have been impregnable if defended by any adequate force, but ... in fact were occupied by a mere skirmish line."[16]

This situation was about to spell disaster for the 18th North Carolina because as spring opened Grant determined that the time had come to return to attempts to break through the center of Lee's line in a more traditional frontal assault. Lee's lines were, he knew, stretched too thin to mass anywhere to defend against a determined attack. The Rebels were most likely thinnest along the Boydton Plank Road position above Burgess's Mill and that was where Grant decided to attack with force. The Tar Heels manning that thin line knew how vulnerable they were and understood that they were likely going to be the target of a massive Union attack very soon as April dawned. "All during the day of the 1st of April," one of the men there wrote, "there was a feeling of unrest and apprehension, not only among the individuals, but even the animals. I have no recollection of having spent a more thoroughly disagreeable day." A North Carolinian posted not far from Lane's brigade likely spoke for many when he wrote to his wife the night of April 1:

> You need not send my clothes, nor flour, nor anything else to me, my dearest, we will either be killed or captured or the road will be destroyed before this letter reaches you. Lee will have evacuated Richmond or be captured before April closes and perhaps before ten days. Our officers and men are all well, but very greatly discouraged, I have kept this letter back to see if the news would change, but it grows worse every day.... Be prepared for bad news from Lee's army. There is no reasonable prospect of good news.

That Tar Heel writer, along with every member of the 18th North Carolina, had good reason to be pessimistic. At that very moment, April 1, 1865, Union Major-General Horatio Wright was massing the Sixth Corps, three divisions, 14,000 men, for an attack the following day against a portion of the Boydton Plank Road Line manned by a mere 2,800 widely spaced Confederates. The unfortunate brigade directly in front of the Federal steam roller was Lane's, who at most had 1,100 men in the entire brigade.[17]

During the final hours of April 1 and first hour of April 2, Union and Confederate artillery put on a great final show before Petersburg. General Wilcox remembered "an almost incessant cannonade, solid shot and shell whizzing through the air and bursting in every direction, at times equal in brilliancy to a vivid meteoric display." The 2nd Rhode Island's commanding officer, Elisha Hunt Rhodes, wrote: "The noise was terrific, and the shriek of the shot and shell gave us an idea of what we might expect in the morning." Another Federal thought that the "whole night was hideous with screaming shells and bombs tracing networks of livid fire over the peaceful heavens [and was something] ever to be remembered by everyone who witnessed it." About 1:00 A.M. on April 2 the artillery quieted down but nobody in the 18th North Carolina slept. Those who were left were veterans who knew very well that all that activity and the buildup directly out in front of their works meant

18th North Carolina's battle flag captured at Petersburg, April 1865. North Carolina Museum of History.

that dawn promised a major assault on their works. Many spent the pre-dawn hours of April 2 reflecting on four long years of service to the Confederacy, a cause that had begun with high hopes and certainty of quick success that now lay in tatters. As they looked up and down the line and saw a mere handful of men where once there had been several hundred, they must have thought of the comrades they had joined up with who were now gone forever. No doubt they also prayed that they would come through the following day — probably be the regiment's last battle — alive so they could return home and rebuild their lives.[18]

Between four and four-thirty the morning of April 2, the Sixth Corps attacked and was an unstoppable wave. Lane's regiment-sized brigade was hit hard and squarely by Brigadier General George Washington Getty's division, which contained three brigades of New Englanders, New Yorkers, and Pennsylvanians. Union Colonel Thomas Hyde's brigade swarmed over the 18th North Carolina's right while Colonel James Warner's Pennsylvania brigade hit the regiment's left as it attacked the gap between it and the 33rd North Carolina. Given the huge numerical disparity between the Federals and Confederates along the Boydton Plank Road Line, the fight was an extremely unequal one. Not surprisingly Wright's Federals quickly had the upper hand and cut the defenses along the road permanently. The 18th North Carolina, along with Lane's other regiments, did what they could but in the face of the numbers brought against them those survivors who were not captured retreated quickly to Fort Gregg on their left. In that last fight the regiment lost its last men and battle flag.[19]

The breakthrough along the Boydton Plank Road Line south of Petersburg along with the Federal success further west at Five Forks sealed Petersburg's and Richmond's fates. The survivors of the 18th North Carolina, which now numbered less than 100 men and officers, retreated through Petersburg and made a dash with the rest of the Army of Northern Virginia southwestward in an attempt to get to North Carolina and join forces with General Joseph Johnston's Army of Tennessee. They would not get that opportunity, though, as Grant's infantry pursued the fleeing Confederates and Sheridan's troopers effectively cut off rail lines that could supply Lee's soldiers and permit them to escape into North Carolina. On April 9, 1865, Lee made the painful decision to surrender the remnants of the Army of Northern Virginia at Appomattox Court House. Given generous and honorable terms by General Grant, Lee told his men they had done well and were as fine a set of soldiers as ever existed and he was proud of them, but the time had come to lay down their arms and return to their homes. Eighty-seven men and officers, some with tears in their eyes, marched proudly to Appomattox Court House and stacked their arms, took the oath of allegiance to the United States, and began the long walk home to southeastern North Carolina.

Appendix A:
18th North Carolina Regiment Members Who Surrendered at Appomattox Court House, April 9, 1865*

Name	Rank	Co.	Name	Rank	Co.
Thomas J. Wooten	Major		A.E. Floyd	1st Sgt.	D
William H. McLaurin	Adjt.		J.P. Innman	Corpl.	D
Thomas B. Lane	Surgeon		A.N. Profit	Private	D
Simpson Russ	Asst. Surgeon		K. Lovett	Private	D
Charles Flanner	Ord. Sgt.		Zack Clewis	Private	D
Willie A. Cornish	Hospital Stewart		William M. Fetter	2nd Lt.	E
Henry M. Woodcock	Chief Musician		Thomas R. Colvin	Musician	E
Benjamin F. Rinaldi	Capt.	A	Stephen B. Costin	Private	E
Marshall M. Tatom	Sgt.	A	Henry Moore	Private	E
William Howard	Sgt.	A	Columbus Barnhill	Private	E
Henry Howard	Private	A	James B. Wall	Private	E
Frank Howard	Private	A	Little B. Wall	Private	E
B.D. Lindsay	Private	A	Alexander E. Smith	Sgt.	F
George W. McDonald	Private	A	John A. Patterson	Corpl.	F
Richard M. Sesene	2nd Lt.	B	W.W. Bullard	Private	F
Snowden Singletary	Corpl.	B	James A. Calder	Private	F
William C. Bray	Private	B	William C. Davis	Private	F
Elconia Austin	Private	B	A.A. Huckaby	Private	F
John Meares	Private	B	James Nolan	Private	F
Owen Smith	1st Lt.	C	M.G. McKay	Private	F
George W. Sherrell	Musician	C	N.Mc.N. Patterson	Private	F
Daniel Greene	Private	C	A.D. Webb	Private	F
D. Klutts	Private	C	John J. Poisson	Capt.	G

*Source: Lane Papers, Auburn University Special Collections and Archives

Name	Rank	Co.	Name	Rank	Co.
John M. Whitted	2nd. Lt.	G	S.W. Wells	Sgt.	I
James R. Dancy	Sgt.	G	J.H. Brown	Sgt.	I
John W. Gordon	Corpl.	G	J.J.F. Heath	Corpl.	I
Joseph J. Leslie	Musician	G	John Care	Private	I
Jesse F. Adams	Private	G	Daniel Brindle	Private	I
Pleasant Dixon	Private	G	L.H. Horn	Private	I
Robert H. Hall	Private	G	David S. Satta	Private	I
C.J. Sasser	Private	G	H.A. Hall	Private	I
Peter T. Smith	Private	G	R.B. Banks	Private	I
Alexander Lewis	2nd Lt.	H	Evander N. Robeson	1st Lt	K
Charles M. Baldwin	Sgt.	H	Saml. N. Richardson	Sgt.	K
Henry C. Long	Corpl.	H	Arch M. McNeill	Sgt.	K
John R. Baldwin	Private	H	Jas. A. Cromartie	Corpl.	K
John J. Chancey	Private	H	Danl. M. Sutton	Corpl.	K
John Creech	Private	H	Jesse F. Bloodworth	Private	K
Abram Minton	Private	H	Stephen T. Buie	Private	K
William Nance	Private	H	John C. Kinlaw	Private	K
John Safrit	Private	H	Wm. Melvin	Private	K
Francis M. Yeltow	Private	H	Jonathan Dunham	Private	K

Recapitulation
Officers — 11
Men — 73
Aggregate — 84

[/s/] Jno. J. Poisson
Capt. Comd 18th N.C.T.

Appendix B:
Biographical Sketches of 54 Men Who Served the Longest with the Regiment

(*Source:* Weymouth T. Jordan, *North Carolina Troops, 1861–1865: A Roster, Vol. VI*)

Jesse F. Adams: Joined the regiment as a replacement from Iredell County on September 6, 1862.

Charles M. Baldwin: Columbus County native who joined Co. H. at age 18 on April 23, 1861, was wounded sometime during the Seven Days, and was promoted to corporal in late 1862. At Chancellorsville he was wounded in the arm. In September 1863 he was promoted to sergeant. The records also show him wounded "accidentally" in the left wrist in late July 1864, which kept him out of service until January.

John R. Baldwin: Columbus County native who may or may not have been related to Charles M., though it seems highly likely. Like Charles, John R. joined on April 23, 1861, and was 24 at the time and listed his occupation as "farmer." He was wounded at Fredericksburg and captured at Gettysburg after which he was confined at Point Lookout, Maryland, until exchanged in early March 1864. Late that spring he returned to duty with the regiment.

Columbus Barnhill: Joined Company E at age 19 on June 18, 1861. He was wounded once in the leg at Second Manassas.

Jesse F. Bloodworth: Bloodworth was originally from New Hanover County and joined the Bladen Guards on April 26, 1861, at age 19. He was one of the few merchants in the regiment. He was promoted to sergeant in April 1862 and 1st sergeant in February 1864. He was wounded at Jones's Farm on September 30, 1864, and returned to duty in February.

Daniel Brindle: Brindle was 32 when he enlisted in Wake County and was assigned to the regiment on August 17, 1862. He was shot in the side and right arm at Chancellorsville.

James H. Brown: A New Hanover mechanic who joined the regiment at age 18 on July 12, 1861, and rose to the rank of sergeant in late 1863/early 1864. He was wounded once at the battle around Jones Farm on September 30, 1864.

Stephen T. Buie: Stephen was one of 3 Buies who served in the 18th North Carolina but was the only one to survive the war. Twenty-seven-year-old Stephen joined on May 20, 1861, and was captured near Hagerstown, Maryland, on the retreat from Gettysburg. He was confined at Point Lookout until exchanged in March 1864. He returned to duty in August. Mitchell Buie, several years younger than Stephen, joined in April 1861 and was wounded at Cedar Mountain and captured at Spotsylvania Court House; he died of "variola" at Elmira on January 23, 1865. Calvin Buie joined the same day as Stephen in 1861 but died of pneumonia at Danville, Virginia on August 14, 1862.

William Washington Bullard: Richmond County native who joined when he was 19 on June 1, 1861. He was wounded once during service at Spotsylvania Court House, returning to duty in either September or October 1864.

James A. Calder: Richmond County farmer who joined the regiment on June 1, 1861, at age 21. He was wounded at Ox Hill on September 1, 1862, and returned to duty at the beginning of 1863, serving with the regiment until Appomattox.

John J. Chancey: Volunteered from Columbus County on April 23, 1861, at age 26 and served with the regiment throughout the war.

Zack Clewis: A Robeson County farmer who joined Company D on May 18, 1861, at age 21. He was wounded at Hanover Court House and was out of service until January 1, 1863. His older brother Augustus also joined the 18th North Carolina in July 1861 and was captured at Spotsylvania Court House and held prisoner at the infamous Elmira prison camp in New York. Fortunately Augustus survived his imprisonment and took the oath of allegiance in June 1865.

Stephen Costin: One of four Costins from New Hanover who all volunteered for service on May 17, 1861, in Company E. Stephen was 24 when he volunteered and was present until Appomattox. John L. Costin, possibly a brother, volunteered the same day and the same place on the Black River and died of disease on November 28, 1861. Gaston Costin, who also volunteered and joined the same time and place as Stephen and John, was wounded at Gettysburg and the Wilderness and was promoted to sergeant in the fall of 1864. He was captured during the massive Sixth Corps assault on April 2, 1865. The youngest of the Costin group, 21-year-old Chancy, joined with the other three and was captured at Malvern Hill and exchanged in November 1862. He was severely wounded in the ankle at Chancellorsville and joined the Invalid Corps on September 17, 1864.

James A. Cromartie: Bladen native who joined at age 20 on March 4, 1862. He was wounded in the right side and taken prisoner at Hanover Court House. He was officially exchanged in November 1862 and returned to duty and was promoted to corporal at Fredericksburg.

James R. Dancey: He was one of four Dancey family members from Iredell County who joined the regiment on September 8, 1862, and was the only one to survive the war. James was promoted to corporal on February 1, 1864, and sergeant on September 1. J.H. Dancey died while at home on June 1, 1863, but the records do not indicate whether it was wounds or disease. John M. Dancey was captured at Spotsylvania Court House and confined at Point Lookout, Maryland, and then Elmira, New York, where he died on January 3, 1865, of "chronic diarrhoea." Twenty-two-year-old W. Dancey was captured at Falling Waters on the retreat from Gettysburg and died of typhoid fever in a Frederick, Maryland, hospital on August 24, 1863.

Jonathan Robeson Dunham: Enlisted at Fort Fisher at age 29 on October 10, 1861, and was captured at Hanover Court House and Gettysburg. He was paroled in September 1863 and returned to duty in March 1864.

Charles Flanner: Flanner was born in Craven County and enlisted as a 19-year-old student in Company G in New Hanover in August 1861. He was captured at Hanover Court House and held at Fort Columbus in New York Harbor until exchanged on August 5, 1862.

Augustus Evander Floyd: Floyd was a clerk in Robeson County when the war broke out and he volunteered for Company D on July 21, 1861, at the age of 20. He was promoted to 1st sergeant at some point before October 1862, but the records are not clear. He was wounded in the Pickett-Pettigrew Charge at Gettysburg, returning to duty in the late fall/early winter 1863/64.

Daniel Greene: Greene volunteered for service in his native Columbus County on August 12, 1861, at the age of 26. The Columbus farmer was captured at Hanover Court House and exchanged on August 5, 1862, and rejoined the regiment in early November. He was wounded in the abdomen and the left hip at Fredericksburg but returned to the 18th NC in March or April 1863. In late August 1863 he was absent without leave and listed as a deserter but like many he returned to duty in January 1864 and served for the rest of the war.

Henry A. Hall: A New Hanover native who joined Company I on July 1, 1861, at age 22.

Josiah J.F. Heath: Heath was born in Duplin County and joined up at age 19 on July 6, 1861. He was wounded at Frayser's Farm and captured at Spotsylvania Court House. He was confined at Point Lookout and Elmira before being exchanged on October 29, 1864. Heath returned to duty in early 1865 and was promoted to corporal on February 28.

Lewis Henderson Horne: Enlisted in Wake County on August 17, 1862, at age 26. He was captured at Spotsylvania Court House and confined at Point Lookout and Elmira before being exchanged in mid–November 1864. He returned to duty in early 1865.

William Howard: Howard was a Catawba replacement who was 23 when he was conscripted into service in mid–August 1862. While initially a reluctant warrior (he deserted in October 1862 and returned before the spring campaigning of 1863), he was wounded in the leg at Gettysburg and ultimately served the 18th North Carolina faithfully until Appomattox.

Alexander A. Huckabee: Richmond County native who was 26 when he volunteered on June 1, 1861. He was wounded in the head at Hanover Court House, returning to duty at the beginning of 1863. He was again hospitalized for a wound, this time to his left hand, received during the Wilderness. He returned to the regiment in late July/early August 1864 and remained with the unit until the end of the war.

James P. Inman: A Robeson County farmer, Inman volunteered at age 28 in Company D on August 14, 1861. He was promoted to corporal on December 13, 1862. He was wounded at Chancellorsville and returned to duty sometime between September 1863 and February 1864.

Davault Klutts: A Rowan County native, Klutts volunteered on September 6, 1862, for service in Company C and served the regiment through the war.

Alexander Lewis: Actually enlisted in South Carolina at Camp Stevens on January 1, 1862, at the age of 20. He was promoted to corporal on April 18, 1863, and captured at Chancellorsville. He was quickly exchanged and returned to duty by the middle of May 1863. He was promoted to sergeant in July 1863. At the Wilderness Lewis was shot in the right thigh and returned to duty sometime before the first of the year. In December 1864 he was elected 2nd lieutenant.

Bazel D. Lindsay: He was a Catawba replacement who joined the regiment on September 8, 1862, and was present or accounted for until the regiment surrendered at Appomattox.

Henry Clay Long: This Columbus County farmer joined the regiment on April 23, 1861, at age 23. He was captured at Gettysburg and confined at Fort Delaware and Point Lookout until he was paroled and ultimately exchanged in either September or October 1864 when he returned to the regiment. He was promoted to corporal in early 1865.

Kinchin Lovett: A South Carolinian who enlisted in Company D in Robeson County on May 18, 1861. He was shot in the left eye and captured at Hanover Court House.

Malcolm G. McKay: Joined on August 1, 1861, at age 23 and was captured at Spotsylvania Court House. He was confined at Point Lookout, Maryland, and Elmira, New York, before being exchanged (no reason given — exchanges had officially broken down by 1864) in mid–November 1864. He returned to duty in either January or February 1865.

William H. McLaurin: McLaurin was born in Richmond County and volunteered as a private in Company F as a 21-year-old student. Recognized for his abilities, he quickly rose in the regiment's ranks from private to corporal to 1st sergeant by the end of April 1862. In September 1862 he was promoted to 1st lieutenant and appointed as the regiment's adjutant. He was wounded at Chancellorsville on May 3.

Archibald M. McNeill: McNeill was born in Bladen County and joined the regiment on May 11, 1861, when he was 18 years old. He was promoted to sergeant at Fredericksburg.

John Mears: Bladen County farmer who volunteered on May 3, 1861, at the age of 22. Wounded and hospitalized in Richmond in June 1864 but records do not indicate where he was wounded or at which battle. He returned to duty that fall and remained with the regiment until it surrendered.

William S. Melvin: One of the older volunteers from Bladen County, William was 36 when he signed on with the Bladen Guards on April 26, 1861. He deserted in June 1862 but returned to duty at the beginning of 1863 and served with the regiment for the remainder of the war.

Abram Minton: Minton enlisted on September 7, 1862 (records don't provide home county), and had an uneven service record. He was missing after Fredericksburg and deserted during the Gettysburg campaign, returning sometime in late 1863 or early 1864. He remained with the regiment after that and was wounded twice, once in the hand at the Wilderness and then in the right shoulder sometime during the Petersburg Campaign.

Henry Moore: A New Hanover native who joined Company E when he was 18 on November 1, 1861. He was severely wounded in the leg at Hanover Court House but returned to duty in early 1863 and served with the regiment the rest of the war.

John A. Patterson: Bladen County native who joined in Richmond County at age 19 on June 1, 1861, and served the regiment until the end of the war, getting promoted to corporal along the way in November 1864.

John J. Poisson: New Hanover clerk who joined the Wilmington Light Infantry on April 15, 1861, at age 29. He entered the company as a sergeant and was elected 2nd lieutenant on June 21, 1861. In August 1862 he became 1st lieutenant and captain of Company G in the second half of November the same year. He was wounded, apparently severely, at Fredericksburg.

Alfred N. Proffitt: Enlisted in late August 1862 in Wilkes County and was shot in the forehead at the Wilderness. He returned to duty by August 1864, suggesting the head wound was superficial; he served the regiment faithfully until the end of the war.

Samuel N. Richardson: Originally from Anson County, he was a student in Bladen County when the war broke out. He joined the Bladen Guards at age 19 on May 10, 1861, and was promoted to commissary-sergeant on April 24, 1862.

Benjamin Franklin Rinaldi: A New York native from Steuben County, Rinaldi had moved to Bladen County to become a merchant. On April 26, 1861, he volunteered for service in Company K and was promoted from private to 1st sergeant on July 20, 1861. At the end of May 1862 he was appointed 1st lieutenant and transferred to Company A. He was wounded sometime during the Seven Days Battles and again in the arm at Ox Hill/Chantilly. On January 23, 1863, he was promoted to captain and led Company A for the rest of the war.

Evander N. Robeson: Joined the Bladen Guards at age 23 on April 26, 1861. He was promoted to sergeant at Sharpsburg and appointed 1st lieutenant on October 17, 1862.

John Safrit: Joined the 18th North Carolina on September 7, 1862, and had a terrifying day at Chancellorsville, being wounded in the face, neck, and hip.

Snowden Singletary: A Bladen County farmer who volunteered on May 3, 1861, at the age of 22. He was wounded in May or June 1864 (probably the Wilderness) and returned to duty that fall. He was promoted to corporal on February 1, 1865.

Alexander E. Smith: Joined the regiment when he turned 18 in July 1862 and was severely wounded at Chancellorsville, being hit in the right hip, leg, and arm. He returned to duty in late 1863/early 1864 and was promoted to sergeant in November 1864.

Owen Smith: At the tender age of 16, Smith, a Columbus County student, volunteered on April 24, 1861, for Company C and was mustered in as 1st sergeant of that company. He was wounded during the Seven Days and discharged when discovered he was underage. He returned and was appointed 2nd lieutenant of Company C in early September 1862. He was wounded in the right leg at Reams's Station and returned to duty at the end of 1864, having been promoted to 1st lieutenant in the meantime.

Daniel M. Sutton: Sutton joined the regiment as a 20-year-old farmer on May 1, 1861, and was wounded at the Wilderness. He returned to duty in December 1864.

Marshall Napoleon Tatom: A Bladen County farmer who joined at age 19 on June 15, 1861. He served throughout the war and was promoted to 1st sergeant in January 1863. Amazingly he was never recorded as being injured despite serving with the regiment the entire war.

James B. Wall: One of the western additions from Rutherford County who joined Company E in July 1862 and served the regiment for the rest of the war except for a brief period of convalescence while he recovered from being wounded in the hand at Chancellorsville.

Achilles D. Webb: An Iredell replacement who joined the 18th North Carolina on August 20, 1862. He was wounded in the left hand at the Wilderness and returned to duty in October/November. Like many, he deserted in February 1865 but he came back to the unit (no date supplied for that) and was paroled with the rest of the regiment at Appomattox.

Shadrick W. Wells: Joined Company I on July 1, 1861, at age 22 and was promoted to corporal on October 1, 1862, and then to sergeant the following month.

John McKay Whitted: Enlisted as a 21-year-old student in his native Bladen County on April 26, 1861. He originally volunteered for the Bladen Guards (Co. K) and mustered into the company as a corporal. The records are unclear as to why, but Whitted ran into some trouble in Co. K. and was reduced to the ranks on July 26, 1861. He transferred to Co. G. on April 26, 1862. He was captured at Hanover Court House and wounded in the leg at Second Manassas. While recovering from his leg wound he was promoted to corporal and returned to duty in time to participate in the Battle of Fredericksburg, where he was again wounded. While recovering he was promoted again, becoming sergeant. The apparently colorful character was again reduced to the ranks in April 1863 (records don't say why) but he was promoted to the officer corps on October 20, 1864, and became 2nd lieutenant, the rank he held for the remainder of the war.

Thomas J. Wooten: Columbus County native who volunteered in New Hanover County on May 22, 1861, at the age of 21. He listed himself as a student and entered North Carolina and Confederate service as a private. He was elected 1st Lieutenant on April 24, 1862, and was promoted to captain of Company K on October 17, 1862. Wooten was wounded at Chancellorsville on May 3 and promoted to major. Upon returning to duty around March 1, 1864, he took command of the regiment's sharpshooters, earning a reputation as "a terror to the enemy's picket lines."

Chapter Notes

Chapter 1

1. John G. Barrett, *The Civil War in North Carolina* (Chapel Hill: University of North Carolina Press, 1963), 4.
2. Marc W. Kruman, *Parties and Politics in North Carolina, 1836–1865* (Baton Rouge: Louisiana State University Press, 1983), 106–107, 180–181; Gavin Wright, *The Political Economy of the Cotton South* (New York: W.W. Norton, 1978), 128–157; William J. Cooper, Jr., and Thomas E. Terrill, *The American South: A History*, 3d ed. (Boston: McGraw-Hill, 2002), 44–45, 194–197, 254–262.
3. Charles B. Dew, *Apostles of Disunion: Southern Secession Commissioners and the Causes of the Civil War* (Charlottesville: University Press of Virginia, 2001), 10–21.
4. James M. McPherson, *Battle Cry of Freedom: The Civil War Era* (New York: Oxford University Press, 1988), 244–245; Dew, 14–15.
5. Kruman, 104–139.
6. *Ibid.*; Wadesboro *North Carolina Argus* (March 5, 1854), (September 16, 1854), (August 15, 1857); Fayetteville *Weekly Courier* (March 31, 1860).
7. *Fayetteville Observer* (July 25, 1859); *Asheville News* (November 10, 1859); George Fitzhugh, *Cannibals All! Or Slaves without Masters*, ed. C. Vann Woodward (Cambridge, MA: Harvard University Press, 1960); McPherson, 56–58; Cooper, Jr., and Terrill, 234–235; Kruman, 104–139.
8. Raleigh *North Carolina Standard* (April 23, 1859), (November 5, 1859); *Fayetteville Observer* (April 6, 1858); Greensboro *Patriot and Flag* (December 3, 1859); Charlotte *Western Democrat* (January 6, 1857), (January 13, 1857).
9. Charlotte *Western Democrat* (June 9, 1857).
10. Salisbury *Republican Banner* (November 29, 1859), (January 1, 1860), (February 14, 1860); Raleigh *North Carolina Standard* (October 22, 1859), (October 29, 1859); *Asheville News* (October 6, 1859), (November 10, 1859); Charlotte *North Carolina Whig* (November 1, 1859); *North Carolina Argus* (May 2, 1861); Charlotte *Western Democrat* (June 9, 1857), (January 18, 1859).
11. Wadesboro *North Carolina Argus* (January 26, 1856), (May 2, 1861); *North Carolina Presbyterian* (September 15, 1860); Salisbury *Carolina Watchman* (November 29, 1859); Raleigh *North Carolina Standard* (December 3, 1859); *Fayetteville Observer* (July 25, 1859); Charlotte *Daily Bulletin* (March 10, 1860); See also John B. Boles, *The South through Time*, Volume 1, 2d ed. (Upper Saddle River, NJ: Prentice Hall, 1999), 260–270; Cooper, Jr., and Terrill, 230–237.
12. *Fayetteville Observer* (July 5, 1858), (August 22, 1859); Greensboro *Patriot and Flag* (February 5, 1858); Salisbury *Western Democrat* (September 15, 1857); Charlotte *Daily Bulletin*

(May 17, 1859), (March 10, 1860); Wadesboro *North Carolina Argus* (September 16, 1854), (September 23, 1858).

13. Salisbury *Carolina Watchman* (January 4, 1859); Raleigh *North Carolina Standard* (August 27, 1859), (October 29, 1859); *Fayetteville Observer* (July 25, 1859), (August 22, 1859); *Asheville News* (November 1, 1860); Greensboro *Patriot and Flag* (November 11, 1859), (November 15, 1860); Charlotte *North Carolina Whig* (July 26, 1859), (November 1, 1859); Charlotte *Western Democrat* (January 11, 1859).

14. Salisbury *Republican Banner* (October 23, 1860); Raleigh *North Carolina Standard* (January 11, 1860).

15. Salisbury *Republican Banner* (June 22, 1855); Salisbury *Carolina Watchman* (November 15, 1859); Raleigh *North Carolina Standard* (April 30, 1859), (October 22, 1859), (October 29, 1859), (November 2, 1859), (January 7, 1860); *Raleigh Register* (January 26, 1856), (June 28, 1856); *Fayetteville Observer* (October 24, 1859); *Asheville News* (October 13, 1859), (July 4, 1860); Greensboro *Patriot and Flag* (November 18, 1859); Wadesboro *North Carolina Argus* (July 5, 1860); Kruman, 187–200.

Chapter 2

1. Joseph Carlyle Sitterson, *The Secession Movement in North Carolina* (Chapel Hill: University of North Carolina Press, 1939), 148–156; William C. Harris, *North Carolina and the Coming of the Civil War* (Raleigh: North Carolina Division of Archives and History, 1988), 26–34.

2. Fayetteville *Weekly Courier* (April 21, 1860); Charlotte *Western Democrat* (January 10, 1860); New Bern *Weekly Progress* (December 6, 1859), (January 6, 1860); Salisbury *Republican Banner* (November 29, 1859), (January 10, 1860), (February 14, 1860); Salisbury *Carolina Watchman* (November 15, 1859); Raleigh *North Carolina Standard* (October 22, 1859), (October 29, 1859), (November 2, 1859); *Fayetteville Observer* (October 24, 1859); *Asheville News* (October 13, 1859); Sitterson, 158–160.

3. Daniel W. Crofts, *Reluctant Confederates: Upper South Unionists in the Secession Crisis* (Chapel Hill: University of North Carolina Press, 1989), 125–126; Sitterson, 160–163.

4. *Wilmington Herald* (January 5, 1861); Charlotte *Daily Bulletin* (November 17, 1860); Sitterson, 174–179.

5. *Wilmington Herald* (November 7, 1860); Greensboro *Patriot and Flag* (November 18, 1860); Sitterson, 180–184.

6. *Fayetteville Observer* (January 7, 1860); Salisbury *Carolina Watchman* (December 4, 1860); New Bern *Weekly Progress* (January 8, 1860); Greensboro *Patriot and Flag* (November 8, 1860); Sitterson, 174–178.

7. *Wilmington Herald* (November 7, 1860); *Raleigh Register* (November 17, 1860), (December 1, 1860); New Bern *Weekly Progress* (November 6, 1860); *Fayetteville Observer* (February 11, 1861); Sitterson, 192–194.

8. *Wilmington Herald* (November 9, 1860); Crofts, 104–129.

9. Charlotte *North Carolina Whig* (November 27, 1860); *Fayetteville Observer* (January 7, 1861); New Bern *Weekly Progress* (January 8, 1861); Greensboro *Patriot and Flag* (November 18, 1860), (November 29, 1860), (January 3, 1861), (January 10, 1861); Crofts, 104–129; Sitterson, 148–180.

10. *North Carolina Presbyterian* (November 24, 1860); Wadesboro *North Carolina Argus* (March 21, 1861); *Fayetteville Observer* (January 7, 1861), (January 28, 1861), (February 11, 1861).

11. *North Carolina Presbyterian* (November 24, 1860), (April 26, 1861); *Wilmington Herald* (January 3, 1861); Raleigh *North Carolina Standard* (April 17, 1861), (April 24, 1861); *Fayetteville Observer* (February 11, 1861), (April 22, 1861); Greensboro *Patriot and Flag* (April 25, 1861); New Bern *Weekly Progress* (April 23, 1861); United States War Department, *The War of the Rebellion: A Compilation of the Official Records of the Union and Confederate Armies*, Series 1, Volume 1

(Washington, DC: Government Printing Office, 1880–1901), 486–487 (hereafter cited as *OR*); Sitterson, 239–249.

12. *OR*, Series 1, Volume 1, 481–486.

13. Weymouth T. Jordan, Jr., *North Carolina Troops, 1861–1865: A Roster*, Volume 6, *Infantry* (Raleigh: North Carolina Division of Archives and History, 1977), 308–412; Walter Clark, ed., *Histories of the Several Regiments and Battalions from North Carolina in the Great War, 1861–'65*, Volume 2, reprint ed. (Wendell, NC: Barefoot's Bookmark, 1982), 16–17.

14. John G. Barrett, *The Civil War in North Carolina* (Chapel Hill: University of North Carolina Press, 1963), 11–12; *OR*, Series 1, Volume 1, 474–478; William Kelsey McDaid, "'Four Years of Arduous Service': The History of the Branch-Lane Brigade in the Civil War" (Ph.D. diss., Michigan State University, 1987), 13–14.

15. Jordan, Jr., 295; McDaid, 14; Clark, 16–17.

16. McDaid, 14; Jordan, Jr., 295; Clark, 16–18.

17. Wooster Family Papers, Southern Historical Collection, University of North Carolina (hereafter cited as SHC); Jordan, Jr., 295.

18. Jordan, Jr., 295; McDaid, 14.

19. William James H. Bellamy Diary, Southern Historical Collection, University of North Carolina (hereafter cited as SHC); McDaid, 30–40.

20. Wooster Family Papers, SHC; McDaid, 30–40; Jordan, Jr., 401.

21. McDaid, 30–40; Jordan, Jr., 295; Bellamy Diary, SHC; Wooster Family Papers, SHC; Barrett, 26–27.

22. McDaid, 17–18, 54–56; Jordan, Jr., 295.

23. McDaid, 47–54; Jordan, Jr., 295, 305.

Chapter 3

1. James M. McPherson, *Battle Cry of Freedom: The Civil War Era* (New York: Oxford University Press, 1988), 423; James M. McPherson, *Tried by War: Abraham Lincoln as Commander in Chief* (New York: Penguin Books, 2008), 65–90; Stephen W. Sears, *To the Gates of Richmond: The Peninsula Campaign* (New York: Ticknor & Fields, 1992), 3–20.

2. McPherson, *Battle Cry of Freedom*, 423–425; Russell F. Weigley, *A Great Civil War: A Military and Political History, 1861–1865* (Bloomington: University of Indiana Press, 2000), 122–126; Jeffry D. Wert, *The Sword of Lincoln: The Army of the Potomac* (New York: Simon & Schuster, 2005), 52–74.

3. Wooster Family Papers, Southern Historical Collection, University of North Carolina (hereafter cited as SHC); Michael C. Hardy, *The Battle of Hanover Court House: Turning Point of the Peninsula Campaign, May 27, 1862* (Jefferson, NC: McFarland, 2006), 38–43.

4. Wooster Family Papers, SHC; William Kelsey McDaid, "'Four Years of Arduous Service': The History of the Branch-Lane Brigade in the Civil War" (Ph.D. diss., Michigan State University, 1987), 55–58.

5. Hardy, 49–51; Sears, 113–114; Wert, 65–72.

6. *Ibid.*

7. McDaid, 58–66; Hardy, 49–90; Sears, 113–117; Walter Clark, ed., *Histories of the Several Regiments and Battalions from North Carolina in the Great War, 1861–'65*, Volume 2, reprint ed. (Wendell, NC: Broadfoot's Bookmark, 1982), 22–24; William James H. Bellamy Diary, Southern Historical Collection, University of North Carolina; United States War Department, *The War of the Rebellion: A Compilation of the Official Records of the Union and Confederate Armies*, Series 1, Volume 11, Part 1 (Washington, DC: Government Printing Office, 1880–1901), 700–714, 740–743 (hereafter cited as *OR*).

8. Joseph T. Glatthaar, *General Lee's Army: From Victory to Collapse* (New York: Free Press, 2008), 123–135; James I. Robertson, Jr., *General A.P. Hill: The Story of a Confederate Warrior* (New York: Random House, 1987), 58; McDaid, 65–67.

9. Joseph L. Harsh, *Confederate Tide Rising: Robert E. Lee and the Making of Southern Strategy, 1861–1862* (Kent, OH: Kent State University Press, 1998), 31–47; McPherson, *Battle Cry of Freedom*, 462–465; Glatthaar, 123–135; Sears, 146–152; Clark, 22–24; McDaid, 67–68.

10. Brian K. Burton, *Extraordinary Circumstances: The Seven Days Battles* (Bloomington: Indiana University Press, 2001), 1–26; Sears, 146–178; McPherson, *Battle Cry of Freedom*, 461–463; Harsh, 47–53.

11. McDaid, 68–69.

12. Robertson, Jr., 68; Burton, 27–38; Hardy, 53–64.

13. *OR*, Series 1, Volume 11, Part 2, 498, 834–835, 881–882; Burton, 58–60; Sears, 193–199; Robertson, Jr., 69–71.

14. Burton, 59–61.

15. Angus Konstam, *Seven Days Battles, 1862: Lee's Defense of Richmond* (Westport, CT: Praeger Publishers, 2004), 28–39; Clark, 24–25; McDaid, 68–73; Glatthaar, 135–137; Robertson, Jr., 68–77; Burton, 69–75; Sears, 200–209; Hardy, 53–64.

16. Sears, 210–213; Burton, 75–80; McDaid, 69–73.

17. Sears, 210–216.

18. *OR*, Series 1, Volume 11, Part 2, 883, 890–891; Clark, 25–27; Sears, 222–226, 249; Burton, 82–99; McDaid, 74–77; Konstam, 40–45; Weigley, 129–132.

19. Sears, 249–254; Robertson, Jr., 78–86; Clark, 25–27; McDaid, 76–77; Weigley, 129–132; *OR*, Series 1, Volume 11, Part 2, 890–891.

20. *OR*, Series 1, Volume 11, Part 2, 883–884, 891; Clark, 26–27; McDaid, 78–79.

21. *OR*, Series 1, Volume 11, Part 2, 883, 891; McDaid, 78–79; Clark, 27; Sears, 293–307; Konstam, 64–68; Glatthaar, 135–150; Robertson, Jr., 78–98; McPherson, *Battle Cry of Freedom*, 462–471; Hardy, 68–79; Gary W. Gallagher, ed., *Fighting for the Confederacy: The Personal Recollections of General Edward Porter Alexander* (Chapel Hill: University of North Carolina Press, 1989), 109–110.

22. *OR*, Series 1, Volume 2, Part 2, 891–892; Weymouth T. Jordan, Jr., *North Carolina Troops, 1861–1865: A Roster*, Volume 6, *Infantry* (Raleigh: North Carolina Division of Archives and History, 1977), 331–332, 345, 415; Clark, 27.

23. *OR*, Series 1, Volume 11, Part 2, 892; McDaid, 81–83.

24. McDaid, 81–83; *OR*, Series 1, Volume 11, Part 2, 884–885.

Chapter 4

1. Walter Clark, ed., *Histories of the Several Regiments and Battalions from North Carolina in the Great War, 1861–'65*, Volume 2 (Goldsboro, NC: Nash Brothers, Book & Job Printers, n.d.), 28.

2. John J. Hennessy, *Return to Bull Run: The Campaign and Battle of Second Manassas* (New York: Simon & Schuster, 1993), 22–23; Robert K. Krick, *Stonewall Jackson at Cedar Mountain* (Chapel Hill: University of North Carolina Press, 1990), 4–7.

3. United States War Department, *The War of the Rebellion: A Compilation of the Official Records of the Union and Confederate Armies*, Series 1, Volume 12, Part 3 (Washington, DC: Government Printing Office, 1885), 473–474 (hereafter cited as *OR*); James M. McPherson, *Battle Cry of Freedom: The Civil War Era* (New York: Oxford University Press, 1988), 501, 525.

4. James I. Robertson, Jr., *Stonewall Jackson: The Man, the Soldier, the Legend* (New York: Macmillan Publishing, 1997), 520–521; Joseph T. Glatthaar, *General Lee's Army: From Victory to Collapse* (New York: Free Press, 2008), 157; McPherson, 501.

5. Joseph L. Harsh, *Confederate Tide Rising: Robert E. Lee and the Making of Southern Strategy, 1861–1862* (Kent, OH: Kent State University Press, 1998), 106–109; Gary W. Gallagher, ed., *Fighting for the Confederacy: The Personal Recollections of General Edward Porter Alexander* (Chapel Hill: University of North Carolina Press, 1989), 122–123; Robertson, Jr., *Stonewall Jackson*, 514–515.

6. *OR*, Series 1, Volume 12, Part 3, 918–919; Robertson, Jr., *Stonewall Jackson*, 513–519; Frank E. Vandiver, *Mighty Stonewall* (Westport, CT: Greenwood Press, 1957), 325–336.
7. Harsh, 112–114; McPherson, 524–526.
8. William Kelsey McDaid, "'Four Years of Arduous Service': The History of the Branch-Lane Brigade in the Civil War" (Ph.D. diss., Michigan State University, 1987), 89–92.
9. James I. Robertson, Jr., *General A.P. Hill: The Story of a Confederate Warrior* (New York: Random House, 1987), 94–98; Martin Schenck, *Up Came Hill: The Story of the Light Division and Its Leaders* (Harrisburg, PA: Stackpole, 1958), 134–135; Robert K. Krick, *Stonewall Jackson at Cedar Mountain* (Chapel Hill: University of North Carolina Press, 1990), 5–7; Harsh, 113–114.
10. McDaid, 89–92; Robertson, Jr., *Stonewall Jackson*, 513–520; Krick, 5–10.
11. Krick, 15–16; Robertson, Jr., *Stonewall Jackson*, 513–525; McDaid, 89–92.
12. Krick, 17–18, 43, 63; Clark, 28–29; Robertson, Jr., *Stonewall Jackson*, 523.
13. Robertson, Jr., *Stonewall Jackson*, 523–524; Robertson, Jr., *General A.P. Hill*, 100–102; Krick, 21–38; *OR*, Series 1, Volume 12, Part 2, 215–216; Clark, 28–29; Schenck, 137–139.
14. Krick, 39–42; Robertson, Jr., *Stonewall Jackson*, 525; *OR*, Series 1, Volume 12, Part 2, 221–224.
15. *OR*, Series 1, Volume 12, Part 2, 180–181, 221–224; Robertson, Jr., *Stonewall Jackson*, 525–526.
16. Krick, 43–45.
17. Krick, 46–53.
18. Krick, 53–74.
19. Krick, 74–84, 104–116.
20. Krick, 104–116.
21. Krick, 202–204.
22. *OR*, Series 1, Volume 12, Part 2, 181–184, 215–216; Krick, 202–204, 211–218.
23. Krick, 220–231.
24. *OR*, Series 1, Volume 12, Part 2, 181–184, 215–216, 220; Krick, 232–237; Shenck, 154; Robertson, Jr., *General A.P. Hill*, 107.
25. McDaid, 92–96; Krick, 264–266; Clark, 28–29; Robertson, Jr., *Stonewall Jackson*, 532–533; Schenck, 155–156.
26. Clark, 28–29.
27. Krick, 211–218; *OR*, Series 1, Volume 12, Part 2, 221–224; Robertson, Jr., *Stonewall Jackson*, 532–535.

Chapter 5

1. John J. Hennessy, *Return to Bull Run: The Campaign and Battle of Second Manassas* (New York: Simon & Schuster, 1993), 21–29.
2. Hennessy, 29–31; James M. McPherson, *Battle Cry of Freedom: The Civil War Era* (New York: Oxford University Press, 1988), 525, 526–527; Joseph T. Glatthaar, *General Lee's Army: From Victory to Collapse* (New York: Free Press, 2008), 150–160; Russell F. Weigley, *A Great Civil War: A Military and Political History, 1861–1865* (Bloomington: University of Indiana Press, 2000), 137–138.
3. Hennessy, 31–33.
4. Hennessy, 40–54, quote p. 54.
5. Hennessy, 55–57; James I. Robertson, Jr., *General A.P. Hill: The Story of a Confederate Warrior* (New York: Random House, 1987), 109–110.
6. William Kelsey McDaid, "'Four Years of Arduous Service': The History of the Branch-Lane Brigade in the Civil War" (Ph.D. diss., Michigan State University, 1987), 96–97; Hennessy, 57; United States War Department, *The War of the Rebellion: A Compilation of the Official Records of the Union and Confederate Armies*, Series 1, Volume 12, Part 2 (Washington, DC: Government Printing Office, 1880–1901), 669–670, 675 (hereafter cited as *OR*).

7. Hennessy, 58.
8. Hennessy, 57–60; McDaid, 96–97.
9. Hennessy, 85–95; Glatthaar, 150–160.
10. Hennessy, 85–95; McDaid, 97–99.
11. Hennessy, 95–100.
12. Hennessy, 96–107.
13. Thomas Purdie letter in the Thomas David Smith McDowell Papers, Southern Historical Collection, University of North Carolina (hereafter cited as SHC); McDaid, 98–109; Hennessy, 96–115; Robertson, Jr., 110–113.
14. Hennessy, 113–115.
15. *OR*, Series 1, Volume 12, Part 2, 675; Hennessy, 116–137.
16. Michael C. Hardy, *The Thirty-seventh North Carolina Troops: Tar Heels in the Army of Northern Virginia* (Jefferson, NC: McFarland, 2003), 88; Hennessy, 135–137; McDaid, 99–102.
17. Hennessy, 138–154; McDaid, 101–102; Hardy, 135–140.
18. Hennessy, 177–200; McPherson, 527–529.
19. *OR*, Series 1, Volume 12, Part 2, 660–671, 675; Hennessy, 195–223; McDaid, 101–103.
20. Robertson, Jr., 121–126; McDaid, 102–109; Hardy, 87–91; John Keegan, *The American Civil War: A Military History* (New York: Alfred A. Knopf, 2009), 157–165; *OR*, Series 1, Volume 12, Part 2, 669–672; Walter Clark, ed., *Histories of the Several Regiments and Battalions from North Carolina in the Great War, 1861–'65*, Volume 2, reprint ed. (Wendell, NC: Broadfoot's Bookmark, 1982), 29–30; Hennessy, 270–282.
21. Hennessy, *Historical Report on the Troop Movements for the Second Battle of Manassas, August 28 through August 30, 1862* (National Park Service, 1985), 254, 292.
22. David Welker, *Tempest at Ox Hill: The Battle of Chantilly* (Cambridge, MA: Da Capo Press, 2002), 50–120; Jeffry D. Wert, *The Sword of Lincoln: The Army of the Potomac* (New York: Simon & Schuster, 2005), 135–137; Hennessy, *Return to Bull Run*, 439–443; Robertson, Jr., 126–127; McDaid, 109–110; Hardy, 89–92.
23. Welker, 123–136.
24. Welker, 137–155; McDaid, 109–111.
25. *OR*, Series 1, Volume 12, Part 2, 672, 677; McDaid, 109–111; Welker, 160–164.
26. Welker, 160–175; McDaid, 109–112; *OR*, Series 1, Volume 12, Part 2, 677; Hardy, 92–94; Robertson, Jr., 126–128.
27. McDaid, 109–112; Clark, 29–30; *OR*, Series 1, Volume 12, Part 2, 669–672, 677; Robertson, Jr., 126–130.

Chapter 6

1. Stephen W. Sears, *Landscape Turned Red: The Battle of Antietam* (New York: Ticknor & Fields, 1983), 59–69; James M. McPherson, *Antietam: The Battle that Changed the Course of the Civil War* (New York: Oxford University Press, 2002), 77–95; Joseph T. Glatthaar, *General Lee's Army: From Victory to Collapse* (New York: Free Press, 2008), 155–173; David J. Eicher, *The Longest Night: A Military History of the Civil War* (New York: Simon & Schuster, 2001), 336–337; United States War Department, *The War of the Rebellion: A Compilation of the Official Records of the Union and Confederate Armies*, Series 1, Volume 19, Part 1 (Washington, DC: Government Printing Office, 1880–1901), 144–153 (hereafter cited as *OR*).
2. William Kelsey McDaid, "'Four Years of Arduous Service': The History of the Branch-Lane Brigade in the Civil War" (Ph.D. diss., Michigan State University, 1987), 115; Sears, 63.
3. McDaid, 115–119.
4. Sears, 65–71, 85–86; James M. McPherson, *Battle Cry of Freedom: The Civil War Era* (New York: Oxford University Press, 1988), 534–535; Glatthaar, 164–165; James I. Robertson, Jr., *General A.P. Hill: The Story of a Confederate Warrior* (New York: Random House, 1987), 133–134.

Notes. Chapter 7

5. Sears, 70–73; Glatthaar, 167; McDaid, 113–120; Walter Clark, ed., *Histories of the Several Regiments and Battalions from North Carolina in the Great War, 1861–'65*, Volume 2, reprint ed. (Wendell, NC: Broadfoot's Bookmark, 1982), 30–31; OR, Series 1, Volume 19, Part 1, 144–150, 951–952, 979; Robertson, Jr., 133–134.

6. Weymouth T. Jordan, Jr., *North Carolina Troops, 1861–1865: A Roster*, Volume 6, *Infantry* (Raleigh: North Carolina Division of Archives and History, 1977), 295–423.

7. OR, Series 1, Volume 19, Part 1, 144–153; 951–952; Ethan S. Rafuse, *Antietam, South Mountain, and Harper's Ferry: A Battlefield Guide* (Lincoln: University of Nebraska Press, 2008) 3–7; Sears, 85–90; McPherson, *Antietam*, 106–107; Robertson, Jr., 133–135.

8. OR, Series 1, Volume 19, Part 1, 951–954, 979–980; McDaid, 115–119; Sears, 94–99; McPherson, *Antietam*, 106.

9. OR, Series 1, Volume 19, Part 1, 144–150; 951–954, 979–981; Hardy, 95–100.

10. OR, Series 1, Volume 19, Part 1, 144–149, 951–954, 979–980; Rafuse, 224; Sears, 91–110, 121–123.

11. Sears, 121–123, 143–154; McDaid, 115–120; Clark, Volume 2, 31–32; OR, Series 1, Volume 19, Part 1, 144–150, 954, 980; Robertson, Jr., 136–138.

12. Sears, 113–121; Rafuse, 6–7; McPherson, *Antietam*, 106–108; Wert, 148–151; Russell F. Weigley, *A Great Civil War: A Military and Political History, 1861–1865* (Bloomington: Indiana University Press, 2000), 144–150.

13. Sears, 156–170; Glatthaar, 165–168.

14. Sears, 156–179; Weigley, 144–151; Glatthaar, 165–169; Wert, 151–154.

15. Sears, 156–179, 196–197, 257; Robertson, Jr., 141–143; Clark, 31–33; McDaid, 115–125; Hardy, 95–100.

16. McDaid, 115–129; Sears, 255–268, 276–290; McPherson, *Antietam*, 124–128; Rafuse, 89–115; Robertson, Jr., 143–151; Norman Stevens, *Antietam, 1862: The Civil War's Bloodiest Day* (Westport, CT: Praeger Publishers, 2004), 72–84; OR, Series 1, Volume 19, Part 1, 150, 981; Series 1, Volume 19, Part 2, 684, 689, 699; Hardy, 92–105.

17. McDaid, 115–129; Clark, 32–34; Robertson, Jr., 148–150; OR, Series 1, Volume 19, Part 1, 35, 204, 345–349, 363–366, 955–957, 975, 981–982, 985–989, 992, 995–999.

18. OR, Series 1, Volume 19, Part 1, 986; Robertson, Jr., 149–151; McDaid, 120–130.

Chapter 7

1. Thomas David Smith McDowell Papers, Southern Historical Collection, University of North Carolina (hereafter cited as SHC); Francis Augustin O'Reilly, *The Fredericksburg Campaign: Winter War on the Rappahannock* (Baton Rouge: Louisiana State University Press, 2003), 9–10; James I. Robertson, Jr., *General A.P. Hill: The Story of a Confederate Warrior* (New York: Random House, 1987), 155.

2. United States War Department, *The War of the Rebellion: A Compilation of the Official Records of the Union and Confederate Armies*, Series 1, Volume 21 (Washington, DC: Government Printing Office, 1880–1901), 1057 (hereafter cited as OR); William Kelsey McDaid, "'Four Years of Arduous Service': The History of the Branch-Lane Brigade in the Civil War" (Ph.D. diss., Michigan State University, 1987), 131–135.

3. William Rufus Barlow Letters, Eleanor Brockenbrough Library, Museum of the Confederacy, Richmond, Virginia (hereafter cited as MOC); Weymouth T. Jordan, Jr., *North Carolina Troops, 1861–1865: A Roster*, Volume 6, *Infantry* (Raleigh: North Carolina Division of Archives and History, 1977), 295–423.

4. William Rufus Barlow Letters, MOC; Jordan, Jr., 295–423; McDaid, 131–148; OR, Series 1, Volume 19, Part 2, 621, 639, 660, 674, 713; Volume 21, 1057; James M. McPherson, *Battle Cry of Freedom: The Civil War Era* (New York: Oxford University Press, 1988), 485–488; Joseph T. Glatthaar, *General Lee's Army: From Victory to Collapse* (New York: Free Press, 2008), 68–73.

5. Robertson, Jr., 154–155; O'Reilly, 10; *OR*, Series 1, Volume 19, Part 2, 684, 689, 699; Thomas David Smith McDowell Papers, SHC; Jordan, Jr., 305–306.
6. Robertson, Jr., 156; Jordan, Jr., 299; William Rufus Barlow Letters, MOC.
7. O'Reilley, 1–2, 13–20; Jeffry D. Wert, *The Sword of Lincoln: The Army of the Potomac* (New York: Simon & Schuster, 2005), 174–183; McPherson, 568–571.
8. Wert, 174–185.
9. O'Reilley, 19–23; McPherson, 569–570.
10. O'Reilly, 11–37; Robertson, Jr., 156–158; McDaid, 149–168.
11. James I. Robertson, Jr., *Stonewall Jackson: The Man, the Soldier, the Legend* (New York: Prentice Hall, 1997), 643–645; Robertson, Jr., *General A.P. Hill*, 155–158; O'Reilly, 40.
12. O'Reilly, 39–41.
13. Robertson, Jr., *General A.P. Hill*, 158–159; O'Reilly, 38–42; McDaid, 149–168; William Rufus Barlow Letters, MOC.
14. Robertson, Jr., *General A.P. Hill*, 159–164; O'Reilly, 128–130; McDaid, 149–168.
15. McPherson, 570–571; O'Reilly, 57–101; William Rufus Barlow Letters, MOC; McDaid, 149–168.
16. O'Reilly, 198–212, 238–243; Robertson, Jr., *General A.P. Hill*, 160–166; McDaid, 149–168; *OR*, Series 1, Volume 21, 547–556, 560, 630–635, 645–649, 653–656; William Rufus Barlow Letters, MOC.

Chapter 8

1. Stephen W. Sears, *Chancellorsville* (Boston: Houghton Mifflin, 1996), 1–25; Ernest B. Furgurson, *Chancellorsville, 1863: The Souls of the Brave* (New York: Alfred A. Knopf, 1992), 29–35; Daniel E. Sutherland, *Fredericksburg and Chancellorsville: The Dar Mark Campaign* (Lincoln: University of Nebraska Press, 1998), 91–108.
2. Sutherland, 111; Sears, 38; Furgurson, 38.
3. Thomas David Smith McDowell Papers, Southern Historical Collection, University of North Carolina (hereafter cited as SHC); James I. Robertson, Jr., *General A.P. Hill: The Story of a Confederate Warrior* (New York: Random House, 1987), 169–170, 175–176; Sears, 38–41.
4. Furgurson, 36–38; Sears, 95, 108–110, 118; Sutherland, 27.
5. William Kelsey McDaid, "'Four Years of Arduous Service': The History of the Branch-Lane Brigade in the Civil War" (Ph.D. diss., Michigan State University, 1987), 166–167.
6. Thomas David Smith McDowell Papers, SHC; Weymouth T. Jordan, Jr., *North Carolina Troops, 1861–1865: A Roster*, Volume 6, *Infantry* (Raleigh: North Carolina Division of Archives and History, 1977), 306.
7. Sears, 54–82, 100–102, 114–120.
8. Sears, 114–135; Sutherland, 125–140; Furgurson, 60–68, 87–100.
9. Sears, 136–171; Sutherland, 125–140.
10. Sutherland, 120.
11. James I. Robertson, Jr., *Stonewall Jackson: The Man, the Soldier, the Legend* (New York: Macmillan Publishing, 1997), 704–707; Sears, 190–224; Sutherland, 120, 125–140.
12. Robertson, Jr., *Stonewall Jackson*, 717.
13. Sears, 225–247; Sutherland, 125–140; Furgurson, 144–171; McDaid, 169–172; Robertson, Jr., *Stonewall Jackson*, 709–712; William K. Goolrick, *Rebels Resurgent: Fredericksburg to Chancellorsville* (Alexandria, VA: Time-Life Books, 1985), 118–154.
14. Sears, 247–272; Robertson, Jr., *Stonewall Jackson*, 716–724.
15. Robertson, Jr., *Stonewall Jackson*, 720–722; Robertson, Jr., *General A.P. Hill*, 182–184; Sears, 270–285; McDaid, 169–173.
16. Robertson, Jr., *Stonewall Jackson*, 720–723; Robertson, Jr., *General A.P. Hill*, 183–185.
17. Walter Clark, ed., *Histories of the Several Regiments and Battalions from North Carolina in the Great War, 1861–'65*, Volume 5 (Goldsboro, NC: Nash Brothers, Book & Job Printers, n.d.), 93–94; Sears, 273–290; Robertson, Jr., *Stonewall Jackson*, 724–725.

18. Sears, 292; Sutherland, 141–159; McDaid, 172–174.
19. Robert K. Krick, "The Smoothbore Volley that Doomed the Confederacy," in *Chancellorsville: The Battle and Its Aftermath*, ed. Gary W. Gallagher (Chapel Hill: University of North Carolina Press, 1996), 107–142.
20. Clark, Volume 2, 36–40, Volume 5, 95–96, 98–99.
21. Clark, Volume 2, 36–40, Volume 5, 93–96; Krick, 125–126; McDaid, 175–185.
22. Clark, Volume 4, 467, Volume 5, 93–99; McDaid, 175–185; Sears, 282–299; Krick, 107–134; Sutherland, 141–159; Furgurson, 196–216; Goolrick, 144–154; Robertson, Jr., *Stonewall Jackson*, 728–736; Robertson, Jr., *General A.P. Hill*, 185–187; *OR*, Series 1, Volume 25, Part 1, 915–918.
23. *OR*, Series 1, Volume 25, Part 1, 889–892, 915–920.
24. McDaid, 169–198; Sears, 308–328; Furgurson, 220–239; Sutherland, 160–170; Goolrick, 144–154; *OR*, Series 1, Volume 25, Part 1, 478, 885–886, 893, 915–917, 919–920, 923–924; Jordan, Jr., 344, 352, 359.
25. *OR*, Series 1, Volume 25, Part 1, 915–918.
26. *OR*, Series 1, Volume 25, Part 1, 805, 918–920; Clark, Volume 4, 467.
27. *North Carolina Presbyterian* (May 30, 1863).
28. Thomas David Smith McDowell Papers, SHC.

Chapter 9

1. Jeffry D. Wert, *The Sword of Lincoln: The Army of the Potomac* (New York: Simon & Schuster, 2005), 253–254.
2. Stephen W. Sears, *Gettysburg* (Boston: Houghton Mifflin, 2003), 18–42; James M. McPherson, *Battle Cry of Freedom: The Civil War Era* (New York: Oxford University Press, 1988), 644–652; Wert, 252–258, 266–269.
3. James I. Robertson, Jr., *General A.P. Hill: The Story of a Confederate Warrior* (New York: Random House, 1987), 196–198; Sears, 40–45.
4. Weymouth T. Jordan, Jr., *North Carolina Troops, 1861–1865, A Roster*. Volume 6, *Infantry* (Raleigh: North Carolina Division of Archives and History, 1977), 306, 322, 400.
5. Sears, 43–58.
6. Sears, 58.
7. McPherson, 649–650; Sears, 1–17.
8. *Ibid.*
9. William Kelsey McDaid, "'Four Years of Arduous Service': The History of the Branch-Lane Brigade in the Civil War" (Ph.D. diss., Michigan State University, 1987), 140–142; Sears, 43–84; Robertson, Jr., 195–203; McPherson, 648–649.
10. McDaid, 140–145; Joseph T. Glatthaar, *General Lee's Army: From Victory to Collapse* (New York: Free Press, 2008), 270–272; McPherson, 649–650; Sears, 82, 110–112, 118.
11. Sears, 117–138; McDaid, 140–148.
12. Harry W. Pfanz, *Gettysburg: The First Day* (Chapel Hill: University of North Carolina Press, 2001), 25–29; Sears, 136–158; Robertson, Jr., 195–210; McPherson, 651–660.
13. David G. Martin, *Gettysburg, July 1* (Conshohocken, PA: Combined Publishing, 1996), 402–403.
14. Martin, 424–425; Sears, 220–225.
15. Bradley M. Gottfried, *Brigades of Gettysburg: The Union and Confederate Brigades at the Battle of Gettysburg* (Cambridge, MA: Da Capo Press, 2002), 641–656; John Keegan, *The American Civil War: A Military History* (New York: Alfred A. Knopf, 2009), 185–203; McDaid, 140–150; Sears, 183–225; Martin, 342–371, 394–429; Pfanz, 91–119, 269–304; Robertson, Jr., 195–215; Glatthaar, 268–288; McPherson, 646–665.
16. Sears, 232–236.
17. Harry P. Pfanz, *Gettysburg: The Second Day* (Chapel Hill: University of North Caro-

lina Press, 1987), 104–123, 390–424; Sears, 264–324; McDaid, 140–155; McPherson, 655–665; Robertson, Jr., 216–220; Gottfried, 646–650.

18. Sears, 341–351, 357–358.
19. Sears, 358–359, 417–419.
20. Sears, 372–383, 396–408; Robertson, Jr., 222–223.
21. Sears, 359–376.
22. Sears, 409–435; McDaid, 150–160; *OR*, Series 1, Volume 27, Part 2, 664–668; Gottfried, 646–650; McPherson, 660–665; Keegan, 190–203; Glatthaar, 280–288.
23. *OR*, Series 1, Volume 27, Part 2, 667–668; Sears, 434.
24. Walter Clark, ed., *Histories of the Several Regiments and Battalions from North Carolina in the Great War, 1861–'65*, Volumes 2 and 4 (Goldsboro, NC: Nash Brothers, Book & Job Printers, n.d.), Volume 2, 42–44; Volume 4, 468.
25. McDaid, 227–230; Robertson, Jr., 230–231.
26. Jordan, Jr., 311–312; Glatthaar, 404–420.
27. McDaid, 246–251; Michael C. Hardy, *The Thirty-seventh North Carolina Troops: Tar Heels in the Army of Northern Virginia* (Jefferson, NC: McFarland, 2003), 165–169.
28. Glatthaar, 419–420.
29. William Rufus Barlow Letters, Eleanor Brockenbrough Library, Museum of the Confederacy, Richmond, Virginia; McDaid, 227–238; Jordan, Jr., 316, 338; Glatthaar, 408–420.
30. McDaid, 238–245; Robertson, Jr., 240–244; Hardy, 170–174; *Fayetteville Observer* (January 25, 1864).
31. McDaid, 245–246; Clark, Volume 2, 46.
32. J. Tracy Power, *Lee's Miserables: Life in the Army of Northern Virginia from the Wilderness to Appomattox* (Chapel Hill: University of North Carolina Press, 1998), 7–8; Gordon C. Rhea, *The Battle of the Wilderness: May 5–6, 1864* (Baton Rouge: Louisiana State University Press, 1994); McDaid, 246–251; Glatthaar, 355–356.
33. *Fayetteville Observer* (January 11, 1864), (February 1, 1864).
34. *Fayetteville Observer* (January 4, 1864), (January 11, 1864), (February 15, 1864), (February 18, 1864).
35. *Fayetteville Observer* (February 22, 1864).

Chapter 10

1. Jeffry D. Wert, *The Sword of Lincoln: The Army of the Potomac* (New York: Simon & Schuster, 2005), 320–322; James I. Robertson, Jr., *General A.P. Hill: The Story of a Confederate Warrior* (New York: Random House, 1987), 240–244; *Fayetteville Observer* (January 25, 1864); William Rufus Barlow Letters, Eleanor Brockenbrough Library, Museum of the Confederacy, Richmond, Virginia; William Kelsey McDaid, "'Four Years of Arduous Service': The History of the Branch-Lane Brigade in the Civil War" (Ph.D. diss., Michigan State University, 1987), 238–245; Clark, Volume 2, 45–46; Michael C. Hardy, *The Thirty-seventh North Carolina Troops: Tar Heels in the Army of Northern Virginia* (Jefferson, NC: McFarland, 2009), 170–174.
2. Rhea, *The Battle of the Wilderness*, 18, 42–46; Russell F. Weigley, *A Great Civil War: A Military and Political History, 1861–1865* (Bloomington: Indiana University Press, 2000), 324–330; James M. McPherson, *Battle Cry of Freedom: The Civil War Era* (New York: Oxford University Press, 1988), 718–721; Wert, 326–327; John Keegan, *The American Civil War: A Military History* (New York: Alfred A. Knopf, 2009), 124–125, 207, 225–234, 322–329.
3. Rhea, 8–59.
4. *Fayetteville Observer* (March 28, 1864); Gary W. Gallagher, "Our Hearts Are Full of Hope: The Army of Northern Virginia in the Spring of 1864," in *The Wilderness Campaign*, ed. Gary W. Gallagher (Chapel Hill: University of North Carolina Press, 1997), 36–59; Gary W. Gallagher, *The Confederate War: How Popular Will, Nationalism, and Military Strategy Could Not Stave Off Defeat* (Cambridge, MA: Harvard University Press, 1997), 36–42; J. Tracy Power,

Lee's Miserables: Life in the Army of Northern Virginia from the Wilderness to Appomattox (Chapel Hill: University of North Carolina Press, 1998), 1–13; Joseph T. Glatthaar, *General Lee's Army: From Victory to Collapse* (New York: Free Press, 2008), 357–363.

5. Rhea, 50–65.
6. Rhea, 60–93.
7. Rhea, 145–208; McDaid, 255–266.
8. Rhea, 222–239; McDaid, 255–266; Robertson, Jr., 251–268.
9. Rhea, 238, 276–287, 310–316; McDaid, 255–266; Robertson, Jr., 251–268; McPherson, 724–726; Keegan, 237–241; Power, 14–24; Glatthaar, 364–368; Weigley, 330–336.
10. James H. Lane Papers, Auburn University Special Collections and Archives, Auburn, Alabama (hereafter cited as AU).
11. Power, 23–24; Gordon C. Rhea, "The Battle of the Wilderness and Its Place in the Civil War," in *The Battle of the Wilderness: Grant and Lee Below the Rapidan River*, ed. Theodore P. Savas (Mason City, IA: Savas Publishing Company, 1999), 1–24.
12. Rhea, "The Battle of the Wilderness and Its Place in the Civil War," 1–24; John Cannan, *The Spotsylvania Campaign, May 7–21, 1864* (Conshohocken, PA: Combined Publishing, 1997), 17–26; McPherson, 725–728.
13. Glatthaar, 367–368; McPherson, 725–726; Wert, 343–344; Gregory Jaynes, *The Killing Ground: Wilderness to Cold Harbor* (Alexandria, VA: Time-Life Books, 1986), 82; Cannan, 15–26.
14. James H. Lane Papers, AU; McDaid, 268–269; Jaynes, 82–93; Glatthaar, 367–369; Keegan, 241–244; Cannan, 33–69.
15. Cannan, 81–111; Jaynes, 88–93.
16. Cannan, 121–138; Jaynes, 95–101.
17. McDaid, 268–283; Clark, Volume 2, 49–53; Cannan, 147–151; Jaynes, 95–105; Keegan, 241–244.
18. James H. Lane Papers, AU; McDaid, 273–283; Clark, Volume 2, 49–50.
19. Gordon C. Rhea, *The Battles for Spotsylvania Court House and the Road to Yellow Tavern* (Baton Rouge: Louisiana State University Press, 1997), 294–301; McDaid, 273–233; Kenneth W. Noe, "'Damned North Carolinians' and 'Brave Virginians': The Lane-Mahone Controversy, Honor, and Civil War Memory," *Journal of Military History* 72, no. 4 (October 2008): 1089–1115; James H. Lane Papers, AU.
20. Power, 30–50.
21. Power, 36.
22. Ernest B. Furgurson, *Not War But Murder: Cold Harbor, 1864* (New York: Alfred A. Knopf, 2000), 59–80.
23. Furgurson, 81–109.
24. Furgurson, 110–127; Jordan, Jr., 306.
25. Furgurson, 226–227.
26. Furgurson, 181–182.
27. Furgurson, 201–206.

Chapter 11

1. Earl J. Hess, *In the Trenches at Petersburg: Field Fortifications and Confederate Defeat* (Chapel Hill: University of North Carolina Press, 2009), xv; Brooks D. Simpson, *Ulysses S. Grant: Triumph Over Adversity, 1822–1865* (Boston: Houghton Mifflin, 2000), 321–345.
2. William Kelsey McDaid, "'Four Years of Arduous Service': The History of the Branch-Lane Brigade in the Civil War" (Ph.D. diss., Michigan State University, 1987), 296–297.
3. Noah André Trudeau, *The Last Citadel: Petersburg, Virginia, June 1864–April 1865* (Baton Rouge: Louisiana State University Press, 1991), 19.
4. James H. Lane Papers, Auburn University Special Collections and Archives, Auburn,

Alabama (hereafter cited as AU); McDaid, 289–295; Trudeau, 19–22; Ernest B. Furgurson, *Not War but Murder: Cold Harbor, 1864* (New York: Alfred A. Knopf, 2000), 248–251; John Horn, *The Petersburg Campaign: June 1864–April 1865* (Conshohocken, PA: Combined Books, 1993), 47–52, 62–68.

    5. James H. Lane Papers, AU; McDaid, 289–298; Hess, xvii–xviii, 38–39; Michael C. Hardy, *The Thirty-seventh North Carolina Troops: Tar Heels in the Army of Northern Virginia* (Jefferson, NC: McFarland, 2003), 200–202.

    6. James H. Lane Papers, AU; McDaid, 289–298; Hess, 38–39; Trudeau, 56–80; Hardy, 200–202.

    7. Hardy, 202–203; McDaid, 299–301; *Fayetteville Observer* (July 25, 1864); Hess, 65–77; Horn, 72–83.

    8. Hess, xviii, 78–82; Horn, 93–107; James H. Lane Papers, AU; McDaid, 300–303; Hardy, 203–205.

    9. John Horn, *The Destruction of the Weldon Railroad: Deep Bottom, Globe Tavern, and Reams Station: August 14–25, 1864* (Lynchburg, VA: H.E. Howard, Inc., 1991), 1–3; James M. McPherson, *Battle Cry of Freedom: The Civil War Era* (New York: Oxford University Press, 1988), 718–737.

    10. Hess, 124–134; Trudeau, 142–157; Horn, *The Destruction of the Weldon Railroad*, 26–113; McDaid, 303–305; Hardy, 205–206.

    11. Weymouth T. Jordan, Jr., *North Carolina Troops, 1861–1865: A Roster*, Volume 6, *Infantry* (Raleigh: North Carolina Division of Archives and History, 1977), 415; *Fayetteville Observer* (September 5, 1864), (October 17, 1864).

    12. Hess, 135–141; Trudeau, 173–191; McDaid, 305–309; *Fayetteville Observer* (September 5, 1864); Hardy, 205–210; John Horn, *The Petersburg Campaign*, 141–151; Horn, *The Destruction of the Weldon Railroad: Deep Bottom, Globe Tavern, and Reams Station*, 122–176; Robertson, Jr., 299–301.

    13. McDaid, 309–315; Hess, 160–166, 174; Trudeau, 212–217; Hardy, 211–214.

    14. McDaid, 315–323; Jordan, Jr., 323–423; A. Wilson Greene, *The Final Battles of the Petersburg Campaign: Breaking the Backbone of the Confederacy* (Knoxville: University of Tennessee Press, 2008), 83–96.

    15. McDaid, 315–323; Greene, 85–89; Hess, 224–228; Trudeau, 294; J. Tracy Power, *Lee's Miserables: Life in the Army of Northern Virginia from the Wilderness to Appomattox* (Chapel Hill: University of North Carolina Press, 1998), 214–215, 237–238.

    16. Hess, 254–256; Greene, 188–190, 212.

    17. Greene, 188–200, 210–214; Hess, 264–272; Trudeau, 366–370.

    18. Greene, 190–202, 210–214; Hess, 271–272.

    19. Greene, 212–226; Hess, 271–273; Trudeau, 369–378.

Bibliography

Primary Sources

LETTERS, DIARIES, RECORDS

Clark, Walter, ed. *Histories of the Several Regiments and Battalions from North Carolina in the Great War, 1861–'65.* Goldsboro, NC: Nash Brothers, Book & Job Printers, n.d.; reprint, Wendell, NC: Barefoot's Bookmark, 1982.
Fitzhugh, George. *Cannibals All! Or Slaves without Masters.* Edited by C. Vann Woodward. Cambridge, MA: Harvard University Press, 1960.
Fox, William F. *Regimental Losses in the American Civil War, 1861–1865.* Augustus S. Brandow, 1898; reprint, Dayton, OH: Morningside Bookshop, 1985.
Gallagher, Gary W. *Fighting for the Confederacy: The Personal Recollections of General Edward Porter Alexander.* Chapel Hill: University of North Carolina Press, 1989.
James H. Lane Papers. Auburn University Special Collections and Archives, Auburn, Alabama. http://www.lib.auburn.edu/find-aid/501.htm.
Thomas David Smith McDowell Papers. Southern Historical Collection. University of North Carolina.
United States War Department. *The War of the Rebellion: A Compilation of the Official Records of the Union and Confederate Armies.* Washington, DC: Government Printing Office, 1880–1901.
William James H. Bellamy Diary. Southern Historical Collection. University of North Carolina.
William Rufus Barlow Letters. Eleanor Brockenbrough Library. Museum of the Confederacy, Richmond, Virginia.
Wooster Family Papers. Southern Historical Collection. University of North Carolina.

NEWSPAPERS

Asheville News
Carolina Watchman
Daily Bulletin
Fayetteville Observer
North Carolina Argus
North Carolina Presbyterian
North Carolina Standard
North Carolina Whig
Patriot and Flag
Raleigh Register
Republican Banner
Weekly Courier
Weekly Progress
Western Democrat
Wilmington Herald

Secondary Sources

BOOKS

Bailey, Ronald H. *The Bloodiest Day: The Battle of Antietam*. Alexandria, VA: Time-Life Books, 1984.
Barrett, John G. *The Civil War in North Carolina*. Chapel Hill: University of North Carolina Press, 1963.
Boles, John B. *The South through Time*, Volume 1, 2d ed. Upper Saddle River, NJ: Prentice Hall, 1999.
Burton, Brian K. *Extraordinary Circumstances: The Seven Days Battles*. Bloomington: Indiana University Press, 2001.
Cannan, John. *The Spotsylvania Campaign, May 7–21, 1864*. Conshohocken, PA: Combined Publishing, 1997.
Casstevens, Francis Harding. *The 28th North Carolina Infantry*. Jefferson, NC: McFarland, 2008.
Cooper, William J., Jr., and Thomas E. Terrill. *The American South: A History*, 3d ed. Boston: McGraw-Hill, 2002.
Crofts, Daniel W. *Reluctant Confederates: Upper South Unionists in the Secession Crisis*. Chapel Hill: University of North Carolina Press, 1989.
Dew, Charles B. *Apostles of Disunion: Southern Secession Commissioners and the Causes of the Civil War*. Charlottesville: University Press of Virginia, 2001.
Eicher, David J. *The Longest Night: A Military History of the Civil War*. New York: Simon & Schuster, 2001.
Frassanito, William A. *Grant and Lee: The Virginia Campaigns, 1864–1865*. New York: Charles Scribner's Sons, 1983.
Furgurson, Ernest B. *Chancellorsville 1863: The Souls of the Brave*. New York: Alfred A. Knopf, 1992.
_____. *Not War but Murder: Cold Harbor, 1864*. New York: Alfred A. Knopf, 2000.
Gallagher, Gary, W., ed. *Chancellorsville: The Battle and Its Aftermath*. Chapel Hill: University of North Carolina Press, 1996.
_____. *The Confederate War: How Popular Will, Nationalism, and Military Strategy Could Not Stave off Defeat*. Cambridge, MA: Harvard University Press, 1997.
_____, ed. *The Third Day at Gettysburg and Beyond*. Chapel Hill: University of North Carolina Press, 1994.
_____, ed. *The Wilderness Campaign*. Chapel Hill: University of North Carolina Press, 1997.
Glatthaar, Joseph T. *General Lee's Army: From Victory to Collapse*. New York: Free Press, 2008.
Goolrick, William K. *Rebels Resurgent: Fredericksburg to Chancellorsville*. Alexandria, VA: Time-Life Books, 1985.
Gottfried, Bradley M. *Brigades of Gettysburg: The Union and Confederate Brigades at the Battle of Gettysburg*. Cambridge, MA: Da Capo Press, 2002.
Graham, Martin F., and George F. Skoch. *Mine Run: A Campaign of Lost Opportunities, October 21, 1863–May 1, 1864*. Lynchburg, VA: H.E. Howard, 1987.
Greene, A. Wilson. *The Final Battles of the Petersburg Campaign: Breaking the Backbone of the Rebellion*. Knoxville: University of Tennessee Press, 2008.
Hardy, Michael C. *The Battle of Hanover Court House: Turning Point of the Peninsula Campaign, May 27, 1862*. Jefferson, NC: McFarland, 2006.
_____. *The Thirty-seventh North Carolina Troops: Tar Heels in the Army of Northern Virginia*. Jefferson, NC: McFarland, 2009.
Harris, William C. *North Carolina and the Coming of the Civil War*. Raleigh: North Carolina Division of Archives and History, 1988.
Harsh, Joseph L. *Confederate Tide Rising: Robert E. Lee and the Making of Southern Strategy, 1861–1862*. Kent, OH: Kent State University Press, 1998.

Hennessy, John J. *Historical Report on the Troop Movements for the Second Battle of Manassas, August 28 through August 30, 1862.* National Park Service, 1985.
———. *Return to Bull Run: The Campaign and Battle of Second Manassas.* New York: Simon & Schuster, 1993.
Hess, Earl J. *In the Trenches at Petersburg: Field Fortifications and Confederate Defeat.* Chapel Hill: University of North Carolina Press, 2009.
Horn, John. *The Destruction of the Weldon Railroad: Deep Bottom, Globe Tavern, and Reams Station, August 14–25, 1864.* Lynchburg, VA: H.E. Howard, 1991.
———. *The Petersburg Campaign: June 1864–April 1865.* Conshohocken, PA: Combined Books, 1993.
Jaynes, Gregory. *The Killing Ground: Wilderness to Cold Harbor.* Alexandria, VA: Time-Life Books, 1986.
Jordan, Weymouth T., Jr. *North Carolina Troops, 1861–1865: A Roster.* Volume 6, *Infantry*. Raleigh: North Carolina Division of Archives and History, 1977.
———. *North Carolina Troops, 1861–1865: A Roster.* Volume 6 Addenda. Raleigh: North Carolina Division of Archives and History, 1990.
Keegan, John. *The American Civil War: A Military History.* New York: Alfred A. Knopf, 2009.
Konstam, Angus. *Seven Days Battles, 1862: Lee's Defense of Richmond.* Westport, CT: Praeger, 2004.
Krick, Robert K. *Stonewall Jackson at Cedar Mountain.* Chapel Hill: University of North Carolina Press, 1990.
Kruman, Marc W. *Parties and Politics in North Carolina, 1836–1865.* Baton Rouge: Louisiana State University Press, 1983.
Livermore, Thomas L. *Numbers and Losses in the Civil War in America, 1861–1865.* Bloomington: Indiana University Press, 1957.
Luvaas, Jay, and Harold W. Nelson, eds. *The U.S. Army War College Guide to the Battles of Chancellorsville and Fredericksburg.* New York: Harper & Row, 1988.
Martin, David G. *Gettysburg, July 1.* Conshohocken, PA: Combined Publishing, 1996.
McPherson, James M. *Antietam: The Battle that Changed the Course of the Civil War.* New York: Oxford University Press, 2002.
———. *Battle Cry of Freedom: The Civil War Era.* New York: Oxford University Press, 1988.
———. *For Cause and Comrades: Why Men Fought in the Civil War.* New York: Oxford University Press, 1997.
———. *Tried by War: Abraham Lincoln as Commander in Chief.* New York: Penguin Books, 2008.
O'Reilly, Francis Augustin. *The Fredericksburg Campaign: Winter War on the Rappahannock.* Baton Rouge: Louisiana State University Press, 2003.
Pfanz, Harry W. *Gettysburg: The First Day.* Chapel Hill: University of North Carolina Press, 2001.
———. *Gettysburg: The Second Day.* Chapel Hill: University of North Carolina Press, 1987.
Power, J. Tracy. *Lee's Miserables: Life in the Army of Northern Virginia from the Wilderness to Appomattox.* Chapel Hill: University of North Carolina Press, 1998.
Rable, George C. *Fredericksburg! Fredericksburg!* Chapel Hill: University of North Carolina Press, 2002.
Rafuse, Ethan S. *Antietam, South Mountain, and Harper's Ferry: A Battlefield Guide.* Lincoln: University of Nebraska Press, 2008.
Rhea, Gordon C. *The Battle of the Wilderness: May 5–6, 1864.* Baton Rouge: Louisiana State University Press, 1994.
———. *The Battles for Spotsylvania Court House and the Road to Yellow Tavern: May 7–12, 1864.* Baton Rouge: Louisiana State University Press, 1997.
———. *The Battles of Wilderness and Spotsylvania.* Eastern National Park and Monument Association, 1995.
———. *To the North Anna River: Grant and Lee, May 13–25, 1864.* Baton Rouge: Louisiana State University Press, 2000.

Robertson, James I., Jr. *General A.P. Hill: The Story of a Confederate Warrior*. New York: Random House, 1987.

———. *Stonewall Jackson: The Man, the Soldier, the Legend*. New York: Macmillan, 1997.

Savas, Theodore P. *The Battle of the Wilderness: Grant and Lee Below the Rapidan River*. Mason City, IA: Savas, 1999.

Schenck, Martin. *Up Came Hill: The Story of the Light Division and Its Leaders*. Harrisburg, PA: Stackpole Books, 1958.

Scott, Robert Garth. *Into the Wilderness with the Army of the Potomac*. Bloomington: Indiana University Press, 1985.

Sears, Stephen W. *Chancellorsville*. Boston: Houghton Mifflin, 1996.

———. *Gettysburg*. Boston: Houghton Mifflin, 2003.

———. *Landscape Turned Red: The Battle of Antietam*. New York: Ticknor & Fields, 1983.

———. *To the Gates of Richmond: The Peninsula Campaign*. New York: Ticknor & Fields, 1992.

Simpson, Brooks D. *Ulysses S. Grant: Triumph Over Adversity, 1822–1865*. Boston: Houghton Mifflin, 2000.

Sitterson, Joseph Carlyle. *The Secession Movement in North Carolina*. Chapel Hill: University of North Carolina Press, 1939.

Smith, Jean Edward. *Grant*. New York: Simon & Schuster, 2001.

Steere, Edward. *The Wilderness Campaign: The Meeting of Grant and Lee*. Mechanicsburg, PA: Stackpole Books, 1960.

Stevens, Norman. *Antietam, 1862: The Civil War's Bloodiest Day*. Westport, CT: Praeger, 2004.

Sutherland, Daniel E. *Fredericksburg and Chancellorsville: The Dar Mark Campaign*. Lincoln: University of Nebraska Press, 1998.

Thomas, Emory M. *Robert E. Lee: A Biography*. New York: W.W. Norton, 1995.

Trudeau, Noah André. *Bloody Roads South: The Wilderness to Cold Harbor, May–June 1864*. Boston: Little, Brown, and Company, 1989.

———. *The Last Citadel: Petersburg, Virginia, June 1864–April 1865*. Baton Rouge: Louisiana State University Press, 1991.

Vandiver, Frank E. *Mighty Stonewall*. Westport, CT: Greenwood Press, 1957.

Weigley, Russell F. *A Great Civil War: A Military and Political History, 1861–1865*. Bloomington: Indiana University Press, 2000.

Welker, David. *Tempest at Ox Hill: The Battle of Chantilly*. Cambridge, MA: Da Capo Press, 2002.

Wert, Jeffry D. *The Sword of Lincoln: The Army of the Potomac*. New York: Simon & Schuster, 2005.

Wheeler, Richard. *Lee's Terrible Swift Sword: From Antietam to Chancellorsville, an Eyewitness History*. New York: HarperPerennial, 1992.

Wright, Gavin. *The Political Economy of the Cotton South*. New York: W.W. Norton, 1978.

Articles

Noe, Kenneth W. "'Damned North Carolinians' and 'Brave Virginians': The Lane-Mahone Controversy, Honor, and Civil War Memory." *Journal of Military History* 72, no. 4 (October 2008): 1089–1115.

Theses and Dissertations

William Kelsey McDaid. "'Four Years of Arduous Service': The History of the Branch-Lane Brigade in the Civil War." Ph.D. diss., Michigan State University, 1987.

Index

Antietam *see* Sharpsburg
Appomattox 208, 210, 213, 215

Barry, John D. 57, 110–111, 115, 141–144, 146, 152, 155, 159–160, 164, 168, 170–171, 175, 181–182, 188, 191, 102
Bladen Guards 1, 30, 32
Branch, Gen. Lawrence 2, 34–37, 39–52, 55, 57, 63, 67, 69, 73–77, 81, 84–85, 87–90, 93–96, 100, 103, 109, 114–115
Brown, John 12, 18, 20–21
Burnside, Gen. Ambrose 33, 60, 108, 116–123, 126–128, 134, 182, 186–187

Cedar Mountain 3, 59, 64, 70–71, 73, 76–78, 88, 98, 107, 111, 130, 135, 162
Chancellorsville 3, 113, 126, 132–137, 143–153, 172, 178–179
Chantilly/Ox Hill 3, 78, 93, 95, 97, 99
Cold Harbor 57, 174, 189–194, 197, 201
Columbus Guards 1, 29–30
Cowan, Col. Robert H. 23, 35–36, 39, 43–45, 49–52, 55–57, 59, 64–66, 71, 81, 99, 101, 115, 152

desertion 81, 113, 168–169, 208, 210

Ellis, Gov. John 20, 23, 29

"Foot cavalry" 2, 64, 69, 80, 82, 91–92, 99, 118–119, 135
Fort Fisher 2, 31–32
Frayser's Farm 33, 37, 55–57, 63, 92–93, 111, 152, 198
Fredericksburg 3, 41, 60, 65, 83, 112–113,
117–121, 124, 126, 128, 132, 136, 147, 150, 155, 162, 165, 172, 177

Gaines Mill 12, 37, 51–54, 57, 111, 191
German Volunteers 29–30
Gettysburg 3, 149, 155, 160, 162–164, 166–170, 172, 178, 182, 184, 208
Grant, Gen. Ulysses 3, 38, 153–154, 173–174, 176–177, 179, 182–186, 188–190, 192–193, 195, 197–203, 206–207, 210–211, 213

Hancock, Gen. Winfield 179–182, 194, 199–206
Hanover Court House 2, 4, 23, 37, 41–43, 46–49, 52, 57, 111, 146
Harpers Ferry 3, 18, 20–21, 102–106, 108–109, 112, 116, 119
Hill, Gen. A.P. 2, 46–51, 55–56, 63–64, 81, 84, 87, 90, 95, 101, 106, 108–112, 114, 128, 135–137, 140–141, 151, 155, 158, 163, 168, 184, 198
Hooker, Gen. Joseph 3, 117, 121–122, 127, 130–138, 145–146, 149–153, 155, 157, 183

Jackson, Gen. "Stonewall" 2–3, 39, 42, 48–55, 61–110, 114–152, 169, 175, 182

Lane, Gen. James 4, 42–44, 95, 109–114, 120–124, 128–140, 142–151, 162–182, 185–188, 190–199, 202–207, 211
Lee, Gen. Robert E. 2–3, 38, 45, 47–48, 51, 54–56, 60, 62, 76, 79–80, 91–92, 97–108, 126, 128–134, 151–152, 167
Light Division (A.P. Hill's) 2, 46–51, 54–

55, 64, 67–75, 77, 81, 84–86, 88, 101, 103, 109, 109, 111–114, 119–120, 134, 136, 138, 151, 168

Mahone, Gen. William 186–188
Malvern Hill 2, 54–56, 59, 63, 198
McClellan, Gen. George 2, 36–39, 41–42, 47–48, 50, 54, 56, 58–60, 62–63, 65, 78–79, 82–83, 91, 97, 102–103, 105–107, 115–117, 126–127, 131, 134, 150, 152, 183
McDowell, Gen. Irvin 41, 60–61, 65, 82, 89
Mechanicsville 2, 48–51, 54, 111, 189
Mine Run 174–178
Moore's Creek Riflemen/Rifle Guards 1, 30

Ox Hill *see* Chantilly

Petersburg 3, 195–199, 201–213; Fussel's Mill 204; Globe Tavern 204–206; Jerusalem Plank Road 199–200, 203–204; Reams' Station 204–206
Pope, Gen. John 58, 60–65, 67, 78–87, 89–92, 95, 98, 134, 183
Purdie, Thomas 3–4, 35–36, 39, 44, 49–50, 57, 59, 64–69, 71, 73–74, 81–82, 84–85, 90, 93–94, 99–101, 106–115, 120–124, 129–134, 139–144, 147–152, 182

Radcliff, Colonel John D. 31, 33, 35
Robeson Light Infantry 1, 30
Robeson Rifle Guards 1, 30

Scotch Boys 1, 30
Secession (North Carolina) 29–35
Second Manassas 3, 78, 86, 90–92, 95, 98, 111, 135
Seven Days' Battles 2, 56–57, 59–60, 64, 91, 98, 113, 115; *see also* Frayser's Farm; Gaines' Mill; Malvern Hill; Mechanicsville
Sharpsburg/Antietam 3, 42, 102, 104, 106–107, 109–111, 113, 115, 119, 125, 129, 135–136
Shepherdstown 3, 107, 109–111, 155
slavery 5–20, 22, 25, 27, 156
Spotsylvania Court House 3, 183–185, 188–190, 197

Wilcox, Gen. Cadmus 167–168, 179–181, 183, 185–186, 190, 194, 199–200, 204–205, 208, 210–211
Wilderness 3, 113, 135, 141, 144, 146, 174, 177–180, 182–184, 189, 192, 200, 208, 218
Wilmington Light Infantry 1, 30
Wilmington Rifle Guard 30, 152

www.ingramcontent.com/pod-product-compliance
Ingram Content Group UK Ltd.
Pitfield, Milton Keynes, MK11 3LW, UK
UKHW041939140426
5217IPUK00014B/571